I AM WHAT I AM

SUNITHA
KRISHNAN

I AM WHAT I AM

A MEMOIR

WESTLAND
NON-FICTION

WESTLAND
NON·FICTION

Published by Westland Non-Fiction, an imprint of Westland Books, a division of Nasadiya Technologies Private Limited, in 2024

No. 269/2B, First Floor, 'Irai Arul', Vimalraj Street, Nethaji Nagar, Alapakkam Main Road, Maduravoyal, Chennai 600095

Westland, the Westland logo, Westland Non-Fiction and the Westland Non-Fiction logo are the trademarks of Nasadiya Technologies Private Limited, or its affiliates.

ISBN: 9789360452988

10 9 8 7 6 5 4 3

Typeset by Ashutosh Jha
Printed at Manipal Technologies Limited, Manipal

Dedicated to the men in my life—
My father Raju Krishnan for trusting me;
My best friend Jose Vetticatil for walking this path with me;
My soulmate and life partner Rajesh Touchriver for helping me see way beyond the horizon.

Contents

Author's Note ix

Prologue: When I Wanted to Kill God 1

1. The Beginning 5
2. Branding for Life 13
3. The Girl Who Did Not Cry 17
4. Snapshots from My Childhood 23
5. Sadbhavana 30
6. The House of Light 35
7. The Development Sector 42
8. Marriage and Celibacy 49
9. A Paper Tiger 53
10. Moving Away for Good 62
11. Early Days in Hyderabad 67
12. The Soul Connection 73
13. Prajwala, the Fire Within 78
14. Those Who Help Themselves 88
15. Rizwana, Kajal and Some Others 107

16. A Home for the Children 119

17. The Daily Bread 133

18. The Power in Partnerships—and the Problems 145

19. A Hard Lesson to Learn 157

20. Palakkad Predictions 165

21. A Funeral and a Wedding 177

22. A Forever Home 183

23. When the Universe Conspired 196

24. Giving Up My Long Tresses 204

25. Why Do Rapists Thrive with Impunity? 210

26. Thamarapadam and the Civilian Honour 220

27. Protectors, Predators, Prey 229

28. From Warrior to Conqueror 247

29. Why Positions Matter 255

30. The Long Game 265

31. I Am What I Am 270

Epilogue: Acknowledging My Debts 276

Author's Note

I guess anyone writing their autobiography has a reason or purpose for doing it. Mine were twofold. One, I wanted the world to understand that everything is possible if you're willing to work for it, and two, for my fellow travellers in Prajwala to understand the past struggles that have shaped this organisation and experience the strength of conviction that sustains it.

Writing this book was hard for me, whether it was reliving difficult memories, confronting mistakes, reflecting on strategies that failed or acknowledging the price that others had to pay for the choices I made. The walls of the room where I shut myself in to sit down and write bear witness to that struggle. Yet, I am glad that I did this. For what it's worth, the five decades of my life that have gone by are now recorded in some shape.

I wrote as honestly as it was within my capacity to do so. Chiefly, there are two conscious omissions. Firstly, I did not name those who have tried to harm me, because the idea was not to shame anybody but only to put on record what I gained from that particular adverse situation, and secondly, the names of all my children and women have been changed to protect their identity.

While I tore through writing the first draft like a tornado, editing it after my husband, Rajesh Touchriver, gave me his feedback was even more intense. As a filmmaker, Rajesh was very clear that a reader must be able to visualise the things, places and events I wrote about. I am not a writer, and descriptions and imagination don't come naturally to me. Being in the practical mould, emotions are not something I factor into my writing either. In any case, I took his comments on board, and without compromising on my reality, I have tried to provide as much clarity as possible, and I hope it will do.

Seetha Natesh and Ajitha, my two editors, were at times my conscience-keepers and at other times gently prodding me to relook at the articulation within these pages. Being passionate and driven can blind one to other perspectives, and one could end up sounding prejudiced or angry without intending to. These two amazing women calmed me down, and ensured that the core of my conviction was not lost in my expression of dissent.

Since English is not the language I'm most comfortable in, the book has needed extensive work from Sanjana Tiwari to both correct and proofread. I cannot thank her enough for her careful, painstaking efforts.

Can't thank my agent, Kanishka Gupta, enough for bringing Ajitha and Westland Books into my life.

Finally, the cover of this book is what readers will first see. And if the cover of this autobiography has a character that reflects my personality, it is thanks to Saurabh Garge who has survived the multiple demands I made.

Finally, *I Am What I Am* would never have seen the light of the day if not for all the divine powers that guide my life, ensure that anger and bitterness do not consume me, and that I keep harnessing all my energies in the right direction.

Sunitha Krishnan
Hyderabad
2 April 2024

PROLOGUE

When I Wanted to Kill God

The shrill ring of the phone jolted me from my sleep. At 5 a.m., this could only be an emergency. It was the police. I could hear the worry in the man's voice. I was to go right away to the railway tracks behind the Falaknuma railway station.

I was ready in under five minutes; my team and I had the drill down pat. So I telephoned Akbar and asked him to bring Jaffer's autorickshaw over. We left immediately. With the streets empty, we reached in about ten minutes. In the distance, I spotted a few policemen huddled together. It must be an abandoned child, I realised. The police wanted to hand her over to us, as they had many times in the past. I had streamlined this process over the last four years of doing this work. The Juvenile Justice (Care and Protection) Act, 2000 was just out, and while it was not yet properly implemented, it provided the legal framework for extending care and protection to children like the ones I served. Our homes for both children and adults were now functional. We had thirty children already in our home, and we had slowly begun to accept children from the newly formed Child Welfare Committee along with those who were referred by police stations.

Ours was the only home in the area, so the police, especially the ones in the Old City of Hyderabad, referred many cases to us. It was always a big challenge to refuse children who had eloped or had been abandoned, but I was very clear about my mandate: I would only take in children of women in prostitution, victims of rape and of sex trafficking and HIV-positive children. It was always a hard decision, but we needed to optimise our limited resources and skills. My team may not have the academic qualifications, but they were trained well. And with many of our own rescued women joining us, we had people with lived experience who intuitively knew what should be done. All this had helped us evolve a comprehensive programme to cater to the needs of the children we served. Anybody who visited our home could vouch for the outcome of our interventions.

To my mind, today would be one of those cases where the police just wanted to hand over the child and fulfil their responsibilities, and congratulate themselves for early-morning productivity. As I approached the police, I went over possible reasons for refusing them and the organisations I could refer them to instead. It was only when I was close enough to see their faces that I registered their horror and discomfort.

I peered at the child and drew in a sharp breath. There was blood all over. The girl, six or seven, maybe even younger, was alive and breathing, though unconscious. The policeman next to me leant over, whispered something in my ear. I couldn't make sense of it. I went down on my knees and gently touched the child.

She woke up, whimpering in pain. I reached out to pick her up. That's when I realised her intestines were trailing out of her vagina. Her insides were torn through. She needed the hospital right away.

I gathered her up, one hand on her shoulder, the other supporting her bottom, and started running. The policemen, shaken out of their stupor, ran with me towards Akbar, waiting by the auto. I asked one of them to get in and told the others to follow.

At Osmania General Hospital, the doctors went still with shock when they saw the child. In seconds, though, their training took over, and they rushed her to the emergency ward.

It was then that I began to talk to the constable who had accompanied me. He told me that one of the beat constables had found the child at 4.45 a.m. near the railway tracks. The child appeared to have been gang-raped and thrown near the bushes. Maybe they thought they had killed her. But the beat constable realised that the child was alive.

This constable, who was posted at the Chatrinaka police station, had sent several children to our home and had my number. His presence of mind and humaneness were definitely greater than his love for duty and protocol. Very often, lower-rung policemen first inform their senior officers and only then raise the alarm and alert agencies like ours. This, of course, means loss of precious time. In this case, though, the intervention was prompt and the police action that followed was diligent. They had arrested six migrant workers, one of whom was the father of the girl. He and his friends had assaulted the child in a drunken rage and left her for dead.

I am a deeply spiritual person. Over the years, my daily routine of prayers and meditation have helped me focus on the task at hand without getting overwhelmed.

But that day, if god had appeared before me, I would have killed them with my bare hands.

The child, Shaheen, just four years old needed thirty-two stitches, several hours of surgery and many, many more in rehabilitation.

For days after, my faith in god remained shaken. I couldn't understand how this all-compassionate being whom I implicitly trusted could let such brutality unfold. Why didn't they stop it? How could a father join five others to gang-rape this young one?

I had felt this way before, when a five-year-old we had taken in died of AIDS the very year she came to us. I had visited her at the hospital, not knowing that those were her last moments. But perhaps she knew. She had clung to my arms as soon as I entered the ward, pleading, '*Madam, mujhe hostel aana hai, mujhe jaane mat dena*' (Madam, I want to come back to the hostel, don't let me go).

Even as I reassured her that she would be fine, that she would recover soon enough and play with the other children, life left her body. I choked with anger. It was not fair. A young soul with hopes and dreams had been crushed, all because of one man's lust.

It would take me several years to understand that the gods were not looking the other way. That they sent people like that constable, like Akbar and me, to act. Why else had that constable happened to walk those tracks at that time? Why had he remembered me immediately and made the call? How did Akbar and I rush to the scene without thinking twice? What gave us the strength to do all that followed?

I realised something else as well. So long as I focused on the pain and trauma of the victims, I risked overlooking their power and resilience. It was crucial to work on the immense potential of human beings to tide over adverse situations and emerge as people who are capable of loving and sharing. I make sure the child understands that they have been wronged, and that they should not be ashamed of being a victim. As their anger, pain, outrage and unbearable sense of betrayal poured out, the child is cleared of the burden of a lifetime. Through unconditional love, empathy and acceptance, they are able to see the beautiful person within. As we take that journey together, the child slowly regains dignity and a spirit to conquer all odds.

If not for that constable and us, Shaheen would not have been found, rescued, rehabilitated. And if not for her own resilience, she could not have moved on and studied law at a reputed institution.

Perhaps it was also god's work that there were people who investigated such crimes, dragged the perpetrators to court and got justice for the victims. That individuals like me started demanding that the silence around sex crimes against women and children be broken.

Could I have done all this without witnessing so many cases? Would I have been moved to action if I hadn't seen these cases at close quarters? There are, after all, billions out there who simply look away. Who else other than the powerful force above us all can compel us to bear witness?

Was there a plan when god chose me and the others to face this reality and fight it? For, each time I see violence and violation, I also see a chance to end it.

1

The Beginning

I was seventeen when I undertook my first rescue. It was so different from our operations today. I was so unprepared, I had no experience, connections or knowhow. But I wasn't unfit. I was resourceful, I had a keen desire to help, with a few good Samaritans pitching in.

It began like this.

My family had just relocated to Bangalore, a city in south India, which was also called in those days the 'garden city'. My elder sister had finished her teacher's training, my younger siblings were studying in the local Kendriya Vidyalaya. I was in junior college and had taken up the sciences. While I worked hard to excel at my studies, I was also very clear that I wanted to understand the gory world of sex crime and prostitution. In this, my job at Kairalee Nikethan English High School, Ulsoor as a guide captain came in handy.

One of my first decisions while starting my pre-university course had been to somehow get back into the Girl Guide movement. I had this vague notion that this would enable me to help others. It was also important for me to get the president's badge, the highest honour for a Girl Guide. So, I convinced my father to take me to the Girl Guide headquarters in Bangalore, and was enrolled in one of the troops. While in junior college, I also attended a lot of camps and finally qualified for the badge.

My job at the school, part-time though it was, was a great blessing. The modest monthly income took care of all my needs, including my college fees. I got to connect with some amazing children. Some of them were branded as 'difficult', and made to join scouts and guides for 'reformation'. Nonetheless, they were great kids. The job gave me a legitimate reason to get back home late, providing me with ample opportunity to explore the dark corners of the city.

My casual interactions with the scout masters that I met offered me a good understanding of the hotspots of prostitution in the city. Most of the street prostitution occurred in the busy Majestic or Shivajinagar areas, which also had some of the biggest bus stations. Majestic was also close to the main railway station. I decided to frequent Majestic and meet the women in prostitution there.

For months together, I walked around and made no progress. My four-foot frame did not help; I came across as a small child. The women would stonewall my attempts to interact with them. They would either look through me or shoo me away. Once, a woman—she looked like a brothel-keeper to me, with her giant frame and the way she controlled all the other women on the street—even spat on me accidentally! I had earnestly asked how I could be of help, and she laughed so hard, she began to cough, spitting betel juice on my face.

But I was persistent. I kept hanging around, hoping they'd get used to me. I couldn't understand why the women were always drunk, why they were constantly chewing tobacco. Their eyes roved constantly, restlessly, in search of a buyer. When they spotted me, their eyes would harden. I think they tolerated me only because I didn't seem to be a threat. Still, I wasn't getting anywhere with them. I understood their hostility. I was an unnecessary distraction, one that could damage their daily business. So, I decided to observe them from a distance, but in a way that they could still see me. I was hopeful that eventually my smile or my friendly demeanour would thaw them.

What I did learn was how the street was organised, the number of women who were prostituting and the men and women who controlled the street. I became intimately acquainted with the smell of the small packets of country liquor everybody drank. It was a funny smell—a combination of perfume, typewriter eraser, liquor, garbage and cigarettes—one that I now associate with Majestic.

I learnt how they operated: the buyers came, chose a woman and went into one of the lodges scattered across the street. They would almost always leave in less than an hour. The hefty woman (sometimes, one of the men) collected the money, either from the sex worker or the client. This would also be used to pay off the police and other characters.

While I couldn't hang around past late evening, I got an understanding of the kind of men who frequented these places: mostly daily wagers, labourers and, occasionally, students. On the face of it, everything looked voluntary and there was no physical force used.

Strangely enough, I never felt any fear or anxiety visiting these places. Somehow, I felt at home, and there was a level of comfort I experienced that I cannot explain. It just felt right. But after a few months just walking around, smiling, with a few hellos here and there, I was getting frustrated.

Honestly, if you asked me what I'd wanted to do there, I couldn't have told you. I didn't even know what exactly it was that I wanted to understand. But an unknown sense of purpose kept me going. Something in my gut kept telling me it was just a matter of time.

And then it happened!

It was a Saturday, a half-day at college. I had completed my scouts and guides session before I got there around 3 p.m. As soon as I reached, some women gestured to me.

This was a first. I ran towards them. It did not even strike me to be cautious, to ask what they wanted or where we were going. There was this feeling of trust that made me follow them blindly.

They took me to a lodge. In one of the rooms was a girl, about twelve or thirteen, sitting on the floor. Beside her, on a chair, was the hefty woman. I looked at her blankly. She pointed at a plastic chair. I sat down. She looked at the child sitting on the floor, then looked up at me.

'You want to help us, right? That's what you've been saying for the last two months you've been coming here. Help this child,' she said, tossing her head. 'God knows where she's come from. Go, find her family and take her back.'

I looked at the child huddled in a corner. After all that silence, this felt like a dare. I knew I had to make the right response. All eyes were on me. I somehow pulled myself together and managed to look confident, my theatre experience in school finally coming in handy. 'What happened?' I asked.

'This child has lost her way, and she's not in her right mind either.'

Some of the other women whispered that a customer had already used the child and left money in her blouse.

I'm not sure where the confidence came from, but I found myself taking charge. I told the hefty lady, whose name I learnt was Laxmi, to keep the child safe until I organised everything. Also, I said, I wanted to speak to the child privately.

My confident air and the authority in my voice seemed to assure them, and they quickly left the room.

I squatted on the floor and began to speak softly to the child. She was obviously scared and reluctant to come close. To break the ice, I offered her some water and biscuits I'd brought with me. She eyed them for a bit, and then put out a trembling hand to accept them. Slowly, we connected. My small frame, and perhaps my earlier experience with the intellectually challenged, helped. Maybe she thought I was her age or younger—she was taller than me.

Eventually, I got her to tell me the name of her village and its whereabouts. The information was quite sketchy: she lived somewhere along the Mysore Road and knew a few landmarks that could help narrow down the actual location.

I learnt a few other things as well: the way she framed her sentences made me suspect that she was somewhat intellectually challenged. But she was certainly not someone who lived on the streets. I'd seen enough street children, and she wasn't one. Her manner of speaking and the way she sat, covering her legs with her frock, indicated that she came from a well-to-do family.

When I emerged two hours later, my status had been elevated. I was warmly offered a small bottle of Gold Spot, a very popular aerated drink in those times. I told them all I'd learnt from the child. One of the women was from same area and identified it as somewhere around Kengeri, which was about 100 kilometres away.

I told them I needed time to organise the transport and that I would accompany the child to her house. Lalita, the lady from Kengeri, instantly volunteered to accompany me. To my utter surprise, Laxmi and two other women said they would join us. I told them I'd finalise all the details and get in touch soon.

On the bus home, I formulated a plan. As I got off at my station, I spotted Rajasekhar-sir on his evening walk. He was a senior officer in the Survey of India where my father worked, and the very man I'd wanted to see. We had a good rapport and often discussed social causes. I told him selective details about the case, omitting the location and the background of the women, and that I needed a vehicle. He immediately offered to arrange an office vehicle on Monday morning.

In those days, we did not have a telephone. So, the next day, which was a Sunday, I made some excuse about an extra class for my students and left. If my mother wondered why I'd scheduled it for 3 p.m., she did not ask.

I reached Majestic at around 4.30 p.m., and met Laxmi and the others. Now, we were no longer antagonists, but allies on the same team. I told them that I would arrive on Monday morning with a vehicle, and we could all take the child to her home. I went with Laxmi to meet the child who had been staying in one of the rooms in the lodge.

To my delight, the child recognised me and rushed to hug me. It was so natural, the bonding. I had carried some food from home, and the three of us ate it together sitting on the floor. Suddenly, Laxmi looked different to me. Until then, I had only thought of her as the hefty pimp who organised sordid operations. Now I saw her as a person I could connect deeply with. I even ended up telling her I was twenty-three instead of seventeen so that she would see me in a more mature light.

That night, I returned with such a sense of purpose that I could not sleep. I tossed and turned, reviewing the plan we had cooked up, pondering over various scenarios, and what my Plan A, Plan B and Plan C would be in each of those situations.

In the morning, I found a jeep waiting near my gate. The driver looked rather confused about why the officer-in-command had sent me an official vehicle, but followed my directions without too many questions. I decided to keep our conversations limited to routes. In any case, I was far too preoccupied with the task at hand and the uncertainties weighing it down.

At 10 a.m., the street in Majestic looked very different from the scene at 5 p.m. Laxmi and three other women were waiting at the street corner with the child. They all looked so different; dressed in simple sarees, flowers in their hair, they could easily pass for housewives. A far cry from their usual get-up: brightly patterned gaudy sarees, their mouths full of paan, kohl-lined eyes, darkened eyebrows, bright lipsticks, all necessary for showing off their 'assets', hoping to catch the eye of passers-by. The child, in new clothes and neat hair, looked refreshed.

In control of the situation, I asked them all to settle into the back seat while I sat in front. With this, the driver's interaction with the rest would be limited. To this day, I can't explain how I got us to Kengeri. I'd never been there, nor was I familiar with any routes. I suppose we were lucky the driver knew the way there. When he was doubtful of the route, I'd seek Lalita's eyes while replying—she was seated right behind the driver, so that I could see her easily—and she'd okay it with a subtle nod. We managed somehow. The women barely spoke, while the child and I chatted about what she'd had for breakfast and her new clothes.

She became animated when we got to Kengeri, pointing out several landmarks, each exclamation slightly louder than before. Despite my worries, it was not very difficult to trace the child's village. As soon as we got out of the jeep, the child clutched my hand and led me to her house. By the time we got to her door, there was a sizeable number of villagers following us, their relief at her return evident.

We learnt that the child's parents had passed away a few months ago. Now, the paternal uncle and his family were responsible for the child. And what a contrast *their* reaction was to that of the villagers! Though they were quick to cover up their shock with loud sobs and hugs, it was obvious that something was amiss. The other women noticed it as well.

When I asked them why her disappearance had not been reported to the police, they became defensive and began interrogating us on where had we found the child. I was taken aback, not expecting such a question, but Laxmi took over effortlessly. She said that the child had been found near my colony and painted me as the child's saviour, telling them how I had given her food and clothes and looked after her as my own.

By this time, the village headman had also arrived. After listening to Laxmi, he thanked me profusely and subtly warned the uncle and his family to take better care of the child. Through his speech, we got a better picture of the situation. The child's father had been a landlord, and the land and property was in the child's name. The uncle's family were just caretakers. A few years ago, the uncle had sold all that he possessed and moved to the city, but had gambled all his money away. When his older brother and sister-in-law died, he had returned to look after the child and the property.

While the family politely offered us some snacks and buttermilk, the village headman insisted that we go to his house for lunch. Over our meal, Thimappa-avare ('avare' is a Kannada word used to denote respect, like 'ji' in Hindi and 'garu' in Telugu) voiced his worries about the child. Most villagers knew that the child was neglected by the uncle's family. He suspected that the uncle was secretly happy that the child had gone missing, as it would allow him to take over the property. All of us nodded in agreement.

Thimappa promised that the village would ensure the safety of the child. He also told me that rural communities are closely knit and could exert a lot of pressure if needed. Most of this speech passed over my head. I was just so relieved that I had completed the first real task in my life. If somebody had given me the Bharat Ratna for it, I would have happily accepted! I was that exhilarated. Even the president's badge hadn't made me this happy. We returned to Bangalore super thrilled with the day's work. The driver, by this time, had understood that we had restored a missing child to her family.

Two days later, when I visited Majestic, I realised Laxmi and the other women had been busy looking into how the child had arrived there. Apparently one of the pimps had found the child wandering on the highway and had lured her under the pretext of taking her back to the village. How she came to be on the highway, nobody really knew. The pimp had sold her for a paltry sum to a buyer and vanished.

It was unclear whether the buyer had raped the child, but he'd left some money in her blouse. Her cries had alerted the lodge owner, who had immediately called Laxmi. They'd tried to keep everything low-key to avoid the police. That's why Laxmi told the women to look out for me.

I think god has strange ways of connecting people. For some reason, Laxmi had felt that I had their best interests at heart, and that is why I loitered around so often in their area. She never once saw me as a threat. She was proved right—I took all the right steps. What she and the other women didn't know was that it was the first time in my life that I was doing any of this. It was as if some force was guiding me, helping me behave the right way. In so many ways, I was slowly becoming aware of the role providence had in my life.

My dad got to know about my rescue at work. Apparently, the driver had spread the story. The office was abuzz with his praise of our undertaking, of how I was a great social worker and how my colleagues and I helped a missing child.

When word got out, I brushed aside any conversation around this. Though people happily mistook it for modesty and humility, it was really reticence. I was not prepared to share a single thing about my interactions with the women in prostitution.

Helping that girl opened the world of these women to me. Now, when I walked on the streets of Majestic, many spoke to me, and I learnt their stories. Some even sought my help for their children's education. Most of them had been trafficked with promises of jobs or marriage. Some continued on this path due to financial compulsions—they had been abandoned by their husbands who had left them with huge debts, or they had urgent financial needs that no other work could help fulfil.

What for me was rape was for them a routine affair. They were all used to rough treatment from their customers. Some drank alcohol to be able to comply with their clients' demands. Every one of them knew many children, ten- or twelve-year-olds, who had been forced into the trade. Though none wanted the same life for their children, they could see no way out for themselves.

I can't tell you what prompted those women to help that child, whether it was to evade the police or protect their own interests. But I can tell you that they were extraordinary people who reached out to a complete stranger to help a child.

Such insights into this murky world of commercial sexual exploitation and the different facets of the many players solidified my decision to work in this area. In many ways, this incident was perhaps the first indicator that I was on the right path.

2

Branding for Life

It was the unfettered curiosity of some of my committed supporters, the puzzled looks about my motives, my passion and drive that first prompted me to share my own past. I could sense people's confusion about me. Is she for real? Why is she so angry? Why is she in such a hurry to get things done? Is there an ulterior motive behind her actions?

When I share my reasons, all the pieces fall into place like a jigsaw puzzle. I don't offer details, just that I survived a gang-rape. The questions cease. Faces flood with sympathy and understanding, an arm or two pat my back, squeeze my shoulder.

But connecting my past with my present had a rather surprising result. My past somehow became a qualification for my work and, many a time, the way I was identified. This didn't really affect me when we started Prajwala, an organisation that battles sex crimes and trafficking. We were a rather small outfit and there were plenty of others doing similar work. But even as the scope of our work expanded and began to be appreciated nationally and internationally, people would not let go of my identity as a rape survivor.

All leaders are stirred to action by ideas or incidents that move them. But it is only in situations of sexual violence that you can never shake off the origin stories. The label is for life. The world refuses to forget it and, as a result, you're unable to shed it. Once a piece of information reaches the public domain, it is out there for the world to rake up at will. I wanted acknowledgement of my skills, my approach and strategies, my social entrepreneurship. I began to resent references to the incident, especially when my entire identity became distilled to someone who had been raped. No doubt a crime had been committed against me, but I considered myself a survivor, not a victim.

Labelling—of any kind—does not help. All experiences, regardless of their impact, are ultimately a phase in time. We should leave it to the individual to decide in what manner they want to remember that phase rather than turning it into a vault they can't escape from.

It is rather pathetic that some rely on labelling as a way to stigmatise someone because of their looks or origin or because of some (usually traumatic) experience. How often have we heard people addressed as 'Shorty', 'Fatty', 'Kalia' (black), or other epithets that body-shame? I myself was called 'Penguin' in school because of the way I walked and 'Kulz' in college because of my (lack of) height. Some such labels are made in jest, or even out of affection, but you never know how they impact that person. When these labels arise out of trauma, or even painful life situations, they turn into nightmares. 'Divorcee', 'kojja' or '9' (for a transgender), 'chinaal' and 'randi' (for women in prostitution, or any woman perceived to be 'easy')—such terminology can have a deep and painful impression on that person.

My children from Astha Nivas (you will learn more about them in the coming chapters) were called 'Prajwala girls' in their schools. Most of them tolerated it, but some deeply resented it and it made them reluctant to go to school. This continues even today. Thousands of children have graduated from our home, but are scared to associate with Prajwala, unwilling to be called a Prajwala girl yet again. Labelling, of any sort, can be unkind.

Coming back to my predicament, anytime a horrendous rape would occur in the country, every media channel automatically dialled my number—not because of my work on sexual violence, but because I can be conveniently labelled as a 'rape survivor'. One time, a national news channel wanted me on their primetime show. I had given explicit instructions on how I should be introduced. But when the programme started, I could see the label 'rape survivor' below my name.

Another time, I was supposed to address police officers on human trafficking. But in his enthusiasm for my work, an officer, while introducing me, graphically described my gang-rape. Perhaps he thought he was doing me a favour. But the result was that my talk on human trafficking, its nuances, laws and limitations, was overshadowed by it, and the participants focused only on asking me questions about my personal life. It was a missed opportunity for learning.

Let me make this very clear—being a victim of sexual assault is not my identity. It is a lived experience that transformed my thoughts, gave my life direction, and became the impetus for what I do. Yet, social media posts that supposedly celebrate my work rarely touch upon the huge milestones that Prajwala has achieved in prevention or advocacy. In their reductive write-ups, I remain the victim who has saved countless others, my work an abridged footnote. Then there is the speculation about my age at the time of the incident. Is this what makes posts popular?

Snide remarks about how I've hogged the limelight with this tag have followed me for years. Most of my relatives think I have no better work than to harp on about an event that happened years ago. An aunt even remarked, 'You talk as if it is a great accomplishment.' A well-known social worker said to my face, 'Nowadays everybody is a rape victim. It's the best way to get more funding.'

The public disclosure of my gang-rape has branded me for a lifetime. My achievements, skills, capabilities, my vision, my accomplishments as a social entrepreneur are all credited to it. Every now and then there are social media posts, especially in March during the week of International Women's Day, or during Dasara, when all female deities are celebrated. They all say the same thing: Sunitha is a gang-rape victim and now she saves children from prostitution. As if being gang-raped is a prior qualification necessary for saving the sexually assaulted!

Once, when we were attending an official event, an elderly gentleman came up to my husband Raj, took his hands into his own and kept saying, 'Thank you for rehabilitating her.' Poor Raj did not know what to do. Since this was a first for me too, I could only smile and move away.

Such experiences, among many others, make victims reluctant to speak about their ordeal in public. For them, it is better if they are nameless and faceless, otherwise closure becomes a lifelong challenge. How is social reintegration possible when your past looms heavily over your present? How can a person move on if you will never allow them to process what happened?

An incident at one of the best hotels in Hyderabad lingers in my memory. One of our young women found employment in the housekeeping section through my request. The human resources manager, who was young and bright, was committed to social causes and had met with me to discuss ways in which she could support the mission. I had requested her to provide employment opportunities for my girls, honouring which she had recruited a young woman with the requisite skills. In less than a week, I started getting calls from the manager suggesting that I provide special counselling to the woman as she was friendly with the male staff. I was taken aback. 'Has something happened?' I asked her. She said, since these girls were from this 'background', she was slightly worried that they would form unnecessary alliances with the male staff. I was both stumped and upset.

What does the world expect? Relocate my women and children to another planet where their background is not known?

None of this, however, has stopped me from citing my life in my work. With my children, especially girls, it is a natural conversation to have to validate their experience and reassure them that I understand them. With other stakeholders, including in the criminal justice system, I talk about it to explain the trauma of emotional exclusion, the impact of being judged as the instigator of a crime of which they are victims.

I have not yet figured out the right way to navigate this matter in my sector. I have often been asked why I play the 'victim card'. Does my sharing this with you mean that I'm perpetuating that impression? How do I balance sharing my motivation to work with the desire to be acknowledged for my accomplishments? I hope to have some answers one day.

3

The Girl Who Did Not Cry

Any sexual assault is a traumatic event and leaves deep scars on the psyche of the survivor. The shame, the guilt, the feeling of being tainted, the self-loathing that it brings in its wake is universal. I was no exception.

I was fifteen when I was sexually assaulted.

It was in a village I'd gone to for a neo-literacy campaign. I'd been visiting this village for a year, interacting with the girls and motivating them to go back to school.

My persistence had borne results, and a handful of the girls I worked with managed to convince their parents to resume their schooling. I'd give them remedial classes to catch up with the syllabus. We'd become friends over time and discussed a variety of subjects, including menstrual hygiene and other intimate issues. Some of my ideas were rather 'revolutionary', I suppose. For instance, when I told them that I didn't believe in physically isolating women during periods, they'd look at me with awe.

On these visits, I'd stay over on weekends to reduce the commute, then return home the following evening in time for school on Monday. My room was some distance from the classroom, and I'd usually cut across some fields to get there. It was usually late in the evening by the time class was over. I was used to the terrain, and the lack of light didn't bother me. A torch was good enough to show me the way. Perhaps my experience in camping as a Girl Guide had helped.

That night, I was walking back to my room after class. It was dark, no street lights around. I had the torch on. The beam caught a group of men coming towards me. I hadn't even heard them. I focused the torch on them. There were about eight men approaching. Yet, they didn't greet me or break their stride. While this wouldn't have made me pause in the city, in the village, that was rather odd. I hesitated for a second, then made to move past.

Out of nowhere came a fist to my face. The blow knocked me to the ground. My screams were crushed under somebody's palm. And then, nothing. I have no recollections, vague or detailed. No faces or other identifying features. Just random impressions—figures and body odours.

Hours later, when I gained consciousness, my clothes, the aches and bruises on my body told me what I had experienced.

When I managed to gather myself, I was filled with anger. Righteous rage. I wanted to fight. The villagers I went to, mostly women, pointed out quietly, 'What has happened has happened. What good could come of making a scene?' They thought it was best to hush up the incident and urged me to return to the city. But I disagreed. I thought, why should *I* be ashamed? It is the creatures who violated me who should hesitate to show their faces.

I met the panchayat, mostly men. Their response was even more humiliating. I got what I deserved, they told me. It was all my fault. I had been swaying the girls and giving them bad ideas. I am not sure what triggered their anger or animosity towards me, but I guess it had been building for some time. Mine was a good lesson to learn from, a warning for those who were a bad influence, they said.

They were treating me as if I was the criminal. I was enraged.

I have no idea how I got home; I was on autopilot by then. My family took the news in complete silence. My parents did not question me, but I could sense their shock and pain. There was no way they would report the incident to the police, and I was not interested in being berated and humiliated once again. Over the next few days, my father held a gentle silence that gave me space, helped me get back to my routine. The rest of the family followed his lead.

In the end, I couldn't take any further action against my attackers. The villagers' reaction, my blackout and, to an extent, my family's response had seen to that. What could I say, really, when I couldn't even remember a single face?

In the days that followed, the anger, hurt and humiliation built up, fuelled by the injustice of it all. I felt in no sense crushed. I had a clear conscience, a deep-seated certainty that I was not at fault in any way. But I had realised that emotions and passion would not get me justice. What they did instead was spark a desire to do something, a spark that turned into a compelling inferno of need, to reach out to other girls who had gone through a similar experience.

There was no moment or day that this realisation dawned. It was gradual, built up over time, the certainty that I would pledge every breath of my life to fight sex crimes against women and girls.

The more I thought about it, the more I started understanding the impact of sex crimes on women. And then it struck me that women and girls caught up in prostitution experience it on a daily—hourly?!—basis.

I started to consider prostitution as the worst sex crime. It is not a one-time violation, but one that continues—often for years—until the woman or girl can liberate herself. I began mulling over what these people go through. If a one-time violation can cause so much pain, what happens when it becomes an everyday affair?

My own experience opened my eyes to the haunting aftermath for the sufferers of sex crimes. I could somewhat relate to the social exclusion they were subjected to. If my experience triggered those reactions, imagine the hostility, the stigma, the ostracism that those caught up in prostitution faced.

What really got to me is how victims of all other crimes are showered with compassion and sympathy—but when it came to sex crimes, the victims receive a healthy dose of judgement, censure, suspicion and whataboutery. The argument is that a man would never commit such a crime without provocation. Its corollary is that women who question the status quo deserve punishment, that rape is a good tool to discipline them—while sending a clear message to all others who wish to walk in their footsteps.

I became obsessed with these thoughts. Every waking moment was taken up in building the skills and attributes that I'd need to help me embark on my mission. That was my sole focus. I became more and more abrasive. I had no desire to be nice to people. Being true to myself was my only priority. This also had its consequences.

There is a template of an ideal victim: one who hides their face, demonstrates fear and trauma, becomes suicidal. That is the behaviour expected of a victim. It invokes the right kind of sympathy, and will perhaps even elicit some outrage on behalf of the victim. But when a person behaves entirely contrary to people's expectations, carrying their self not only with strength and confidence but also a certain disdain for public opinion, the tide turns against them. This was how it was for me. In the eyes and gestures of those around me, the message was crystal clear: 'My god, look at that attitude! Even after all this she has not learnt her lesson.'

I focused on my present and worked to realise my future. My old preoccupations no longer interested me. Where once I'd been keen on participating in all extracurriculars in school, now I was indifferent to anything other than successfully finishing my academic requirements. I had a clear purpose and I studied hard to achieve it. Academically, I continued to be a high achiever. It was still important to me that I did not disappoint my parents, especially my father.

In the meantime, whispers about me kept going around. How my parents had given me too much freedom, how that can end up becoming a problem, how girls should be taught to behave. Suddenly, my status took a nosedive. From an all-round achiever and role model, my 'downfall' turned me into a cautionary tale. I even heard some parents tell their children not to hang out with me as I was a 'loose' character. My parents handled all this and more gracefully, never bringing it up with me.

All this while, I had been trying to present myself as hard at work. By day, my parents saw me as a bold and courageous child who didn't allow anything to deter her, who focused wholeheartedly on her education. At night, however, all the suppressed trauma, the pain and shame manifested as nightmares. Each night, I would run towards the door, crying in my sleep. Sometimes, I would even hurt myself in the process. My parents held me silently, giving me the space to speak if I wanted, never prodding me.

My trauma was my silent companion, an ever-present shadow. Crowds alarmed me, I would get panic attacks all the time. Still, I couldn't bring myself to share my turmoil. I thought that if I ever put it into words, I would never find the strength to pursue my goals. And I was determined not to allow any of this to shape my thoughts or discourage me. Some of these symptoms, which I now know are part of post-traumatic stress disorder, haunt me even after all these years. I still shudder when the shadow of a tree falls over me, sometimes a certain body odour can make me feel nauseated. But back then, I would experience this all day, and it was more intense at night-time.

I evolved my own means of healing. I truly believed—then, as now—that I am not to blame for what happened to me, and I was determined to not allow this to crush me. I felt nobody could truly understand the gamut of conflicting emotions I was going through: feeling soiled and at the same time untainted; feeling the shame and yet standing straight and proud; feeling helpless but also powerful. I decided not to disclose what happened to me to anyone I met from then on. I felt I could take care of my inner world on my own. My conversations with my gods were perhaps the only time I expressed my shame and pain, where my mask of imperturbability came off fully. Of course, it was hard, often excruciatingly so. Over time, bit by bit, my nightmares and panic attacks reduced, reassuring my parents that there was no deep damage. I realised I could depend on my own strength to heal.

No doubt the love and backing of your near and dear ones is important, but if you don't receive it, or if it isn't expressed in a way that you understand, then you must dip into your own reserves. And in my experience, unleashing the power within you is more sustainable than leaning on others. After all, that external encouragement may be gone someday, but you'll always have yourself. This was especially true for me because I did not understand my family's silent support. For the longest time, I thought that they did not support me. Today, after meeting thousands of victims, I can see how extraordinary my own family was, especially my parents. Their unconditional love and non-judgemental attitude helped me see my true strength and eventually heal.

I think life is all about choices. When I was gang-raped, I had two choices: be subdued and hide my face in shame, or be a survivor and move on. I chose the latter. While moving on, I chose to pledge my life to fighting sexual crimes. I chose to focus on making my dream real. I worked on all aspects that would make it come true. So, at the end of the day, I am simply the sum total of all the choices that I have made.

Sometimes I wonder what my life would have been like if I had not been raped. I still think I'd be in the development sector, maybe in the education sector. Much before all this happened, I had already deeply committed my life to the welfare of others and had taken baby steps towards it. This incident merely changed the field of the action.

So, can dreaming, fantasising, pledging to embark on a mission bring about change? Obviously not. What brings change is action.

4

Snapshots from My Childhood

As a child, I was allowed free rein at home. Perhaps this is because I have always been a person of action. *Doing* has always come naturally to me. So has telling others what to do. Perhaps this is because my elder sister Sumathi lived in her own world as a child. I've also always been protective of people in my care, constantly doing something for them. These tendencies were strongest when it came to my younger siblings. Though my younger sister Sujatha, whom we all called Sujji, did not fall in line, my brother Sukumaran, Suku to me, was my devoted follower. I'd make him do all the household work, threatening him with dire consequences—once, when he had a gum infection, I conveniently interpreted it to him as clear evidence of his demonic instincts. My parents noted this in quiet amusement, as my end goal was 'noble'.

I was also a driven student and brought home prizes in a range of extracurriculars—singing, dancing, elocution, poetry recitation—as well as in academics. Our house was filled with my medals, cups and trophies. Such accolades were important to me; they were proof of my hard work, a record of my progress, a testament to my worth. I was competing with my own self, not with my peers.

Everyone was proud of me—the child that neighbours and family considered a role model. But even before these accomplishments, I was special. You could even say I was born special.

I was born with a clubfoot, a rare condition—so, I was literally one in a thousand. Fortunately for me, right before my birth, my grandmother, Muthiamma, as we called her, dreamt of a beautiful baby born with something amiss. It spooked her enough to insist on accompanying my father to see me in the hospital. My father, who was stationed in Shillong at that time, a small town nestled in the mountains of north-eastern India, collected Muthiamma from Palakkad, Kerala, located in the south. They arrived in Bangalore, where my mom's family lived, on 23 May 1972, a day after my birth. As soon as she reached the hospital, Muthiamma rushed to my mother's bedside. She picked me up and unbundled the swaddle, her movements jerky, her face betraying her fears.

To everyone's utter shock, her nightmare had come true. My left foot was turned upside down. No one had noticed, not even the hospital staff. Everyone panicked, my mother began to cry. The doctors declared that I had a clubfoot, a rare congenital anomaly where the foot does not develop properly, but that it could be corrected.

Over the next two years, I was in and out of hospitals and underwent corrective surgery. I'm told I rarely cried during treatment. I became known as the child who could take pain, who was brave in spite of it. I think my love for myself began back then. Though I had small, uniquely shaped feet (they are practically rectangular, with all my toes of equal size), I could walk normally. As I grew older, I needed orthopaedic footwear that supported my midfoot. I use this kind of footwear even now, as it gets painful otherwise. But, thanks to my grandmother, I am an able-bodied person.

With all this going on, my parents' attention remained focused on me for the next few years. Perhaps it was partly this that turned Sumathi, my elder sister, cranky and difficult. Her interest in school was minimal. When I was two, I was sent to Shanti Kunj, a small day-care centre at Amberpet, Hyderabad. My father was now posted at Survey of India, Uppal, Hyderabad. My parents tell me that I delighted in learning and in sharing my knowledge with the neighbourhood children. Slate in hand, my plastered foot dragging behind me, I'd play at being teacher, boss them around and dispense advice to all.

My father's job at the Survey of India meant frequent transfers. When I was three, he was posted to Bangalore. It was here that my younger sister was born. Now we were three daughters, and my parents yearned for a son. Three years later, their yearning was fulfilled with the birth of my brother.

With Daddy travelling for as long as six months at a time on work, my mother looked after us and the house by herself. We couldn't afford any help. Nor did she have the time to pick us up or drop us off at school. So, from the very start, we were taught to be self-reliant. We travelled alone by public transport to school, which was two kilometres away. My mother was an extraordinary homemaker who didn't let the lack of resources affect us. She could turn a few wooden luggage boxes into a sofa or a diwan. She would cook small portions of two or three rice dishes, and that would be our full-course breakfast. We always had fruit after dinner, even if it was a few pieces each from a banana. The entire family would clean and tidy the house and wash the bathrooms on Sundays. Then we would troop out together for a long walk, and if it was the beginning of a month, maybe watch a movie. Life was beautiful and we were happy in our togetherness. Small joys like eating fried groundnuts as we all walked and talked still linger in my memory. Another cherished memory is of our train rides. We travelled by second-class sleepers, fighting one another for window seats, snacking on a variety of local delicacies, sipping chai from kulhads. When we didn't have reserved seats, we sat huddled near the toilet, mom ready with all her newspapers. We didn't consider any of this a hardship, we would just settle down and enjoy the journey.

When I was seven years old, my father was transferred to Bhutan on deputation to the Chhukha Hydroelectric Project. The Indo-Bhutan Central School in Tsimalakha had an entrance exam for admission to the third standard. I fared exceedingly well in all subjects, except Hindi. My father, who was a Hindi Visharad (a course conducted by Dakshina Bharat Hindi Prachar Sabha which aimed to popularise Hindi in non-Hindi speaking states), told me he was sure I could easily master it if I put my heart into it, but his disappointment was clear to me. I couldn't bear it, I had always been my father's pet. In the next few years, I not only mastered Hindi but also ensured that I won all competitions in Hindi in school and college.

When I was in the sixth standard, my father was transferred to Visakhapatnam, popularly known as Vizag. We moved with him. Sumathi was with us for two years before she went to Bangalore for a teachers' training course.

It was in Visakhapatnam, at Kendriya Vidyalaya Nausenabaugh, that I discovered the Girl Guides. I was deeply inspired by the movement, and saw in myself all qualities that made me worthy of serving others. So, I participated in all the camps, went to the jamborees and moved up the ranks to become a guide leader. Two years later, when I joined Kendriya Vidyalaya Waltair, I automatically declared myself a guide captain, as there was no guide teacher in the school. I cannot begin to describe the atrocities I committed on my siblings in the school, strictly controlling their every desire to participate in any activity.

By this time, I had realised that I wanted to work with the disadvantaged. Very close to our house was a home for special children. I'd visit it on the way from school; the coordinator, Ms Molly, allowed me to interact with the children. In the early days, I recited small poems, but slowly, I realised that they responded better to rhythm. So, I started choreographing short dances for them, basing them on the dances we were taught at school.

I had also started visiting a small slum on the sly, stopping there for one hour or more after school, teaching the dropouts in the community hall. It was my secret, and I was happy to do it quietly without anyone noticing. I did, however, feel guilty about not telling my father. To change this, I wrote an article for the Sunday magazine of the popular daily *The Hindu* about my little world. Everybody thought it was a story, I even won a small prize for it. But my father knew the truth. His silent endorsement was a great support.

Life was good, but trouble was brewing. One evening, I came home to utter chaos. Neighbours were gathered around whispering among themselves, my mother was in tears, wailing, while my father clutched a telegram. Sumathi, we learnt, had a nervous breakdown. My distraught parents had to rush to Bangalore, while my siblings stayed in my care in Vizag.

That night, I ransacked the house, but could not find the cash that my mother had mumbled about as she was leaving the house. It was the end of the month, so we were low on groceries as well. Fortunately, I had some money saved from the tuition classes I took, and that could last us a few days.

Now, when I look back, I find it strange that no one, including our immediate neighbours, bothered to check on us. At the time, I was fourteen, Sujji was eleven and Suku was eight. Perhaps it was because we rarely socialised, being content in one another's company. Of course, moving every few years did not help form lasting friendships. In any case, it became my responsibility to look after our family, and for me it was very important that I did not fail my siblings. I'd never cooked before but managed somehow. I tried to keep to the routine, making several dishes for breakfast, packing lunch and eating fruit at dinner. My siblings never complained. We made do.

In a few days, I'd spent all my savings. We were out of oil, but I had nobody to turn to. Maybe if I had talked about my situation in school, my classmates or teachers would have helped. But I couldn't overcome my pride, or my driving need to be self-reliant. With great reluctance, I went to the old lady next door and requested her for a little oil. She gave me four teaspoons of it in a small bowl. Scarcely had two days passed before she came over and requested I return that quantity, scared that her daughter-in-law might come to know she'd lent me some. Not knowing what to do, I sold my books, bought half a litre of oil and gave the lady eight teaspoons.

While such painful incidents evoke bad memories, there were also acts of kindness that I cannot forget. I hold them especially dear, because these people had no clue about what we were going through, but still reached out. They were a healing balm on our wounds. My classmate Mercy Molly Mathews, for instance, got me lunch boxes from home without my ever asking for it. There was a woman whose name I forget, she lived down our lane. One evening, I was coming back from school with a bag of vegetables, and she stopped me and asked why I was the one doing the shopping. I just told her that my parents had gone to Bangalore, so the task had fallen on me. This lady told me to wait, then went into her house. When she returned, she had a steel vessel filled with dosa batter. I was overwhelmed. My only regret is that I never kept in touch with her, for my life was going to change dramatically in the coming months.

Looking back at those twenty days, I fondly remember how the three of us worked as a team to manage the house. We lived on the first floor, and drinking water had to be fetched from the ground floor on alternate days. Suku, who was just eight years old, would help Sujji carry small vessels filled with water multiple times until we had enough. They cheerfully assisted me in every household chore. Money was the only thing that I was solely responsible for, and I made sure that my siblings never lacked anything.

Meanwhile, the doctors were slowly learning the reason for Sumathi's breakdown. From her therapy sessions, they learnt that she resented me strongly, that she believed she had been denied parental love because of me.

After my birth, my parents had left my sister in the care of my mother's elder sister, who had no children of her own. They didn't want their elder daughter neglected while they were busy ferrying me to and from hospitals while my foot was being treated. This backfired rather spectacularly.

Valliachan, which is how I referred to my uncle, was a chronic alcoholic and womaniser, and physically abused my aunt every day. My parents had given my aunt some money for my sister's expenses, but as she didn't receive any money from Valliachan, my aunt kept it for herself. Sumathi, a witness to the daily violence, was also treated badly and her studies suffered.

Once my parents understood the situation, they brought my sister home right away, but the damage had been done. Sumathi had come back to a house full of people where I was the centre of attention. On my part, I treated her with extra affection to make up for the neglect. It was natural for her to reject this patronising attitude, but my parents saw me as the good one. It was the same at school. I was elected as an office-bearer and was very popular among the teachers. Constant comparisons were inevitable. Stifled and crushed, Sumathi resented me.

After she completed her tenth standard, Sumathi had wished to pursue a teacher's training course. As Bangalore had the closest reputed teacher's training institute, my parents were forced to send Sumathi back to my aunt's house, exposing her once again to the same toxic environment. This was what had triggered a nervous breakdown.

The doctors told my parents to reflect on their parenting, asking them to pay more attention to my sister and not overly focus their attention on me. Thus started a new phase in my life. Now my accomplishments, though definitely acknowledged, were never celebrated. Daddy had told me what had transpired, so I ensured that Sumathi was adequately pampered and supported. I became the de facto elder sister, tutoring her, even taking her for haircuts and paying for them with my pocket money.

There were times when this new set-up upset me, especially when I had to receive prizes alone and no one from the family accompanied me. Fortunately, I found the strength to never let that fester into resentment. Years later, when all my siblings were settled, I made it a point to invite my parents for every award function—a small compensation for the years I had lost earlier!

This experience made a deep impression on me. In the running of Prajwala, we take care never to pay undue attention to any one child lest others begin to resent them.

5

Sadbhavana

Because of Sumathi's situation, Daddy opted for a transfer to Bangalore. I could not move with them as I was in the tenth standard and had to sit for the crucial board exams. I stayed back in Vizag in the care of my father's colleague Vishwanathan Uncle and his wife; they took care of me for four months until I completed my board exams. I think that that four-month break was good for the family. Sumathi recovered and got back to completing her teacher's training. At fifteen, I too had that time to heal on my own and carve out my future goals.

I chose to complete my eleventh and twelfth standard in Junior College and not in Kendriya Vidyalaya. By this time, I was also haunted by the ghosts of my past and needed a new setting to revive myself. St Anne's Junior College gave me the perfect opportunity to explore my thoughts until they slowly came together as doable actions and thereafter shaped my mission.

After finishing college, I spent some time considering my options. Medicine and engineering were the obvious choices, but they didn't appeal to me; I wanted to take up something that dealt directly with society. In the end, I chose environmental science. I decided against a bachelor's degree in social work; the idea was to understand multiple subjects before I took up a narrow specialisation.

Back then, the only college in Bangalore that offered environmental science was St Joseph's College of Arts and Science. Admission was a simple enough affair. I had the marks needed, and I was able to cover the fees with a scholarship and some savings from my part-time job as a teacher.

St Joseph's was a culture shock. There were students from all backgrounds—the uber rich and the middle and lower classes. I couldn't believe my ears when a classmate mentioned that she'd come directly from a horse-riding class. I didn't even know such a thing existed! My classmates also largely spoke in English. While I could read and write without a problem, I wasn't very confident while speaking the language. I adjusted soon enough to all of this by sticking mostly with Hindi-speaking students. That I loved my course helped greatly. I'd still get panic attacks, but I'd pass them off as an illness; I didn't want to share my past with my classmates or teachers.

There was another area of my life that troubled me, especially because it was so important to me. My 'extracurricular activities' with the women in prostitution had slowed down quite a bit. My relationship with the women of Majestic had taken off after the rescue of the young girl when I was still in Junior College. After that, I'd meet them regularly and help them in whichever way I could. Much of this involved helping them enrol their children in residential schools. But I was now busy with my final exams, college entrance exams and admissions for my undergraduate course. I continued to stay in touch with a few women, but it wasn't a regular affair. I had no plan, knowledge or skills, so I was wary of overpromising and underdelivering. This was about to change.

My college classmates Sandeep and Satchidanand introduced me to a few of our seniors who wanted to set up a community development initiative in the village of Mudalodu in Gauribidanur taluka, eighty kilometres from Bangalore. The village was being overseen by Dr Vasudev, founder of the Bharat Health Mission Trust and a family friend of one of my seniors, Srinivas. Learning to run a non-profit organisation and working on developmental activities with a small group of like-minded people was right up my alley.

And that's how I came to be a founding member of Sadbhavana, a society for rural development. I was the only woman among six men. We operated on goodwill: our office was a spare room in Satchidanand's house, and we used Dr Vasudev's ambulance to reach Mudalodu. We would go on Saturday and return on Sunday. My parents, in spite of what had happened in the past, had no objection as all the others were from very respectable families, and for once, I was doing something as a part of a group, not as an individual.

The extraordinary beauty of my family was they never created an obstacle in anything that I wanted to do, in spite of my past experiences. My father, especially, had ensured that my decisions would be respected. In many ways he also subtly taught me to take responsibility for my choices. Immersed in my own world, I did not consider any of this as a great blessing back then. It is only now that I see the amazing grace with which my siblings and I were bestowed. I do not remember any instance in our life when we were discouraged or questioned about our choice of education, career or even life partner.

Being part of Sadbhavana allowed me to understand the power dynamics at work in a village. At the same time, I experienced the power of collective action.

We didn't really do any great development work in Mudalodu. The Bharat Health Mission Trust was taking care of the health needs of the villagers. Sandeep and the others were trying to organise the youth, while I focused on women and children. It was a delight to connect with the adolescent girls, to talk to them about literacy, menstrual hygiene, economic empowerment and how to deal with violence.

I even helped organise a ten-day camp at a school in Mudalodu through St Joseph's Centre for Social Concern. Father Ambrose Pinto, who was in charge of this unit, had just hired an assistant, Shoba Veigas, who had completed her master's in social work (MSW) from Roshni Nilaya. It was the first time I had met an MSW student. Shoba and I hit it off right away, so working out the details of the camp with her was a smooth process. We had fifteen students sign up for the camp. In the ten days we were there, we completely transformed the school, constructed a playground and conducted a theatre workshop for the children.

Sadbhavana also taught me a few good lessons that would come in handy when I started Prajwala. The foremost of these was to cut your coat according to your cloth—particularly in financial matters. Unfortunately, I learnt this the hard way. We'd organised a national youth conference with a ministry. While I can't recall any details about the conference itself, the humiliation of being unable to reimburse the participants' travel expenses several weeks after the conference stings even today. However, our hands were tied: Sadbhavana had no money of its own and had to wait until the ministry disbursed the money. I ended up asking my father for a loan, promising a high interest, handing it to the organisation under someone else's name, unwilling to bring my family into it. I was never able to return the money to my father—though it was less than Rs 15,000, it was a huge amount for a family that lived on one person's salary.

Sadbhavana continued after this misadventure for some time, but not very actively. For me, Sandeep's death changed things. He had been one of the sweetest people I knew, soft-spoken with a droll sense of humour, a wonderful friend, a great singer. We enjoyed working together. I felt his absence keenly. I kept wondering what had made life so unbearable for him that he'd taken his own life. Eventually, Sadbhavana organically dissolved. As time passed, I lost touch with these friends. Perhaps it is true some friends come for a reason, some others for a season and only a small few for a lifetime.

College life was about classes, participating in Hindi competitions, attending youth festivals, standing for college elections and losing miserably, making enemies of one's own classmates and being absorbed in Sadbhavana the rest of the time.

I did make some lifelong friends in college though. Shoba Veigas was one of them. By this time, I had decided to pursue my master's in psychiatric social work, but I wanted to study somewhere that gave me more than academic understanding, that helped me understand the ground realities. It was Shoba who suggested Roshni Nilaya, located in Mangalore, as an option.

While it sounded just right for me, I wanted to go see it for myself. Shoba had arranged for me to stay at her friend's place. The eight-hour bus journey to Mangalore was totally worth it. Roshni Nilaya was all that I had dreamt of, and more. I'd fallen in love with the campus. I got back excited, impatient to apply.

I went to the interview armed with a recommendation letter from Father Ambrose Pinto, as per Shoba's suggestion. I'd had a sumptuous breakfast courtesy D'Costa Uncle, the father of a college junior. I'd turned up at his doorstep assured of a welcome—which

I did get, once Uncle learnt that his son had promised me room at their place but neglected to inform his father about the whole plan!

With all this going on, I'd had no time to dwell on the interview. But as I walked towards the building, the nervousness bubbled in my stomach. I don't remember the questions; I suppose I must've answered adequately enough. Then, I handed over the letter from Father Ambrose Pinto to the principal, Philomena D'Souza. She opened the envelope, unfolded the paper and went through the recommendation. Then, raising her gaze, she asked, 'Tell me, what do you think of nepotism?'

I was stumped. I'd never heard that word before. My English was still limited in terms of vocabulary. I didn't understand the question at all. I decided to hazard a guess, unwilling to appear 'less than' in English. But the minute I said, 'I really don't mind it,' I realised it was the wrong response.

D'Souza's face stilled, some of the others looked disapproving. One lady actually shook her head in dismay. They asked me to leave. As I made my way to the door, I knew I'd messed things up. I decided to take one last step—damage control.

I turned around, walked back to the centre of the room while the others looked, most of them confused. I took a deep breath in and said, in a bold, clear voice, 'You won't regret it if you give me admission.' With that, I left.

On the way back home, I brooded. I was surely doomed—I'd looked up the meaning of nepotism. So, when I received a letter from Roshni Nilaya sometime later, I opened it with dread.

I read that letter twice just to make sure I wasn't imagining things. Roshni Nilaya, school of social work, welcomed me as a student!

6

The House of Light

A new chapter in my life had begun. I was starting work in a field I had always yearned to be part of. I was determined to work hard, to listen, learn, to do. Sow the seeds, guard my crops steadfastly, reap the harvest, so to speak.

I knew that I wanted to rent a room, be independent. My father accompanied me for the admission, to get to know the faculty and to help me with my accommodation.

When Philomena D'Souza, the principal, learnt of my plans, she questioned me to make sure I knew what I was getting myself into, the responsibilities I would have to shoulder. Then she referred me to the Álvarezes, a couple who lived close to campus and were willing to rent a portion of their house. We visited their house, an old Portuguese structure with a lovely garden, and learnt that Mrs Álvarez was a nurse, that the couple didn't socialise much and that they wanted to let out a small outhouse on their property. My father liked the house and the outhouse, and thought the family appeared safe. Mangalore had been exposed to a lot of Portuguese influence, and most old houses had spacious porticos with lots of fruit trees. One could easily fall in love with the place. The house owners, on their part, liked that my father was calm and exuded quiet grace. I suppose it matched their own personality. They agreed to let me rent the outhouse.

The reason I wanted to live off-campus was to have the freedom to work part-time, to polish my spoken English and resume my mission. Since that awful interview, it had become a priority to learn English. To my mind, life in a hostel was full of rules and restrictions, leaving little scope for outside activities. By this time, I had fallen out of touch with all the women in prostitution that I knew, and I was keen to find ways to understand prostitution better in Mangalore. I knew living in a hostel would not allow me much freedom or mobility.

The first six months in Roshni Nilaya were full of deep reflection and inner silence. I had reached my learning destination, and I was soaking in every bit of knowledge that my teachers imparted. It also made me introspect. I could compare what I was learning with my past experiences in development work. The mistakes I had made, individually and as part of Sadbhavana, became clearer. This inner churning completely absorbed me, leaving little or no time to make friends in the first few months. I would spend a significant part of the day reflecting on and assimilating the knowledge I was gaining. Another reason I didn't socialise much was to hide my lack of proficiency in English. My father used to always say, 'The more you speak, the more you betray!'

I found a part-time job as a tutor. Once I got home, I'd turn on the radio while cooking, especially the English news, and practise my English. If they ever heard me, the Álvarezes must have thought I was mad, talking to myself. Soon enough, I realised that this wouldn't work out—I didn't have the time or energy to work, cook and pursue my course.

Roshni Nilaya, true to its name, had become a place of worship and enlightenment for me. With each class, I learnt something truly new, opening my eyes to fresh perspectives on social change and transformation. Rita Norohna, Hilda Rayappan, Madhav Rao and Ramila Shekhar, my teachers as well as the principal, were slowly addressing all the questions I had been carrying for years. I don't think they understood what a monumental impact they had on my life.

Roshni Nilaya changed the way I connected with people. D'Souza, with whom I connected at the level of soul, became my greatest confidante. She listened to all my escapades with such interest that I felt compelled to seek her out and share my day with her. Ramila Shekhar was more like an elder sister, motivating and pushing me to consider other perspectives. In the second semester, I also made some lasting friends among my classmates, who all came from different backgrounds. Some had taken their religious vows and had good prior experience, while others had come straight out of college. But what all of us shared was a common vision to make the world a better place.

Ours was a six-day workweek, three days each of theory and field work. This schedule allowed us to apply what we learnt in the classroom. We gained a lived understanding of what constituted social change, the rationale of strategic planning and how to design a results-based programme, and we applied that in our field placement every week.

In my first year, I was placed in a Muslim community in the port of Bandar. The impoverished community had multiple problems—unemployment, illiteracy and high rates of domestic violence. The organisation I was placed with worked with women and girls and assigned me several cases per week. My knowledge of Hindi, Kannada and Malayalam really helped. These practicals taught us valuable lessons we'd need in the real world. I learnt to plan, to identify problems and course correct, and to shape my learnings into the programme to ensure lasting change. I learnt to build professional relationships and to attach myself to the problem, not the person.

This last bit was a real challenge—one that I struggle with even today. In 1992, many parts of the country witnessed communal tension as a reaction to the Babri Masjid demolition. This was true of Mangalore as well. I was working with the Muslim community during those turbulent times, and I remember none of them made me feel like an outsider and always found ways to protect me and ensure my safe passage to college. How could I not get attached to the people?

These experiences strengthened my commitment to the course. I decided to drop my part-time job and my English practice and moved to the college hostel. It was mostly a smart decision, but financial viability became a big question. I had to ask my father for money a few times, which he gladly gave. Shoba too came to my rescue, giving me small amounts of money for my hostel fees, and I also took up assignments on holidays as a tourist guide for cruises that landed in Mangalore.

In my first year, the students of Roshni Nilaya embarked on a massive AIDS-awareness campaign in Mangalore through street plays. Performing those street plays brought us together. This was perhaps the first time I felt a sense of camaraderie and unconditional acceptance, of working as a part of a team with a clear vision. It remains one of my most cherished memories from that time.

In my second year, I was placed in the psychiatric ward of Wenlock District Hospital and in the gynaecology ward of Lady Goschen Hospital. I met people with mental health conditions as well as one of the first AIDS patients in the country. My resolve to work towards the care and protection of HIV/AIDS patients started then. I even played a major role in a theatre production about HIV directed by Vimala Lobo, a well-known theatre enthusiast in Mangalore.

Working with people from different walks of life—students, teachers, patients and their families, my outreach communities—for the first time, I realised that I didn't need to compartmentalise different facets of my personality, keep them in different silos. In the large universe of social change and social transformation, everything could converge. For the last few years, I had been living different lives with different people. Now I could finally be myself, completely, in every moment of life. I could apply all my talents, be it my theatre skills, the poet and the writer in me, the singer and the dancer in me and my organisational abilities to one singular purpose: social change. It was the most divine experience to live without constantly compartmentalising.

In my last semester, we had to work on our dissertation. Mine, of course, was on prostitution and I decided to do it in Bangalore. After all, that was where I'd started, and it was the area I wanted to work in.

A classmate of mine, Sophia Lewis, joined me to study the awareness women in prostitution had about HIV/AIDS. She came for fieldwork despite her parents' disapproval. My own family never got to know what I was up to. We took official permissions and went to the state home, a government-managed protective residence that housed women who were arrested for prostitution. Sophia got most of her data here. She came twice or thrice with me to the field, but couldn't continue as she found it rather daunting. But for me, the experience was quite the opposite: I felt like I was among friends. I met Laxmi, Lalita and all the other women in Majestic. Through Laxmi, I also met bar dancers and women who prostituted in big hotels. Prostitution could be many things and done in many ways, I realised. I decided to write my thesis on the socio-economic profile of women in prostitution: the causal factors that lead to it, the working conditions, its financial aspects and what these women thought about leaving prostitution.

With my training in social work, I could now plan and carry out better interventions, and completing a scientific study gave me a lot of new insights. It was years later, after I had worked closely with hundreds of victims and survivors, that I realised how research studies on prostitution can be very limiting, and perhaps misleading as well, since it is done (mostly) by researchers who have no prior working knowledge of the situation and depend on tools to gather and interpret data in a given context, which may not reflect the true facts. While research is possible with empirical data in any setting, when it comes to traumatised individuals living with complex realities, a prior understanding of the target group has great relevance. In a context like prostitution, the researcher's data will depend on where their informers are located at the time of research. For example, if a woman has been housed in a government home, she will speak of some realities, or if she is part of a group on the field which favours rights for 'sex workers', her story will be different from another who has exited prostitution and identifies as a trafficked survivor.

Most research is conducted in a limited frame of time. This means the researcher will get only a superficial response, one that may be empirically true, but absolutely false in the real sense. This is especially the case in prostitution, as it involves traumatised souls who will bare only a speck of their lives to a researcher. It is foolish to consider the little information they reveal as an absolute truth and build theories around it. That is what life has taught me. But it would take me years to confront this and many other uncomfortable truths. Having said that, my college thesis did give me some deep insights that would help my work in the future and serve as a point of reference from which I could review a situation and gauge the pitfalls I might face.

The last component of my postgraduation was the block placement. This is akin to a six-week internship in any organisation. My classmate and friend Rashma Alva wanted to go to Rajasthan. There were multiple reasons for her decision, but chief among them was to gain exposure in a northern state in India. I liked the idea, and after my emotionally depleting research, I felt it would give me the right kind of break. We were placed at the Rajasthan University Women's Association, Jaipur. This was my first exposure to a safe home for women and girls in difficult circumstances. For the first time, I met many severely traumatised young girls in the same place and had the opportunity to closely engage with them.

One incident had a long-lasting impact on my mind. It was about 11 a.m. when a woman was referred to us by Sawai Man Singh Hospital for a short stay. The woman was badly bruised and what caught my attention was the six-month-old baby in her arms whose lower lip had six or more stiches. The woman told us that her husband had cheated on her and was in an illicit relationship with another woman.

In Rajasthan, like in many other states, this is a socially legitimate practice called 'natha'. The man, enraged at his actions being questioned by his wife, beat her and also threw their six-month-old child at a wall. The child's upper teeth had plunged into his lower lip, tearing it open completely.

I was writing down the case notes. Completely enraged, I advised the woman to file a complaint against her husband. The case worker in the organisation also endorsed my suggestion. The complaint process turned out to be a complicated affair. The woman was new to Jaipur and had arrived there only to confront her husband who had shacked up with the other woman. She could not clearly tell us where exactly the incident had occurred. The entire day went in tracing the right police station to file the complaint. Finally, at 6.30 p.m., we were able to do so.

The inspector was cooperative, albeit a little cynical. To his credit, he did not discourage us and promised to file the complaint as soon as the husband was located. After an hour or so, the man was brought to the station. Perhaps because I had been rather vocal in pushing for a complaint, the inspector looked at me twice before he started the interrogation. Things were going smoothly when suddenly, in the middle of questioning, the inspector delivered a tight slap to the man's face.

That action changed everything. The wife, who had been sitting next to me on the bench, just tossed her child to the side and rushed to the inspector. Kneeling at his feet, she begged him to stop hitting her husband. I was totally unprepared for such a reaction. When I tried to pull her back, she shrugged me off, her whole attention on her 'poor' spouse.

For one whole day, we had wandered from station to station trying to file a complaint against the man. And now, this woman was pleading that the source of her misery be spared from hurt. The incident opened my eyes to how deeply ingrained patriarchy is in the system, how it plays havoc with the lives of women. In later years, I would see many such instances where patriarchal values were the main obstacle not only in reporting a crime but also, when it came to victims of sex trafficking, in actually normalising the exploitation. We stood like mute spectators as the woman happily left with her abusive husband, the child in her arms.

With the block placement completed, I had fulfilled all the requirements for my master's degree. I had spent these two years fully absorbed in my studies. The gold medal I received at my graduation ceremony was proof of my hard work. Those two years of intense learning were also among the most spiritually satisfying phases in my life. I had been working towards my vocation—I had grown as a person, as a researcher and as a field worker. It had sharpened my hunger for social change and honed my skills and capacity to effect it. I was ready to go out into the real world, a qualified professional. I had laid, I believed, a strong foundation to become a social entrepreneur.

7

The Development Sector

What I needed now was a job in the development sector, I told myself on the way home. I shoved two bags stuffed with all that I had amassed over the last two years under the bus seat, settled in for the journey, and spent the whole ride home, eight hours of it, planning my next steps. I considered all the rungs I'd need to climb to reach the end goal—my own organisation.

I had a fairly objective view of my own skills. The passion needed, I had in spades, but you need more than that to start an independent initiative. Since it was a necessary component of the course, I had acquired some experience working in the field. I'd had long field placements, mostly in hospitals, and had completed my month-long block placement in Jaipur. But I still lacked the knowledge and skills to set out on my own. So, for the moment, I decided to stay away from the women in prostitution that I knew. I didn't want to make them empty promises. Either I would go to them with a plan, or not at all.

Besides, I lacked funds. As a family, we did not have any great financial resources; my father was the sole breadwinner. In any case, I had always been reluctant about accepting money from my family, and I was already heavily indebted to Shoba for her support, financial and otherwise, during my master's. While she had not asked for a paisa, it weighed heavily on my mind. Of course I was not the only beneficiary of her generosity. Shoba was born with generosity in her spirit, and she gave away whatever she had without any thought for her own comfort.

Considering all these factors, a job made the most sense. And I got one through my friend Geeta Menon, an activist with a left-leaning ideology. Geeta made me feel extremely comfortable almost from the very moment we met. Our friendship was organic and has sustained for over three decades now. Like in any relationship, there are some things that we cannot agree on. Chief among these has been leftist ideology. Geeta would gift me books by Marx and Engels and, honest to god, I tried to read them, but most of it just went over my head. My English had improved vastly by then, so I did get the gist. But I quickly realised that the ideology was not for me. Not wishing to disappoint Geeta, I kept accepting the books she'd gift me. They're still part of my library. My later experiences with the right-wing would show me that I didn't agree with that philosophy either. All in all, I prefer to respond to humanitarian needs with my own moral compass. I suppose you could say being a humanist is what I most identify with.

While the books unnerved me, Geeta herself did not. I related to all that she'd talk about. At that time, my own understanding of caste and class was just evolving, and I was immediately able to connect her ideas on those topics with what I already knew about prostitution. As I'd learnt while working on my thesis, most of the women in prostitution belonged to the lower castes or were minorities.

Geeta, who headed the Stree Jagruti Samiti, an organisation that worked with domestic workers, was well connected in Bangalore to all the non-profit organisations. That's how she helped me land my first job as a paid intern at Samvada, an amazing organisation that worked with students to mould their understanding about the development sector. At that time, Samvada's office was located in a flat in Wilson Garden. Three people managed the organisation: Anita Ganesh, the founder, Arun Khotenkar and Lucy Kumar. Initially, I was a glorified office assistant. Most days, I cooked for the team or read in the library. Gradually, I began to interact with the students who dropped by. Samvada also had a fellowship programme for activists working in different people's movements. It was a treat to meet them and learn about their work.

I was given a chance to visit several people's movements. I went to the backwaters of Kerala, where activists like Father Thomas Kocherry and the Samvada Fellows were trying to bring the government's attention to the damage caused by some of the larger projects related to prawn aquaculture and the impact of coastal bans on the fishing community.

It was here that I learnt the impact government policies could have on the lives of people. Any structural adjustment plan undoubtedly benefited some, but it also harmed many others. For instance, a new policy can give big industries free access to the market without considering the lives and livelihoods of millions of smaller workers. The coastal ban restricted the fishing community from deep-sea fishing but allowed bull-trawlers of big, international companies access. These trawlers took away most of the fish, leaving nothing for fishermen on the coast. Similarly, prawn aquaculture on paddy farms by big companies destroyed the soil with salinity, making it completely impossible for farmers to grow any crops in the next two decades. I do not feel, at any point, that the activists are against progress, but their agenda of equitable development is one that is easily misinterpreted. Many movements, I believe, suffer from this problem. Further, activists tend to focus on the problems rather than on a balanced resolution, so they end up looking like adversaries of the state. During this trip, I met many agitating fishing communities who were convinced that the government had no ears at all, and felt compelled to react in a 'do or die' mode. The government, on the other hand, appeared to believe that its knowledge is complete, and therefore, saw any other perspective as working against it.

My work in Saharanpur in Uttar Pradesh with the Gujjar movement gave me new insights into the lives of nomadic communities. Gujjars are cattle-herding tribal nomads who live in the Shivalik ranges of Saharanpur during winter and travel during summer to Jammu with their cattle.

The organisation that I visited was fighting for the basic rights of the Gujjars. The forest department had made life difficult for them by issuing new rules regarding permits necessary to enter the forest, which restricted their natural nomadic movements. It impacted their livelihood by limiting their basic human rights and entitlements, and barring their access to minor forest produce. Their livestock, a special breed of buffaloes, required cold climates to survive and they usually grazed in the forests. The Gujjars were now battling an identity crisis since they were being categorised as encroachers and barred from entering the forest.

When I began working with them, I was taken aback by the fact that the entire community was illiterate, and wondered why the government hadn't arranged access to mobile schools on the lines of Kendriya Vidyalayas, where all branches follow the same curriculum. This way their children would have access to education even when they travelled. But what bothered me almost as much as the lack of access to education was the attempt by the government—and society at large—to alter the very nature of the community, pressing them into settling down in one place. For Gujjars, herding cattle was a sustainable means of livelihood. If they had access to education, perhaps they could come up with new, innovative techniques regarding herding. It also bothered me that forest officials could think that the tribal community would destroy the forests. The government had banned the sourcing of minor forest produce—fibre, fodder, food, medicinal plants, non-timber firewood, honey, wax, lac, herbs, roots and tubers—by these communities, disrupting their daily sustenance. How can communities who have been custodians of our forests for centuries damage them?

From my time with the Gujjars, I could see how they nurtured the forests, the deep respect they had for nature. In fact, if anybody has the potential to destroy forests, it is those who live in settlements—villages, towns, cities—or the government. The former has no innate respect for forests and the latter often prioritises major development projects that benefit a significant population of people in the short term, at the cost of harming a larger group that is already impoverished and marginalised. In the long run, this usually backfires on everyone, even those who benefited in the beginning. A good example is Joshimath, Uttarakhand. It is a cautionary tale of how unplanned construction and the obstruction of the natural flow of water, along with hydel power activities, have contributed to increased landslides, endangering the lives of all residents.

My stay with the Gujjars was also personally very satisfying. The families were very loving and their hospitality was heart-warming. They fed me simple but very tasty food. I still remember the taste of the hot rotis served directly from the fire, and the spinach curry they made when they learnt I was vegetarian, serving it with raw onion on the side. No other spinach curry has ever come close to that. Truly, some flavours can never be replicated, like this one, or Muthiamma's chammanthi, a kind of chutney we make in Kerala that is ground on an ammikal, or a stone mortar.

I also tried beedis for the first time with them. While I didn't take to the smell or taste, I loved holding them. It gave me a thrill to clutch it between thumb and index, butt turned inwards. It was the exact opposite of smoking a cigarette. I smoked as many beedis as I could—the cold weather a silent support to my new pastime—and I always kept one or two on me. In fact, when I visited home, I'd fully forgotten about the beedis, so it came as a shock to my parents when they found a few in my pockets. Like with all other jolts in life, they took it rather calmly, waiting to see if I used them. Once they saw that I didn't, they were reassured.

By this time, my siblings were established in their own paths. Sumathi was married and had a child. Sujji and Suku were in high school.

I continued to selectively share what I learnt on my travels. Other than some superficial stories that only my parents listened to, I didn't disclose much about the political understanding I was gaining. My parents were simple folk who weren't greatly concerned about such things. Daddy, an avid radio listener, was aware of all current issues, but had no strong opinions about them. His ears were mostly tuned to gathering news about increments in the dearness allowance or a change in salary scale by the government. At heart, his political affiliation was to the Congress. I remember him crying when Indira Gandhi was assassinated. Both Daddy and I sat the entire afternoon listening to the funeral relay on the radio.

For someone fresh out of college, Samvada was perhaps the best sort of exposure to social work and the people in it. I was gaining valuable knowledge every day that would help in the coming years. But I couldn't appreciate it then. While I really enjoyed my outreach trips, being in the office was another matter. I was highly uncomfortable around Anitha and Lucy, and though I couldn't tell you why, I felt constantly lacking around them. When my alma mater St Joseph's invited me to speak to the sociology class, Anita and Lucy also came along. I noticed them writing furiously while I spoke. I wondered what they were doing—after all, nothing I said would have been new to them.

I learnt soon enough. After we got back to office, the two asked to talk to me. They analysed every aspect of my talk, from the content to my diction to my body language. The incident left me thoroughly shaken and angry. I realise now that they were genuinely trying to help me improve my work. But blinded by my own insecurities, I developed a strong aversion to them.

The greatest exposure Samvada gave me was a workshop conducted by Sakshi in Kasauli, Himachal Pradesh. Sakshi, India's first women's violence and crisis centre, was established in Delhi in 1992. This workshop on child sexual abuse was also the first of its kind in India. The founders, Jasjit Purewal and Naina Kapur, were facilitating it. We were around fifteen women in the workshop. None of us actually spoke about our experiences, but bit by bit, there was a silent acknowledgement by everyone of the world of pain and shame that we had endured. Whether at the hands of a 'safe' family member or a stranger, all of us had experienced being violated. The workshop was the most stimulating healing space I had ever experienced.

The workshop reassured me that I had no reason to be ashamed, that I was not at fault for what had happened to me. Even though I had always believed that intellectually, I had never managed to shake off the guilt and self-loathing that came with the trauma of the sexual assault. The workshop struck at the foundations of the protective walls I'd built around myself over the years. My next steps in personal healing had started.

It was also a novelty for me to understand sex and sexuality and learn about gender and sexual orientation—I had never known that one could be sexually attracted to others of the same sex. Further, I came to understand patriarchy and power dynamics in gender-based violence, especially in sex crimes. It helped me understand better the mindset of that victim of domestic violence whom I met in Jaipur. All of these ideas were very interesting to me. While I loathed ideological books, I was open to reading as much as possible about these aspects of human beings. I learnt about the impact of pornography on men, and the ways in which that could shape how a man views the body of a woman or child.

When I returned from the workshop, I was more than ready to leave Samvada. My discomfort with Anita and Lucy apart, I was restless. By then I had completed a study, with help from student volunteers, that looked at the impact of pawn brokers on the lives of slum women. This meant I had started contributing to Samvada's body of knowledge. Once the six months of my internship were over, it was time to renew my contract and take me on as an employee, but I politely declined.

Around this time, I met Dr Subha K. from the Institute of Social Sciences (ISS), a premier institution for research and training on local governance, gender equity, human rights and other socio-cultural issues. She offered me a small research project titled 'Women, Violence and Religious Fundamentalism'. ISS was headquartered in Delhi, and Subha was heading the Bangalore office. This was my ticket to leave Samvada. While I did depart eagerly, I want to place on record that every moment of those six months was worth the experience and had a lasting impact on my life and work.

8

Marriage and Celibacy

Most ponder over the question of marriage at various points in life. For me, this was after I returned from my post-graduation. My parents hadn't brought it up yet, but I felt compelled to let them know that I was not interested in marriage.

The way I saw it, marriage may have its benefits, but it also comes with responsibilities and adjustments. I was not ready for those. Does this mean I was not attracted to the opposite sex? Was I put off by men entirely? That was not the case. Fortunately for me, my father had a huge influence over me. Had it not been for him, I might have sworn off all male company. But his quiet support and encouragement had given me the strength I needed at the time while also reassuring me that, truly, not all men are abusers. Admittedly, I had my fair share of infatuations and attractions growing up, but at that point of time, I was too preoccupied with trying to understand the dark world of sexual exploitation. I wanted to be free to focus on my larger mission, to work with women in prostitution.

At Roshni Nilaya, there had been many Catholics who were from different orders, and were ordained as brothers and sisters. There was also a woman from a secular order—she had taken all her vows as a nun but was not obliged to wear a habit. This identity appealed to me. I had always been spiritually inclined and had a deep faith in my family deities. But Hinduism didn't seem to have anything along those lines. Hindu sects were structured units with rules concerning dress code, prayer practices and life choices. My parents themselves followed the Brahma Kumaris, and every Thursday, my dad's colleague Ranga

Rao Uncle, who was a Brahma Kumar, would lead a small group in meditation at our house. I studied these practices too. But I found organised spiritual practices to be restrictive and claustrophobic. I wished to experience divinity through my mission, not by wearing a robe or performing rituals. My search led me to a small, loosely threaded group who called themselves Pratidhwani, which means echo. The members were professionals who were committed to listening to the call of their souls. After a few interactions, I decided to join the group.

I chose my own vows, and one fine day, I started wearing a rudraksha mala, prayer beads usually associated with Shiva in Hinduism and with religions like Buddhism, Jainism and Sikhism. Only my close friends and my family knew. I usually wore it under my clothes, a private symbol of my decision to live a spiritual, celibate life without marriage. In essence, I was self-proclaimed Hindu nun. My family got the message. And if they were unhappy or opposed to it, they did not say anything. The only person to react was Muthiamma, who had a knowing smile when she heard the news.

It is with this clear personal identity that I started my micro-research project, 'Women, Violence and Religious Fundamentalism' for the ISS. This research took me to various religion-affiliated groups in Karnataka and Maharashtra. I got to interact with the Rashtriya Swayamsevak Sangh (RSS) and the Durga Vahinis of Maharashtra, right-wing Hindu nationalist organisations, and engaged directly with their members. I also used my contacts to meet with Muslim organisations. My primary aim was to understand the information and narrative that women in such clusters received. What was clear was that, across all groups, there were subtle efforts to polarise the community. All parties felt the presence of an enemy and the need to be alert and suspicious. I could very well imagine how this kind of indoctrination could be used to easily provoke people to violence if the situation arose. After all, religion is a very tricky matter. It can persuade the sanest person to do the most unreasonable things. Over the course of my research, I came to understand religion as a tool which can be used to persuade people to commit horrors; that people could be made to believe, genuinely, that violence was the only answer to safeguard the community.

My report was candid and sharp, and I must say the ISS did not like it very much. Understandably so, as these matters are delicate and volatile. Any research should be done with care, ensuring a balanced viewpoint lest it cause more harm than good. I think Subha rewrote it in the end. In any case, I never got to see the final document.

As soon as I finished this assignment, I got a field-based job as coordinator at Janodaya. Founded by Santosh Vaz, Janodaya conducted community development activities in the urban slums and villages around Bangalore. It was a purely welfare organisation and did not really align itself with a specific ideology. Janodaya undertook a lot of livelihood projects for the poor and ran a crisis intervention centre for domestic violence as well as a small shelter. The programmes were linked to government projects, and their quality depended largely on the funds received. Vaz used her wealth of connections to keep the projects going. My role was that of a programme coordinator who worked with a large team involved in various interventions.

This was the first time I had people working under me, looking to me for guidance and directions. I quickly realised that leadership came naturally to me, but team-building was a different ball game. My first few weeks absorbing the staff dynamics and resolving interpersonal issues were a nightmare. I had never before seen people fight for power and position. Over the next few months, I figured out how to manage and lead my team.

During this time, I also began to interact with other groups, mostly women's groups, in Bangalore. Geeta also connected me to groups working with domestic workers. I began to understand community-based interventions in education, vocational training and livelihood generation. This was the time that I began to be attracted to the ongoing women's rights campaigns. I keenly observed the anti-arrack movement, where women activists physically shut down all toddy shops and succeeded in implementing prohibition in Andhra Pradesh.

My stint at Janodaya and interaction with these movements gave me the confidence to go back to the women in Majestic. By this time, I truly believed that 'exiting' their way of life was a possibility. This was in 1996. I slowly began to get back in touch with the women, confident that the rural and urban livelihood projects that Janodaya ran for the poor could be easily adapted for them.

However, there had been a few changes in the six years that had passed. There was a noticeable increase in the number of very young women on the streets and few familiar faces. Another very apparent change were the several non-profit organisations that had launched targeted HIV/AIDS interventions. They were teaching women in prostitution about behaviour change and condom usage. Back then, my friend Laxmi had controlled the streets. Now she was putting those formidable managerial skills to other uses: she'd become a peer educator and was on the payroll of an NGO. She even had an identity card.

Despite the years, Laxmi's love and affection for me hadn't fizzled out. Reconnecting with her and the new set of women on the street was fun, and a sort of homecoming. I still felt that old sense of kinship with them. What's more, spending time with them revealed to me a totally new pattern—something I would have never imagined, something which would steer my life in a different direction in the coming months.

9

A Paper Tiger

As I spent more time with Laxmi and other women at Majestic, I noticed some new, worrying patterns. More lodges had come up in the area, and many girls from across the country were being continuously brought in. This was mid-1996. The chief minister at that time, a flamboyant man, had openly proclaimed his love for wine and women. I wondered if it was his attitude that had encouraged the sudden spurt in the industry.

I did not have to wonder for long. The Miss World Pageant was set to be held in Bangalore. Lakhs of tourists were supposed to land in the city for the twenty-day event which would end on 23 November. The lodges and the women inhabiting them had risen in anticipation of the flood of tourists at the time—and the corresponding increase in demand for paid sexual services.

This was the first time I saw how prostitution was directly connected to tourism and other industries and events. The visible presence of very young girls was troubling. While I collected the data on the streets on these newer trends, anti-pageant protests broke out in Bangalore with activists across all ideologies joining in for their own reasons. Right-wing activists felt it was against Indian culture, the left felt it was an onslaught of multinational companies. Feminist groups, women's groups, farmer's groups, everybody from all corners participated. Bangalore became a war zone, with protests in every part of the city. Every day there were marches, roadblocks, strikes and gheraos. The government came under fire for overtly supporting the pageant and allowing Amitabh Bachchan to speak from the Vidhana Soudha, the state legislative assembly. (Bachchan's Amitabh Bachchan Corporation Limited and Godrej were the main sponsors of this edition of the Miss World pageant.) All this forced the government to impose heavy restrictions on the pageant itself.

For my part, I had developed a strong revulsion to an event that had spiked a manifold increase in prostitution. I was also strongly opposed to the very construct of beauty that such pageants promoted. My work in Samvada had required me to oversee a child sexual abuse helpline. I had spoken to hundreds of teenagers suffering from anorexia nervosa, a psychological condition which compels sufferers to adopt disordered eating practices for the sake of becoming thin.

Who defines the right shape and size? Who decides what is a beautiful skin tone? What are the rules that define physical beauty? I felt these pageants helped create a false construct of attractiveness, aided by various cosmetics brands. And so, I decided to join the protests against the pageant. I remember how, in one of the open forums, a tall and beautiful model was trying to defend the beauty pageant by giving a detailed explanation of the beauty with brains argument. I asked her, 'I am four feet and six inches in height, my body parts are proportionate, I am reasonably intelligent and received a gold medal in my master's. Do you think I can compete in this pageant?' The stumped look on her face was, for me, all the more reason to deepen my involvement in the protests.

In the beginning, I participated in a few marches and public protests. Some of the women's groups planned the protests together to ensure a continuity in the events and place sustained pressure on the government to cancel the pageant. I wanted Janodaya to be part of these protests. Vaz was not very keen initially, but eventually gave her reluctant consent.

At one such meeting, a woman called Lalita from a left feminist group proposed a picketing protest against Godrej. The plan was to picket the showroom located opposite the Cubbon Park police station. This was close to Chinnaswamy Stadium, the venue of the pageant. It was sure to garner attention and maybe even international coverage. Everyone approved the plan.

Apart from the leftist women's group, there were three other volunteers from other women's groups. Me, Gayatri, a women's rights activist I had met and befriended during the protests, and Ranjini, another activist from a left-leaning feminist group involved in the labour movement. All of us had been taking turns to join different protests as our time permitted.

This was my first picketing protest ever, and I didn't know what that entailed. Gayatri and I were asked to speak to the public that was sure to gather outside the showroom because of the commotion. They also made it abundantly clear that we should court arrest. That we should not worry, as the group would have lawyers on call who would ensure bail right away. It would go exactly like the arrests of hundreds of protesting activists who had been let go in a few hours. Thousands of freedom fighters had courted arrest and so could I, I thought naively. It was necessary for me as an emerging activist to know what arrest meant.

The day of the protest dawned, 28 October 1996. I got ready like any other day. As usual, I did not tell my parents about my plans. I went to office, completed some filing work and requested a colleague to drop me off just before Cubbon Park, where we were to gather. It was 11 a.m. Ranjini and Gayatri were already there, as were some folks from the women's group. Gayatri and I were briefed about our speeches. Ranjini would accompany the group's team into the showroom. I didn't know of their plans, but I'd spotted cow dung in someone's hand and commented to Gayatri about how strange that was. She had no clue either about it. Hindsight is, of course, 20/20.

We were told to hand our bags to some men to avoid losing them in the inevitable melee. I wasn't convinced, but didn't want to protest since I only had a notebook and some money in my purse. Nothing of value to worry over. At around 11.30 a.m., we were told to move towards the showroom. The idea was to get it started quickly for maximum impact. At the appointed hour, Gayatri and I took position outside the showroom while the others rushed inside. Passers-by were shocked. Gayatri began her speech on why we should oppose the pageant, and I followed suit when it was my turn. The police realised our plan, and began rapidly approaching the showroom. There was no time to check on what the others were up to. I'm sure that I could have easily slipped away in the ensuing chaos, but I chose to stay and court arrest. I was following instructions in good faith, thinking it was the right thing to do.

Gayatri and I were bundled into a jeep by a policewoman. The others were already seated and were yelling slogans even as the vehicle turned into the station. All of this was fun, and I was really enjoying the experience. I even began to feel like a real activist. We just needed to wait it out until we were released.

I began to worry after a few hours had passed, and asked Lalita if she knew what was taking so long. She told me that their lawyers were waiting in the court and trying to round up media persons for more attention. This made sense as not many journalists had followed us into the station.

As time passed and we remained in the police station, I grew more and more uncomfortable. Something didn't feel right. I couldn't understand what was going on and information from the women's group was scarce. It was only much later in the evening, when we were taken to court, that I realised they had more to the plan, something that we'd not been privy to. There was a barrage of media persons outside the court. So I wasn't surprised by the sloganeering when we entered the court campus. After all, we had wanted this attention. But what raised my antennae was the strange and insolent way in which the members of leftist women's group behaved in court. Some squatted down on the floor; the leader of the group even shouted at the judge. I was so taken aback by this behaviour that I couldn't even register what she was saying. All that I could see was a fuming judge who ordered us to be remanded.

I was numb with shock. They were taking us to jail. The walk to the police vehicle was surreal. There were women shouting slogans, journalists pushing their mikes into our faces, lawyers swarming around—it was a circus. I just wanted to find someone who could tell my parents that I was safe and would be back soon.

We were led into the women's barracks of Bangalore Central Jail. I was tearful and anxious, but could not cry. I wondered how I could tell my family about what had happened. Gayatri and Ranjini were both from the development sector. Babu, Gayatri's spouse, was also an activist. Ranjini's entire family was left-leaning. All of them had somehow found out what had happened and reached the court. Ranjini assured me that her uncle would inform Geeta Menon, who would inform my parents. I was perhaps the only real outsider, as I had no familial affiliation with the development sector.

The thirteen of us were placed in one block. The child who had been with us was sent to a juvenile observation home. This was the first time since the morning that I had the chance to observe the other women. Most of them were older than me and, from the way they talked, had been in such situations before.

Ironically, that night, I worried more about my parents than the protests. I slept badly, stressed about what they must be going through. Still, I held onto hope. Maybe the lawyers would get bail tomorrow.

It was only on the following day that I realised that the others didn't mean to get bail. They were hoping to create as much commotion as possible so that the protests got heavier coverage. Caught in their plans unwittingly, I felt dizzy with shock.

The jail superintendent, a Mr Abbai, came to meet us early next morning. As soon as he entered with the warden, the women from group started screaming. They demanded to see the jail manual and the diet chart that should have been shared with all the undertrials. Abbai lost it. He'd brought us breakfast from a restaurant, perhaps as a courtesy or an olive branch. He ordered the warden to serve that to the officers and to feed us the usual prison fare instead.

Drama unfolded both inside and outside the jail after this incident. A large group of protestors, mostly from left-wing groups, gathered outside demanding our release. The courts refused to entertain our bail application. I was told some judges even went on leave for short periods to avoid reviewing the bail application. All this was speculation, of course. I sometimes wonder whether an application for bail was even made in the first few days. The plan, as I learnt far too late, was to have people gather outside the jail demanding our release to gain more focus on the protests.

It had been over twenty-four hours, and I still hadn't heard from my parents. The others had met their parents in court and received a change of clothes from them. They all knew the drill as they were from activist families: undertrials don't get uniforms in jail and must bring their own clothes. Though Ranjini and Gayatri hadn't been aware of the larger plan either, their families had done the needful the very next day. I felt isolated.

Days had passed, with no news from my parents. I wore the same clothes every day, washing them at night in our barracks and wrapping myself in a bedsheet while sleeping. I lost interest in the protests. I wanted to stay far away from the group's women; they were a closed group. And I didn't want to dwell on the lack of news from my family. I decided to focus on the other undertrials. There were over 200 women undertrials and convicts in the jail. Most were murder-accused in dowry cases. The rest were here for theft, burglary or prostitution.

It was a new experience interacting with them. They were inquisitive about us and why we had been remanded. I tried to satisfy their curiosity as much as I could. I also spoke to the warden and told her I would like to conduct yoga and meditation sessions. She readily agreed. A small number of convicts and undertrials participated. We used the front courtyard for our meditation sessions. For me, that one hour was the most engaging time of the day: my mind would calm down and give me a temporary break from overthinking.

Thanks to that performance from our group the first day, we were served only jail food. In the morning, we'd wait in a single file, plate in hand, to be served. When our turn came, the server, usually a convict, would toss the food onto our plate. In the afternoon, we got rice, some randomly cooked vegetables and a large bucket of spicy water that passed for dal. This was served in our barracks—special treatment, I think, as some high-profile activists/leaders were constantly trying to meet with us, and perhaps the jail authorities felt compelled to treat us with care. The women in my barracks would make a great show about the food. They'd allow the dal to settle and then spoon out the bit of lentils at the bottom and divide it amongst us. I didn't care. I needed food only to stay alive. I was least bothered whether it had taste, whether it was a balanced diet. Jail reform was definitely not on my agenda.

What really bothered me was that nobody from my family came to visit. The jail was filled with people who had committed grievous crimes, and they had visitors practically every day. Mulakat or visitation time was from 10 a.m. to 3 p.m., and it was a strange ritual. From 10 a.m. onwards, the gong would ring and there would be pin drop silence so we clearly hear the number or code called that indicated there was a visitor. I waited and waited for my number in vain. It is not that we lacked visitors; most days there were activists and protestors trying to meet us. Now and then some high-profile activist would get access, and we'd be herded to meet them. Once, a small group of women activists from Vimochana were allowed to meet us inside the women's barracks (not sure how they managed that, maybe because of their interventions with the prison ministry). They had got some idlis for us, albeit sorely mutilated. Anything taken inside is thoroughly checked and we could only discern through taste that the mush they presented us with was idli.

We came to be known as the Cubbon Park hudigiaru (Cubbon Park girls). I came to understand that our bail was strongly opposed by the state on the grounds that we were Naxalites from some Green Tigers group. God only knew what that is. The news from outside was more reliable, as Gayatri's husband, Babu, and Ranjini's uncle were also monitoring the court proceedings. I also learnt that Janodaya had put up a public advertisement dissociating from and disowning me, stating that my actions did not reflect the organisation's views and that they were mine alone.

Six days into my incarceration, Geeta and Daddy came to visit.

They'd brought me a change of clothes. I couldn't look my father in the eyes or even speak to him. Seeing him through the grills of the mulakat room, my heart was in my mouth. I was choked with guilt; he looked haggard. Much later, I learnt that Geeta, Shoba and Daddy had been detained in the police station for many hours the first few days, questioned about my antecedents and connections. Apparently, they found pamphlets with radical information in my bag and wanted to know my affiliations. This was the same bag that I had reluctantly handed over for safekeeping to the men who had accompanied the women's group on the day we were picketing. I cannot imagine the anguish and humiliation my father must have felt when he was subjected to interrogation. The guilt consumes me even today. That was the only time anyone from my family visited me in jail.

For the first time in my life, the words 'rejection', 'belonging' and 'loneliness' held meaning. I cared nothing for my visitors. All I wanted was my own people, those who mattered to me. I realised that this experience was going to change my life forever.

Throughout, we kept receiving snippets of news from our visitors. It went from bad to worse. Apparently there really was a group called the Green Tigers. They'd even thrown a small bomb into Chinnaswamy Stadium, aiming for the stadium generators. Fortunately, they'd missed by fifteen yards and had caused no actual harm. Someone called Suresh had self-immolated, and other women were threatening to immolate themselves. We were doomed. I was actually a paper tiger, but there was no way we were getting bail now.

Such news, the group's secrecy and my feelings of isolation and betrayal began to affect my health. Ranjini and Gayatri were also depressed, but they met their families practically every other day, and were physically coping better. I started getting panic attacks and suffered from low blood pressure. The jail doctor was summoned, and I was given intravenous fluids. As soon as I recovered, Lalita started acting up. She claimed she had a heart ailment, but refused to go to the hospital, and wanted her personal doctor to treat her.

By this time, Abbai had realised that I was the odd one out. In all probability, he had investigated us and monitored the way we all behaved inside. I was the only one who did not have any personal visitors. Perhaps it also helped that I was trying to engage with the prisoners with meditation and yoga.

He sought me out and asked if Lalita's condition was real. Honestly, I had no clue. The group were really disciplined and kept mum before us. I told Abbai it would be better to summon her doctor rather than create another opportunity for publicity. He agreed, and asked me to get the doctor's phone number and speak to him. Dr Pugazhendhi seemed to be expecting the call. Much later, I came to know that the newspapers had reported that we'd all been ill, and the government hadn't taken any action.

We were arrested on 28 October. I'd now spent twenty-three days in jail, with no word of bail or release. Then, three days before the pageant, with no indication at all, we were suddenly free to leave. It was 20 November. Strangers celebrated our release with fireworks and garlands. Yet, I felt no happiness, just trepidation. All the others had someone to receive them, but there was nobody waiting for me.

My heart sank. I didn't know where to go, what to do. Taking pity at my plight, Ranjini's uncle offered to drop me home. I accepted. I don't know what else I could have done, for I had no money; my bag was still in police custody.

At home, I was greeted with utter silence. My father opened the door. My mother, resting on the diwan—she'd fractured a toe—simply looked at me sadly. My siblings couldn't even meet my eyes and avoided me. Their silence felt laden with accusations. If they'd actually said something, I'd have fallen at their feet and begged forgiveness. But nobody spoke a word. I walked to my room and had my first proper bath in twenty-four days—one day for each year of my life.

It was still early evening and the gloomy silence in our house was rather uncomfortable. No one, including Daddy, was taking any initiative to ask me any questions. I decided to go for a walk in the colony. It was definitely to escape from the stifling situation, but I also felt that, if I hid at home, avoiding the world, I'd do that forever. The annual Ayyappa puja was going on and almost the entire colony was in the pandal, which was located right in the centre of the colony. I walked in and went straight towards the deity. All eyes were on me, I could feel it. Their voices died down, the music from the loudspeakers blared on. Not a single soul greeted me or spoke to me. I bowed before the idol, thanked him for my liberation and then, with my head held high, I walked out.

But then, what could they have asked me anyway? What would you say to someone who's been released from jail? Hello, how are you? When did you come out? How was your experience there?

I will never know what my family went through in those twenty-four days. I never asked, and they never told me. Suku, my brother, was a teenager then. What would he have heard from neighbours, from his friends? I have no idea what my sisters had to face, the censure my parents endured. Much later, I heard that an uncle my father looked up to had said something like, 'Once, only freedom fighters went to jail, now only criminals do!' This time I had truly shamed my family.

10

Moving Away for Good

I knew I had to deal with the consequences of my actions. But it stung that my family suffered by association. Maybe being out of sight, out of mind was the solution—that might cut down on the gossiping and baseless rumours. I made up my mind to leave Bangalore. But where would I go?

Back in late 1995, around the time that I had just completed a project for the Centre for Education and Documentation (CED) and was about to join Janodaya, I'd attended a conference organised by the Peace and Justice Forum in Mumbai at the invitation of some Catholic sisters involved in development work in Bangalore. While the conference itself wasn't of great significance to me, I had met some interesting people, one of whom had been Brother Varghese Theckanath. He was the founder of the People's Initiative Network (PIN), an organisation which worked in the slums of Hyderabad.

We had ended up chatting, and after learning about my interests, he'd invited me to work with him. It had been over ten months since we'd last spoken. I mulled over it for a while and decided to give it a shot. Going to Hyderabad made sense. I contacted Brother Varghese, asked him if his offer still stood. 'Of course,' he replied.

Over the next few days, I quietly made arrangements to leave Bangalore. Only when I was ready to leave did I tell my parents. They voiced no objections. So preoccupied was I in my own misery that I failed to check what they really thought about it. In retrospect, maybe just relief, as the current atmosphere in our closely knit colony did not feel even close to positive.

It felt like a permanent move and was a big price to pay for my actions. This was the first time I'd faced rejection at home. I could have handled the rejection from my neighbours, from the world. But together, it was all too hard to bear.

It was an important life lesson, and I took it to heart.

I knew what it was to be trapped in a situation not of my own making. I knew what it felt like to face the consequences as well.

I'd also learnt what a person in custodial care needs. Jail had taught me that. I knew the processes that stripped away the dignity of a person. The loneliness and the need for belonging that isolation creates. I'd take all these lessons and turn them into cornerstones of my care and protection programmes later.

Importantly, I had also learnt the value of standing up for what you truly believe in and facing the repercussions thereafter. And I'd learnt not to blindly believe in others. I also decided that I wouldn't ever get involved in any agitation or protest organised by others—any activity, for that matter, that I didn't fully understand. For years to come, I didn't participate in any protest organised by others, even as a mark of solidarity for causes that I knew and understood, such was my loss of faith. If I did participate in a protest, I was the organiser, wholly aware of all the stakes involved.

Thirteen days after my release from jail, I left Bangalore. I had one bag. In it were three sets of clothes, a few utensils, two bedsheets and a picture of my favourite deity, Ayyappa, along with two small lamps. That was it, the sum total of my belongings.

I bid my family goodbye at home, asking them to not come to the station. There was both sadness and relief in my parents' eyes. My siblings didn't say much. I'm not sure even today what they thought about my departure. As I became more and more engaged in my mission, my interactions with Suku and Sujji had greatly reduced. Sumathi, I barely communicated with after her marriage.

I boarded a bus for the railway station. Geeta had come to see me off. She looked worried, but I assured her that Brother Varghese would take care of me.

For the next few years, I was a virtual outcast. I was obliged to go to Bangalore every two months—all of us who had been jailed had to appear for the case hearing. This allowed me to see my family. Otherwise, the only news I'd get about them was through my father's occasional letters. Though I looked forward to seeing them, eager to know what they'd all been up to, I shared little of note in my own letters. I didn't really want to expose them to my work.

At the court, I'd meet Gayatri and Ranjini—I was truly fond of them—but steadfastly avoided the others. Once the hearing concluded, I'd rush to Safina Plaza near Commercial Street where my dear friends Geeta and Shoba would be waiting. We'd spend hours talking, window shopping and indulging in all kinds of street food. In two days, I'd be back in Hyderabad. Fortunately for me, my modest salary and my frugal lifestyle—helped in great measure by Geeta and Shoba, who took care of my annual requirements for clothes—meant that I could afford the train tickets. In the end, it would take twenty-four court hearings over four years to acquit us all for lack of evidence. But that was all in the future.

My train entered Hyderabad's Kachiguda railway station on 4 December 1996 at 6.30 a.m. I'd lived in Hyderabad briefly as an infant, and that gave me a sense of familiarity and comfort. A new phase of my life had begun.

Brother Varghese had come to receive me. He was a Catholic brother from the order of the Montford Brothers of St Gabriel, and lived in the Old City of Hyderabad, in Moosanagar, right below the Chaderghat Musi Bridge, a slum he worked in, to best serve the community.

He had arranged for me to temporarily stay with the sisters working with him until my own place was ready. They were from the order of the Sisters of Charity and lived in Kamalnagar, adjacent to Moosanagar. The sisters lived in a small house. Sister Bridget received me with great warmth and made me comfortable. I was told there was another sister, Lissy Joseph, who also lived there. She'd be moving out in a few days to pursue her master's in social work.

Brother Varghese was keen for me to get involved right away. Perhaps he sensed my turmoil and felt that immersing myself in work would help. And rightly so. It was a small team: aside from Brother Varghese, there was Brother Peter, Brother Bal Reddy, Brother Suresh, Anthony, a layman, and the two sisters. In less than an hour, they had pulled me into their planning. That afternoon, there was a convergence meeting with the district collector. Brother Varghese asked me to go with Anthony for the meeting.

This was the first time I was seeing a district collector in person. Bhanwarlal, IAS, had summoned all the district revenue officials and NGOs working in Hyderabad to plan the pulse polio campaign to be held on 6 December. Polio-drop booths were to be set up in locations across the city, and he wanted the NGOs to help monitor them and ensure that the operations went smoothly.

Each NGO stated their preferred booth based on the area they operated in. When the collector asked for volunteers to monitor polio booths in the Old City, I sensed a strange reluctance from all of them. PIN operated in these areas, so I happily volunteered. Anthony did not react at that moment, but I could feel those present do a double take. When we were returning from the meeting, Anthony casually mentioned that Sister Lissy will join me to monitor the polio-drop booths in the Old City, and finally explained the implications.

Now for the context: having landed that very day in Hyderabad, I didn't know the significance of 6 December for the Old City of Hyderabad, a Muslim-majority area. Four years ago, on that very day, the Babri Masjid in Ayodhya, Uttar Pradesh had been demolished, and the wounds of it were still fresh. The Muslim community observed it as a day of mourning and had declared it as 'black day'. Essentially, I had agreed to visit a sensitive area during a period when the chances of disturbance in law-and-order were high.

I wasn't bothered by this information. My logic was simple: I was available to work, and if I stuck to my role, no one would do me any harm. That two-hour meeting had introduced me to the district officials of the Hyderabad Collectorate as well as the NGOs, and I was happy to get involved in work so quickly.

The next day was spent with Anthony, who took me around so I could observe the work that PIN did. He was young, reserved and very committed to his work. He'd also completed his master's in social work. Anthony, or Tony as I started calling him, was recently married and lived with his wife in the adjacent colony, a slightly better settlement with pucca houses. Tony and I formed a good team. He would take me on his cycle to visit all the slums where PIN had set up some kind of learning centres or bridge schools. He also introduced me to several basti, or slum, leaders. I spoke both Hindi and Telugu, and that helped me quickly connect with people. Ashwaq Bhai was one such leader who warmed up to me instantly.

On 6 December, I went with Sister Lissy to the Old City on her two-wheeler. We visited all the polio booths there. As expected, there was hardly any traffic, and all the shops were closed. I saw the majestic Charminar and all the other beautiful old structures in the area. Perhaps it was the best time to see them, with no crowds barring me from soaking in the grace of the time-worn buildings.

Other than a few instances of stone pelting in the Old City, nothing untoward had happened. Everywhere we went, we were met with friendly eyes.

Our last stop was Boys Town, a sprawling five-acre campus for the most deprived and needy, located in the Old City's Jahanuma. The Nizam had donated this land to the Montford Brothers to set up an orphanage, school and industrial training institute, and the missionary brothers were doing a great job in managing this institution.

Sister Lissy parked her bike near the gate, and we slowly walked towards the polio booth.

I could see a tall, well-built man in his late thirties looking at us. As we walked towards him, my vision began to blur. Everything went fuzzy. Superimposed on that was an image of this man running towards me with a child on his shoulder. I blinked in surprise and realised I was standing right in front of him. Lissy introduced him to me as Brother Jose Vetticatil, the director of Boys Town.

As soon as we spoke, I felt as if I knew him from before, and by the easy way he interacted with me, I sensed he also felt the same. The connection was instant and felt deep-rooted. Brother Jose accompanied us to the booth. I did my work in a daze. He then invited us for tea, and we followed him to the refectory before getting back.

The entire affair lasted less than thirty minutes, but I knew something profound had occurred. I'd met someone who would be one of the greatest influences on my life.

11

Early Days in Hyderabad

I moved into my room in Shoba's house as soon as it was ready. The house was in Moosanagar, where Brother Varghese lived. We were on the banks of the Musi river, which was more the city's sewerage than a river. The slum, with its labyrinthine network of tiny lanes and overcrowded shanties, was one of the most congested places in the city. Children were everywhere, and unfortunately so was filth, always accompanied by the obnoxious smell from the Musi and tornadoes of mosquitoes and flies. Largely populated by the Muslim community, everybody conversed in the very distinct dialect of Urdu spoken in Hyderabad. There were a few Hindu homes here, Shoba's among them. She worked as a teacher in one of PIN's bridge schools for the children living in these slums. The PIN team of the brothers lived in an adjacent lane, and Tony's house was in the adjoining slum, a ten-minute walk.

My room was tiny; if I took a couple of steps in any direction, I'd touch the wall. I organised it into three areas: the kitchen, a puja room-cum-study and a bedroom. All I had was a small mat to sleep on. There was no scope for any furniture—I did not possess any, nor was there any space for it. Life was simple, with zero maintenance worries. The rent was Rs 400, manageable with the small honorarium of Rs 4,000 that Brother Varghese had promised. I had already decided that, sooner or later, I would send some money home as a small compensation for the pain I had caused as well as to prove that I was striving to be a better daughter.

Shoba and her husband Shiva annaiah ('elder brother' in Telugu) cared for me as if I were family. Their kindness made up for all the discomforts—the small room, the shared bathroom, the 3 a.m. walks to the common tap to store water for the week, the swarms of mosquitoes courtesy the Musi, which remains a glorified drain till date.

I lived like a queen in the slum. I'd wake up at 6 a.m., switch on the radio and do my ablutions. By the time I emerged from the shared bathroom, there'd be a steaming hot cup of tea waiting by my door. Breakfast would follow in the next half an hour, usually prepared by Shoba or one of the neighbours. The food was simple, usually idli or lemon rice. But the thought behind the gesture made it a delicacy. Lunch would be at the office, courtesy of PIN, typically dal and rice, which all of us took turns to cook. The office had a decent bathroom, which was an added attraction. At the end of the day, I'd prepare the occasional dinner, some one-pot meal like vangi bath (a spicy rice dish made with brinjal), curd rice, pulihora, or tamarind rice, but most times, I'd eat at someone's house after I had returned from work. Bedtime was around 11 p.m.

It was a true blessing that the people of the basti chose to adopt me, following Shoba's example. The fact that a small gas cylinder donated by an acquaintance lasted eight years should give you some idea of how much I cooked. I accepted all this love as my due, and put in all my efforts to ensure that the government's welfare schemes meant for the people in the slum reached them.

Hyderabad was proving to have been a good decision, except for one thing. My time in jail had given me great gifts, life lessons that are relevant even today. It had also given me a very real, tangible one that would plague me for years: head lice. These squatters, which had grown big and fat feeding off my blood, didn't even have the decency to stay hidden. They'd shamelessly wander in and out of my hair, drawing remarks from my team about it. But as much as I wanted them gone, there was nothing I could do. Washing my thick, knee-length hair already took a lot of water, a truly scarce commodity in Moosanagar. We shared the bathroom with so many families, and there was no way I could spend even more time trying to get rid of the lice. My hair, everybody's envy from afar, was really a nightmare.

By this time, I was good friends with Brother Jose. Our close camaraderie had me calling him Jo-etta (a confusing word in Malayalam used to address both brother and husband). I would readily accept Jo's invitations to visit him on Sunday, which allowed me to spend time with him and to indulge in a luxurious bath in their guest room and wash my hair to my heart's content. Boys Town, therefore, became a favourite hangout, and I'd try hard to make it a weekly affair. Unfortunately, I wasn't very successful. So, lice became my constant companion.

The other problem I faced was the one of repeated urinary tract infections (UTIs). I'd drink very little water throughout the day so as to use the community toilet as little as possible. I still don't drink that much water. Poor vaginal hygiene, the physical stress of the work, lack of sleep and my tight jeans all contributed to chronic UTI. Again, there was no clear solution in sight. I just lived with it for many years, managing the condition with barley water as and when it worsened, handling the discomfort and pain.

In the meantime, I had become deeply engaged in all the activities that PIN organised, particularly with the adolescent girls in the bastis. Anthony and I conducted a series of life skills workshop for the girls; we sorted them into smaller groups for talks on empowerment, brought them together for cultural festivals to nurture their collective strength and motivated them to continue their education.

I was also working with the youth for self-employment, helping them access small loans from the banks and connecting them with opportunities at the Hyderabad Collectorate, where I was now a regular visitor.

I believe this work was accelerated by the path-breaking innovative community development project that the visionary chief minister of the time, Chandrababu Naidu, initiated. The Janmabhoomi (birthplace) Programme, started in 1996, was a fantastic project that focused on people in slums and villages to reconstruct and revitalise society.

In the first phase, local committees were formed in all villages and slums to prepare proposals on areas they wanted work to be done or improved on, such as access to education, drinking water, health, hospitals, family welfare, environment protection, etc. These proposals were handed over to the officer responsible for that place, who then had to execute the proposals on a war footing and ensure that all the concerns were addressed. This was done through a multi-departmental convergence every quarter.

Bhanwarlal, the district collector, had formed a small group to help monitor the committees and the inter-departmental convergence. I was part of this core group. Being the state headquarters, Hyderabad was a prominent point of focus. If the scheme failed here, there was no hope elsewhere in the state. The collector took it up as a personal mission, especially since the chief minister was directly monitoring progress across the state.

It was during this time that I met Vasireddy Sarat Babu, the project director of the National Child Labour Project or Balajyothi, located at the Collectorate. He was also part of the project's core group. We were in one team and would travel together in an auto to the slums to monitor the Prajala Vadaka Palana (PVP) or the people's committee. This was also an opportunity for me to meet district officials from various departments. I did my best to ensure that the people in my slum and all those that PIN focused on got the benefit of all my connections. I also made sure that the Janmabhoomi project was a success in the slum that I was staying in.

Two things happened that changed the course of my work in the slums: one was a torrential rainstorm that wreaked havoc on property and practically submerged our basti in the Musi river. I had no expensive belongings, but my things were still of value to me. Books, clothes, mats, provisions—all that is necessary for living were drenched, rendering them unusable. The second was the announcement of the Nandanavanam beautification project, which entailed the razing of all the slums along the river.

Suddenly, the lives and livelihoods of everyone living in these areas were at stake. Most slum dwellers were daily wagers, and depended largely on the city for sustenance. Uprooting them to a faraway place would endanger their livelihoods. Our team decided we had to do something about it. Senior basti leaders like Ashwaq Bhai and many others joined hands with us. I was selected to get all the information from the collector's office as I was the only one who had penetrated the inner layers of the district administration.

When I shared our predicament with Collector Bhanwarlal, I was speaking not only as an activist, but also as a slum dweller myself. He understood my objections and concerns but confessed that he had no powers to stop the chief minister's special project. To protest the Nandanavanam beautification project, we formed a core group from all the affected slums and called it Nandanavanam Basthi Samrakshana Samithi.

The next few months were hectic, I went basti to basti, informing residents about the project and mobilising them for the people's movement to follow. I also suggested to Brother Varghese that performing street plays would help increase awareness and recruit sympathisers. He suggested that I take charge. I didn't know much about it, but I had done a fair bit of street theatre in my college days, and so agreed.

I contacted Uday Bhanu, a railway employee and well-known theatre director in Hyderabad. He was very gung-ho about it, and came down to Moosanagar with his two assistants, Jolly Puthuserry and Biju Sridharan. We went to all the affected slums, selected people from there, and shaped them into a powerful street theatre troupe. This group would perform in all the slums and complement our mobilisation efforts.

Another initiative I took was to design a photo exhibition. I felt strongly that just getting the slum dwellers to participate wouldn't be enough. We needed all of Hyderabad to support us. If people knew the repercussions of this project on the lives of the poor, they'd surely support our protests. Brother Varghese left it to me to find my way.

I reached out to Bharath Bhushan, an ace photographer, and Anantha Krishnan, a well-known journalist, for help. Getting the funds to pay for their work was a challenge, but Brother Varghese managed to find a way via PIN. I knew our finances were spread thin, but this was an important—even necessary—expense.

All these campaigns and projects went on simultaneously with the protests. I managed to take the photo exhibition to a national conference organised by the National Alliance for People's Movement (NAPM) in Delhi. The street theatre group also got an opportunity to perform before prominent activists, including Medha Patkar.

We had mobilised a large number of slum dwellers who were committed to the fight. One of our first 'attacks' on the Nandanavanam project was a massive public protest, preceded by a rally attended by thousands of people. It was a tremendous show of strength. The government did not expect this. We followed that up with a 'rasta roko' protest (halt the way), where we blocked a main road with heavy traffic by lying down on it and undertaking a relay fast. During the 'relay fasting', as one of the main protesting leaders, I sat in the front, adorned with garlands presented by our basti dwellers. Brother Jo and some others of the Montfort congregation found all of this amusing, especially the relay fasting. In fact, Jo was among the few who did not visit us to express solidarity. He firmly believed that strikes and protests were tokenistic strategies that were photo-ops to serve the self-interest of protestors, that they didn't really help effect a solution. I was the butt of his jokes for months to come.

But I knew what was at stake. This was not something where I had a tokenistic presence; I was involved in the planning and execution. And this affected me and my newly adopted family of slum dwellers directly.

As it happened, the government did take note of our protests and immediate work on the project was stalled. But I knew from my contacts that nothing had changed. The government was just biding time, waiting for us to get tired and abandon the protests. And we were getting tired. For the residents of the slums, abandoning work that would provide daily wages to protest indefinitely was proving untenable.

It was then that we hit upon the idea of a Public Interest Litigation (PIL). Brother Varghese and I met the highly respected advocate K.G. Kannabiran, who took on the case pro bono. K. Balagopal, another amazing advocate, also pledged his support. And so, we filed a PIL in the Andhra Pradesh High Court to stall the Nandanavanam beautification project. While the high court did not stall the project, it directed the government to prepare a comprehensive relocation plan and provide proper housing to all the slum dwellers before proceeding with their eviction.

It wasn't a great judgement, but it wasn't a terrible one either. As for the beautification project, it somehow never got off the ground. Till date, the Musi looks much the same, and most of the illegal encroachments continue. The government did, however, create a relocation colony on the outskirts of Hyderabad where some residents relocated. Now, Nandanavanam Colony, as it is named, has become a part of the weaker section housing scheme.

12

The Soul Connection

I've already talked about the connection I felt with Brother Jose. The bond felt more real each time we met. He was the first person outside my family that I spoke to about my sexual assault, and the only one who now knew all the details about that fateful day. My family had never asked, and with Jo, it felt like the most natural thing to share even without his asking. We only talked about it once, but with that, a burden I'd expected to take to my grave was now in the safe custody of a trusted friend.

I do not know whether I can give my relationship with Jo a label. Some relationships cannot be explained. Much like how you cannot really explain your relationship with your gods. If people around us noticed our easy familiarity with each other or speculated about it, I didn't care. I know there were some nasty rumours doing the rounds. But for Jo and me, we were immersed in our work, and he believed he could join me whenever I took the first step to do something for women in prostitution.

I was working hard to become an integral part of PIN, but I also managed to carve out some private time. Only Jo knew about it. In 1996, soon after I met Jo, I began to visit Mehboob ki Mehendi on my own. Mehendi, as it was popularly known, was the red-light area in Hyderabad located bang opposite the high court of Hyderabad. As I walked its streets over and over, I knew with absolute certainty that my destiny lay here, even if I didn't know what it was I would do.

Interestingly enough, like Mehendi, most of the red-light areas in the country are located in the centre of the city, like Kamatipura in

Mumbai's Grant Road, GB Road just adjoining the Delhi's Kamala Market police station, Delhi, Sonagachi in Kolkata or Baina in Goa. If brothel-keeping is a crime as per the Immoral Traffic Act, 1956, why then did stakeholders in the criminal justice system, the police or the judiciary, never close these places down? That is something that I struggle to understand even today.

Mehendi was nothing like Majestic in Bangalore or Mumbai's Kamatipura. This was the Old City, with traditional buildings that had chhajjas (intricately designed awnings over the windows). The women, young and old, would sit at the windowsills to display their attractions. From down below, the windows and chhajja acted as a sort of frame, showcasing, perhaps even emphasising, all they had to offer. Some days, music from the houses spilt onto the streets, adding to the atmosphere. There were mehfils and mujras, the women's voices drifting into the streets. The hijras (eunuchs), who were usually the gatekeepers, invited customers in. There was a certain grace to the place that words cannot describe. Perhaps the Hindi movie *Mandi* comes close to capturing the atmosphere. But the place was much, much more than that.

Mehendi was also lively. Crowded with shops, it was busiest in the evenings. Like Majestic, there were policemen everywhere. Unlike Majestic, I did not try to meet any of the women. I'd decided that I wouldn't do anything until I was clear about the modalities of my intervention. There were also many children about, either playing or ferrying small packets to the houses. Later, I came to know those were packets of a country liquor called gudumba.

I did once try something just for the heck of it. Since I had some loose change in hand one day, I entered one of the brothels with live music and sat down—the only woman in the audience. I saw a scene right out of the movies. It was an average-sized room with high beams. In the corner sat a woman singing, and in the centre of the room was the tawaif, the dancing girl. She was quite graceful, but I wouldn't call her performance a dance as much as a sort of shuffle accompanied by a few foot and hand gestures. I kept my eyes on the girl, threw the cash I had towards her and subtly watched the room. Not surprisingly, the attention soon shifted to me. I could feel the pinch of their gaze on my neck. After throwing the cash, I had no clue what to do next. Sitting there indefinitely was not an option, and the room was getting slightly suffocating with the mix of various bodily odours. I stuck out like a sore thumb and felt like I was making them all uncomfortable. When I left, a bunch of men followed me until I reached the bus stop. I never went back.

Jo didn't think well of my visit to the brothel—he told me off immediately and at length. He felt it was pure recklessness and even insinuated that I had a hero complex. For my part, I didn't regret it; I'd truly wanted to see what a brothel looked like on the inside.

At this time, we were all working on the protests against the Nandanavanam beautification project. There was no way that I could abdicate my responsibilities and start something anew. And I didn't yet know what I could do. But the yearning to do something—anything—was not to be gainsaid.

Just ten days after my brothel visit, Mehendi was raided. There was mayhem in the area. Though most ran for their lives, some sixty-five women were detained by the police. Practically all the main organisers were arrested, and some people with vested interests vandalised the whole place. They even burnt all the clothes and property of the women in a bonfire right in the middle of the street to celebrate their victory against the 'bad women' and to 'cleanse' the area.

I was shocked and scared—will someone who had seen me there connect me to this eviction? Jo had an 'I told you so' look on his face. My journalist friend Anantha Krishnan, who was very interested in this story, was my main source of information. Apparently, there was complete chaos. Women had been thrown into Chanchalguda Jail and the state home located in Yousufguda. Several of them were diagnosed as HIV-positive.

The high court was monitoring this case, and it was the only place to get authentic information. I took advantage of the fact that I was already there practically every other day because of our PIL against Nandanavanam. Coincidentally, court number one was hearing both cases. I was only too happy to walk around the historical corridors, nosing around for information on both cases. The high court is among Hyderabad's finest buildings. It was built by Mir Osman Ali Khan, the last Nizam, or ruler, of the princely state of Hyderabad, with red-and-white stones in the Indo-Saracenic style.

But even in this regal court, there was complete chaos. The government had no plans for rehabilitation, and women were being moved from one place to another. First, they were put in the jail, and when the civil liberties groups intervened, they were shifted to the government-run state home at Yousufguda where, I believe, they were creating a big ruckus.

The judges were livid. There was a barrage of lawyers, and the amicus curiae made some superficial contributions about at least getting the women released from custodial care and getting a state advisory committee in place.

The reputed social worker Malladi Subbamma also intervened. To me, her proposals felt quite removed from reality. She advised that all detained women be released immediately and offered individual or community rehabilitation. But what about the fact that they needed to be assessed for emotional, social and vocational preparedness to survive in mainstream society? That was a vital step; only then could a phased plan for their release be executed.

What I found valuable was the report submitted by IPS officer Tejdeep Kaur, who headed the Women Protection Cell of the Crime Investigation Department wing at that time. She had led the rescue operation and the closure of Mehendi—what I'd term eviction. Her report in court highlighted the organised nature of the red-light area, the network of the organisers and the revenue generated. It also profiled the women and girls, including the numbers forced into prostitution. I found this report quite in sync with my own understanding of the situation.

Observing the court hearings, I realised there would be no going back now. Hundreds of residents from that area had also pleaded for the eviction, citing how Mehendi had caused long-term damage to their families. Some even claimed that their daughters could not get married, that no decent family considered them suitable. They were damned by proximity. It was then that I began to have strong suspicions that land sharks were behind this case. After all, the entire area is just opposite the high court and considered prime property.

The case dragged on, and finally, my friend Sarat Babu, who had now founded the NGO Pratyanmaya, came forward and offered to set up a safe home for all the HIV-positive women if the government was willing to fund it. The government was already on the backfoot—it had been unable to offer a convincing rehabilitation package, and some eight officers had been found guilty of colluding with the prostitution ring. So, budgetary commitments were made and Pratyanmaya set up a home for twenty-one HIV-positive women in the outskirts of Hyderabad.

What happened to the other women? Most of them were let off without any plans for future. They ended up back on the streets with nothing but the clothes they wore. None of them could go back to Mehendi; it had been cleared out. So, the women moved to different parts of the city and started to set themselves up in prostitution on their own. The brothel madams who had constructed houses in the outskirts of the city gathered as many women as they could and moved out to start fresh operations in a more decentralised fashion. Since they no longer had a brothel in a red-light area, they now sent women to trusted buyers in other locations.

Throughout this time, I was frustrated with my helplessness. There was nothing I could do. I had no locus standi in that area, no organisation of my own. PIN did not do any kind of rehabilitation work with women in prostitution—preoccupied with the rights of slum dwellers, they would not find this mission interesting. As the people's movement gathered enough steam to keep on going without me, I started to emotionally wean away.

But what could I say to Brother Varghese? He had come to rely on me, valued my contribution in what was a small team. I thought citing health concerns would be the best way to avoid an argument. I already had UTI and had also developed cysts in my uterus. I made it look like a big health crisis because of which I had to urgently go to Bangalore for treatment.

Brother Varghese, who was a wonderful person, actually called up my father on our neighbour's phone and offered all the necessary financial help for my treatment. My father, poor man, could not understand a word. His blank response was enough for Varghese to intuit my white lies. I sheepishly talked to him about it many months later. He was too nice a person for me to mislead this way. But I had my reasons too. I had to do what my soul yearned for, and time was running out. And so, that was the end of my work in slums.

13

Prajwala, the Fire Within

After a two-week break in Bangalore, during which time I resolved my health problems, I returned to Hyderabad. I had already shifted my meagre belongings from Shoba's house and left it in storage at Boys Town. I needed to move out of the area because the Nandanavanam movement had brought me close to a lot of the residents there, and they looked to me with a lot of expectations. A clean physical break would allow me to completely focus on my mission.

Jo, in the meantime, had his staff scout for a house for me. It was a small two-room affair with a private bathroom in the heart of the Old City, in a place called Shah Ali Banda, right next to the Charminar. The landlord had some kind of steel business, and the landlady was a teacher. The couple had three children, one of whom was partially visually challenged. The rent was slightly higher at Rs 700, but the money I'd saved from my work at PIN was enough to give me some semblance of security for the present, and I did not break my head over how to sustain it in the future. The fact that my decision felt right was good enough at the moment.

Moving from what had been a virtual matchbox to this place felt like a great luxury. I managed to acquire a few bits of furniture. A small wooden bed (in case I had a guest), a mat with a cotton mattress for myself and two plastic chairs. For the first time, I set up a proper kitchen. The small house had adequate cross-ventilation, but light only seeped into the first room; the rest of the place required harsh electrical lighting even during the day. I also had a special place for my gods; by now, their numbers had expanded. I called the owners Annaiah and Bhabhi (elder brother and sister-in-law), and while they affectionately showered me with food, I still had to cook. Archana, their visually challenged daughter, developed a strong devotion towards me and would insist on cleaning my house on Sundays as she felt she had superior skills in mopping. Then we would share lunch, and I would hear about her entire week and all the news of her college and friends.

The fact that I was referred by the director of Boys Town made a huge difference. Boys Town, with its reputed school and industrial training institute, was one of the most respected establishments in the Old City. I would stay in this place for the next few years until life took me elsewhere.

I quickly plunged into my mission. The first thing I did was contact Anantha Krishnan, who knew many of the people evicted from Mehendi. He introduced me to Akbar, formerly a pimp and the chief electrician of the brothels, who could no longer return to his old job. He had just married Jyothi, a woman who had exited prostitution. Through Akbar I met Jaffer, another former pimp who now ran a cycle repair workshop. I told them that I'd like to connect with all the women.

Both were eager to help. Akbar even wanted to work with me. I told him plainly I did not have much money. In the end, we agreed upon Rs 600 per month. Akbar and Jaffer organised a meeting with all the women they were in touch with.

Khatoon and Masoom Bi were the first two brothel-keepers they introduced to me. These two sisters had ruled the Mehendi area for over three decades and still held a small room there. I was told they had properties in Barkas and Kalapather, but they insisted on meeting in Mehendi. Perhaps they did not want to be recognised as brothel-keepers in other areas or they had some other motive.

At the time, it did not bother me. I was happy to meet them wherever they wanted; I just wanted to start as soon as possible. Back home, when I reflected on it, it struck me that the residents in that area had opposed the presence of these women and fought a legal battle to evict them. How would they react when the same women returned?

On the day of the meeting, the entire street was on alert and the shopkeepers were on guard. This was apparent to me, especially when

I saw people patrolling the street where the small room owned by Khatoon and Masoom was located. Thankfully, I had anticipated this, and requested Akbar and Jaffer to inform the people of the area about my motives. As a result, the meeting went off without complications.

Over twenty women attended it. All of them had been recently released from the state home at Yousufguda. It was a hellishly uncomfortable experience for me. First, I had to listen to all their frustrations against the court, government, state home, jail and the police. They were angry with Tejdeep Kaur and spoke very poorly of her, accusing her of all kinds of atrocities, including kicking a pregnant woman. I listened patiently, but in my opinion, what Tejdeep Kaur lacked was the support of the Department of Women and Child Welfare. If the police and the welfare department had joined hands, much confusion, frustration and violations could have been prevented.

In any case, my job was not to defend anybody. I heard the women out, and then I told them about myself, that I wanted to help them and was willing to go to any extent. That I was just an individual with a friend, the director of Boys Town, who was also interested in helping them. There was no agency and nobody else backing me.

Masoom Bi's eyes swept over my face and then down at the rest of me, as if my body could disclose my intentions. They ran back to my face and held my eyes for a bit. Then, she spoke up, 'Do something for our children.'

Right away, all of them nodded. They'd been forced to operate in different parts of Hyderabad, on the streets, and didn't know how their children, left behind wherever they'd been staying, fared. I told them I'd get in touch in three days.

I rushed to Boys Town right away to meet Jo. Finally, after all this time, I could do something of value for those women. I tripped over my words in my excitement, unable to share it fast enough with him. He heard me out patiently, and then asked me, with an absolute lack of enthusiasm and perhaps some outrage, 'So, what's their contribution? Why are they dumping their children on us?'

I was taken aback. These women had lost everything; why—how—what should—*could*—they contribute? Wasn't that *our* job, of people who are privileged, to reach out and provide everything? What was the point in them seeking help if we put them to work? And finally, most fundamentally, we were the ones who had approached them. It was our need—rather, my need—that had sent me to them in the first place. Instead of taking this as a great start, he was raising unnecessary objections.

Jo was adamant. For the first time, our arguments turned personal. I was angry. After years, I was finally on the verge of starting something significant, and he was blocking my way. When I saw neither of us budging, I walked out in a huff and refused to speak to him any further.

When it was time for my next meeting with the women, Jo and I were still not talking. I went in a subdued mood, for this had now become my personal initiative. There was no way I could go back to Jo, we'd been that harsh with each other.

But Jo clearly wielded great influence over me. I found myself parroting exactly what he'd said. I told the women they couldn't dump their children on us. If they wanted something done, they should also contribute. There was an ominous silence for a second after that, then, a thunderous commotion. They were all talking all at once, with their mouths and their hands. I couldn't follow a word. My bewilderment must have been apparent. Khatoon Bi shushed them all and then looked at me, spitting fire, 'Who told you we're slinking out of our responsibility?! We'll obviously contribute for our children!'

I then realised that each of the women had been taking off jewellery—rings, anklets, chains, bangles, nose pins, earrings, even cash—and passing it on to a pile in the centre. Masoom Bi pulled out a kerchief, tied all of it into a bundle and handed it over to me. My hands were shaking, I was struck dumb. With an effort, I collected myself, then handed the collection back to Khatoon and Masoom Bi, and told them we could start a school for the children. They could use this money to get a room somewhere, and it would be my responsibility to get the teachers.

The women began to talk excitedly, making quick plans. They all wanted the school to be in Mehendi itself, which they felt was the safest place. Something to the effect of a known devil being better than an unknown angel. Within minutes, they'd even selected the place—an independent building off Qamar Hotel, which used to have a brothel on the first floor along with a few rooms on the ground floor and shared a common wall with a house where some hijras lived.

Masoom Bi and Khatoon Bi summoned the hotel owner, who arrived right away. The owner had lived on their earnings for decades and was reasonably subservient. They told him that they wanted to use the room adjacent to his hotel for a school for children. The two women clearly still wielded a lot of power in this area. Frankly, I don't think he had much choice in the matter, and was elated to see him agree. I announced that we'd start the very next day.

Once again, I headed straight to Boys Town. Jo heard the entire story without offering any opinion. That night, I stayed back at Boys Town. Jo and I talked for over two hours, walking about in the school grounds, going over what would work, what wouldn't, what I needed to arrange, so on and so forth. That's when I told him I wanted to call it 'Prajwala'. He had no problem, even though he did not really understand the meaning. I had decided on the name in December 1996, when I had first visited Mehendi. 'Prajwala' means eternal flame. For me, it symbolised what we set out to be, a flame to guide these women and girls in their journey towards the light. And so it was that Prajwala was born!

The next few days were hectic. There was no way I could find a teacher overnight, so I became the first teacher at Prajwala. There were five children in that first batch. All my tutoring and Girl Guide experience came handy. I created a timetable for six hours and taught them everything I knew. The subjects ranged from numeracy, English and Hindi alphabets, music, dance and various types of knots (a key skill in the Girl Guides).

I had asked Akbar to spread the word about the need for a teacher. In the meantime, he was himself both a student and a teacher. He'd taken up a class so as to give me a break and taught basic electrical work. As he was also unlettered, I made it mandatory for him to sit in on all my classes. In any case, there was no other work for him at that time.

Word of my school/tuition centre spread fast. Soon, I found my first teacher, a young Marwari girl just out of her teens. What her motivations were—to see if it was really a school and not a front for nefarious activities, or if she genuinely wanted to serve—I'm not sure. Shweta came to us after graduating from high school, looking for a job. I gladly offered her one, with a promise of Rs 400 as salary.

Now, I had two staff members, and an outflow of Rs 1,000. Soon after Shweta began working, we accepted fifteen more children, taking the total number of students to twenty. We needed another teacher, and Vijeta joined the team. There were only two rooms and a small bathroom, so we could only accommodate two teachers. The Mehendi centre became fully functional, and my overheads increased to Rs 1,400.

While I wasn't very good as a teacher, I was a capable administrator. I worked out a proper curriculum, a lesson plan and a weekly plan with Shweta and Vijeta. What bothered all of us was the way the children behaved. I knew first-hand what a herculean task it was to keep them engaged for the entire day. Their attention span was limited and few of them liked all the subjects. And even when they did, they were interested only for the first few minutes before they got bored and started distracting the others. I was wary of disciplining in case they dropped out. It was critical that we did not lose any of them.

Of course, they'd been exposed to a lot, and it was evident from the language they used and the crass jokes they made. This was rather hard for Shweta and Vijeta to take as they'd had a very sheltered upbringing. Even our youngest, at three years old, knew a lot about the adult world. Once, a seven-year-old asked a five-year-old for oral sex, thrusting a rupee at her right in front of me and the teachers. The child said it so comfortably, but had no clue what it meant. In all probability, this is what they regularly heard in their homes.

The oldest of the children, Aju, eleven years old, had deep burns on his stomach. His mother had pushed him onto the balcony to escape police custody when Mehendi was getting cleared out. He was supposed to have jumped onto the next terrace and escaped, but had fallen onto an electric pole and received the burns.

All twenty of the children had disturbing stories about jail, about police violence and about what the customers did to them. We had six slightly older boys between eight and eleven, and many of them had couriered drugs and country liquor for the women. They had additional responsibilities such as collecting money from the customers and running other errands in the brothel.

These children had no idea what a balanced meal looked like. For them, food meant biryani and a lot of oily, fried food. The mothers had asked Khatoon Bi and Masoom Bi to sort out the children's afternoon meal. I did not get involved. The small nest fund with which I was managing the organisation did not allow for meal plans.

Friday was their jumme ka namaz, and thus their weekly bath, their 'pani nahana' day. They'd all turn up late, but neat and clean, surma in their eyes.

I designed a curriculum that not only looked at the children's scholastic needs but also their psychological needs—my degree in psychiatric social work finally coming in handy. Both Vijeta and Shweta were eager to absorb more knowledge. They had just finished high school and were flexible and willing to learn from mistakes. With a proper curriculum and teaching aids, the school became a fun place and the children wanted to come in every day. We told them clearly that we were preparing them for eventual admission to regular schools.

To help them understand what that entailed, we introduced uniforms for students and sarees for teachers, and followed all other protocols usually enforced in schools. The day would begin with an assembly, and on Saturdays, there would be a march-past. Akbar's sessions on electrical work continued, although I no longer allowed him to attend classes. Both my teachers were young girls, and I did not want unnecessary complications.

Soon, the children were liberally using English words and could even sing hymns, and word spread on how effective we were. The mothers were getting glowing reports from their children. Women who had moved to other parts of the city would visit and ask us to start something similar in their areas. I was greatly enthused. Prajwala would be expanding its operations.

Among those who'd asked me to start another school was Padma. She had offered me a part of the house she lived in, a rented two-bedroom, for a modest sum of Rs 300. She was even willing to do away with the rent if necessary. I was overwhelmed.

Akbar and I went to see the house, which was five kilometres away, in Kishanbagh. As always, we travelled by cycle, with me riding pillion. It was convenient, and saved us a lot of money.

It was a big house and had two large rooms, a smaller room with a kitchen and a bathroom. Padma would stay in the smaller room. We could use the two larger rooms; they could easily accommodate around forty children. The was even a nice courtyard with a neem tree—just the right setting for a school assembly! The house had two separate entrances, one leading to the two larger rooms and the other to the smaller one. In all probability, the owner had designed it like that to rent out multiple portions that shared a bathroom. Padma was renting the entire building. In my enthusiasm and excitement, I did not wonder why a single woman needed such a big house when she used only the smaller room. The drive to expand Prajwala was all-consuming and did not allow space for such logical questions.

I found two new teachers, Subhasini and Tahseen, without much trouble. We had twenty children enrol almost immediately, and used the same curriculum that we had at Mehendi.

Once the centre opened, I thought it would be good to meet the mothers, so we invited them to the school. That was when we felt the first prickles of alarm. Over thirty women attended the meeting, and during the session, we heard a commotion outside. A huge mob with sticks had assembled on the road in front of the house. We were all unnerved, and the women fled. Later I'd learn that a few men in that area had recognised some of the women and instigated the community.

Tahseen, Subhasini, Akbar and I stood our ground. Tahseen, who had some clout in that area, spoke to the mob and introduced me. I told them that we ran an education programme for deprived children, omitting the background of the women. Tahseen and Akbar added that the director of Boys Town was supporting this venture. Suddenly, everyone calmed down. Jo was nowhere, and yet he was everywhere! The community was impressed that a bridge education programme for deprived children was being set up here.

The Kishanbagh centre was now a full-fledged one, with twenty-six children enrolled. But I felt a strange unease. At our Mehendi centre, there was absolute transparency with the community about the background of the mothers. Here, we had to present half-truths and were operating on the credibility of another institution. And something about the new centre just seemed off. I couldn't say what it was, but something niggled at me.

My fears turned real in less than two weeks. I got a call from a panicking Tahseen at 7 a.m. one day. By now, I had a landline telephone installed at home. She had gone early to school to prepare for an activity and found condoms in the classroom. I rushed to the centre and asked Tahseen and Subhasini to keep away before cornering Padma in her room. At first, she mumbled that she'd had some relatives over and allowed them to use the room for the night.

Until then, I hadn't know there was a don hidden inside me. My voice changed, along with my entire demeanour. I did not even raise my voice, and I don't remember what I said but she was soon falling at my feet in tears.

Padma had been using the school as a front to run a brothel. That was why she'd offered us the room and that too at a modest rent. What a betrayal! I quickly called Tahseen and Subhasini to brief them.

There was no way we could stay here. The question was, where would we go now?

Tahseen took me to her house just two streets over. I don't know what she told her parents, but her father offered his vacant house on rent to the centre. He was one of the most respected leaders in that area. We were able to avert a major calamity before the local community came to know. In a few days, Padma vacated the building.

What would I have done if Padma had been caught red-handed? I have no idea. I had once again fallen into the same trap—assumed that others' motives were the same as mine. This was another big lesson for me not to take anyone at face value, especially those who demonstrate support that appears to be too good to be true.

Thanks to Tahseen, Kishanbagh had a safe place for the children to study. Both the teachers were fully aware whose children our students were, and had met the mothers at our Mehendi centre. I will be forever grateful for Tahseen and Subhasini's commitment towards the children; they could have got into real trouble if the background of the children had been leaked. I'm fully aware that they were with me not because they couldn't get a job anywhere else, but because they both felt compelled to support my mission. God was sending me, in ones and twos, the right kind of people who'd help bring it to life.

Prajwala was fumbling, falling and getting up every day!

Once the second centre was up and running again, we started two more, at Kalapather and Pahadi. While most of our students were children of the women who had fled Mehendi and lived and operated incognito, we allowed other children to join, especially those of the pimps and others who worked for the brothels in Mehendi. A small percentage of other children also enrolled in the centres. This helped us avoid too many questions from the community.

But Prajwala's rapid growth in this first phase was turning into a challenge for me. I had to the pay salaries of ten teachers and Akbar, and then there were the overheads—rent, travel, teaching materials. At Mehendi, the mothers had initially paid the rent, but over time had found it difficult to spare the money. As we expanded, community partnership was restricted to identifying a place for the centre, a little money for its maintenance and purchase of some school materials such as a blackboard, writing supplies, etc. The women found it hard to part with money; the times were hard, and they had to also provide roti, kapda and makaan for their families.

I had learnt financial planning during my Sadbhavana days, but not really paid it much mind so far. In fact, I had confidently told Jo that Prajwala's financial affairs were my concern and he should not interfere. I was sure that the savings from my work would make for a good start, and that the mothers would be able to continue making regular contributions. I was clearly wrong.

Jo and I had already agreed that we would not bring Boys Town or any of Jo's connections into the conversation about Prajwala's financial needs. As a renunciate, he had no income whatsoever and did not even have a personal bank account. My savings from PIN were gone, so I sold the bit of gold I had. It was not much, just three pairs of earrings and a ring. Our greatest achievement at that time was that all the staff got their modest salaries on the first of the month, and our landlords their rent on the third. We had not missed even a single deadline, an ethos that we follow to this day.

But back then, Prajwala had not yet been registered. We weren't prepared to bring outsiders into the organisation at a time when we were still trying to understand the dynamics of its operations. But then how could we make Prajwala financially sustainable? Would I have to go knocking on people's doors for donations?

14

Those Who Help Themselves

There came a point when I couldn't pay the salaries, let alone the rent. It was the twenty-fifth of the month, and I knew no way to raise the amount. Sitting in the office at Mehendi, I'd been unable to think about anything else the whole day. I decided to leave for home; I'd not been of much use anyway.

Back home, I lay on the floor, wondering if I had anything of value to sell. When we'd started, we needed less than Rs 1,500 for the entire operation. Now, with five centres, staff and overheads, I needed far more. What could I do? The ceiling had no answers.

At around 2 p.m., there was a knock on the door. I opened the door to find the postman. He usually dropped the letters from my father outside. I wondered why he'd knocked this time. Shrugging, I extended my hand to receive the letter. He shook his head, and asked me to come to the post office to receive a money order.

What money order? Who was sending me a money order? I could only think of my father. But why was he sending me money? I hadn't told him anything about my work, much less my financial challenges. I locked the door and walked with him to the post office, five minutes away.

There, the postmaster took out a bunch of notes and asked me to count them. It was Rs 12,500, which was just around what I needed! Eagerly, I looked at the accompanying note for the sender. It said Ranjit V., and there was a line: 'You had helped me in college, just returning with interest.' For the life of me, I could not remember who this person was. And how was it that they were so meticulous as to seek me out and return the money? This mystery remains unsolved. In college, I had given money to college mates who'd needed it, but it had really been without any expectation of having it returned. Working part-time during college, I paid my own fees, and always had something spare that I could share. This was another aspect of me that baffles my near and dear ones—the ability to give away whatever I possess with ease.

At any rate, the arrival of the money was truly divine intervention, and I'd see many, many others over the years. It made me believe that the gods above were watching over me and wouldn't allow me to fail.

But while they had taken care of this month through Ranjit, bless his soul, I couldn't rely on the gods to cover my monthly outflow. I had to help myself. It was time to act.

The Boys Town model of functioning had always been an inspiration to me. It was one of the largest industrial training institutes for deprived and marginalised boys. What was unique about this institution was that it was a training-cum-production institute that was completely self-sufficient. It not only gave people technical training in various areas—book-binding, printing, fabrication, fitter, welding, carpentry—but also did production work.

So, I decided to explore setting up a production unit. I had met many middle-aged women for whom prostitution was no longer a viable option. They didn't earn enough from it any more: there was far too much competition and the buyers preferred younger women. However, these women hadn't ever operated on their own and, even on days when they earned little or nothing, the brothel had at least given them a roof over their head and food for their bellies. This was particularly true for women who had operated in traditional red-light areas. There was something about the old areas—'class' perhaps fits best—that the other operators, with their desperate revenue models, did not possess. Such older establishments, in fact, had a system in place to take care of older women in prostitution, even ones who were dying. After experiencing the comforts of a brothel, it was difficult to cope in the open market on the street.

Since I'd met them, Akbar and Jaffer Bhai had introduced me to a number of former pimps who had turned to making plastic toys. Akbar, in particular, took great pride in introducing me to all his past acquaintances. Perhaps it was his way of showing them that he now led a dignified life. The fact that he was in awe of me and genuinely respected me only added to this pride. Akbar, in fact, was the only person who knew the day-to-day challenges I faced running Prajwala—most of the time, I set forth riding pillion on his cycle to tackle these problems!

Akbar and I met some of these former pimps and shared my plan for setting up a plastic toy-making unit with women who were formerly in prostitution. While many were sceptical about the women's ability to do such work, they didn't dissuade me. Rather, they connected me with two craftsmen, or karigars, as they are called.

Ahmed was a timid guy, unused to speaking to blunt women or taking orders from them, and perpetually wore a grumpy face. Baba, much younger than Ahmed, was an open chap. His easy smile and friendly demeanour charmed people. The two were willing to work with me, but needed daily wages as per the market rate.

While I was clueless about the viability of such a venture, I agreed. Baba, who was the more proactive one, took me to a workshop, or karkhana, near Hassan Nagar that was looking to sell their second-hand machines and replace them with newer ones. While the new machines cost about Rs 60,000, I'd get two second-hand machines for Rs 30,000.

Baba inspected the machines on sale and assured me that they were in good condition. Ahmed concurred. Together, we calculated that we needed around Rs 45,000 to set up a complete unit, including the machines and the raw material.

The million-dollar question was how many women we'd need to work in such a unit. Baba reckoned that if we operated for eight to ten hours, we'd need at least four women. Ahmed really did not care about working with women.

Baba, I was realising, was perceptive and clearly understood my aim. His enthusiasm and go-getter attitude were a great inspiration and asset. He understood that I wasn't in this for money, but was genuinely trying to help the women. Baba sought me out privately and told me that if this took off, we could actually generate a lot of revenue which could be channelled into Prajwala. I was touched. By this time, I had a fairly good idea that he had thoroughly researched me and knew all about our education centres.

The machines we had selected needed electricity to heat the plastic granules, which would then flow into the moulding die. Once the product rolled off the machines, they had to be painted and made beautiful. I was told both dolls and balls were a good idea, being in high demand at jatras and melas and other regional fairs. I was even given to understand that the karkhanas couldn't meet the market demands.

It seemed like a good business plan, and I was enthused. I shared my thoughts with Jo; he was supportive but wasn't sure how it would pan out. Selecting women was not a great problem. Instead of four, I hired seven, three of whom were HIV-positive and had escaped from the Pratyanmaya, the home run by my friend Sarat Babu. They felt stifled there, unable to do anything productive. From their account, it seemed like the shelter had only provided for their basic needs in a custodial setting.

I decided to meet Sarat Babu, whom I had worked with during the Janmabhoomi community programme. We had got along. I knew his wish to serve was the motivation behind establishing Pratyanmaya. I'd learnt from my contacts that over twelve of the women at the shelter had escaped, and three of them were with me now. Women living in brothels over a period of time normalise a lot of things, including alcohol and a certain narrative of free life which is rather subjective. Living in a shelter would be like detention to them, and the natural tendency would be to attempt to escape. Many then fell back into the same trap of prostitution. Of the twelve who had escaped, only three did not want to return to their old line of work and had sought me out for an alternate livelihood.

I used that as a pretext to meet Sarat at the Collectorate. He was thrilled to see me, and was genuinely happy to hear about my plans for the toy-making unit to help generate income for women. Unprompted, he asked me how much money I needed. I'd carried my notes, what I suppose you'd call a business plan. He waved it aside and asked me what I foresaw as the sum total of expenses. I told him I needed around Rs 45,000. This figure included the machines and the raw materials. He asked me to wait, since he had other people waiting to see him. Sarat was now coordinating the entire Balajyothi programme, a child labour project, and was obviously a busy man.

I wanted to be prepared to discuss further nitty-gritties of the unit. So I went to Akbar, who was waiting outside, and asked him to somehow contact Baba, since he could explain the details with more authority and better knowhow. Akbar, who always felt important inside the Collectorate, was positively radiating with pride at my faith in his ability to get things done. For those who have only lived with stigma and been treated as scoundrels, acceptance is transformative.

Fortunately, pagers were common during those days, and Baba had one. As soon as Akbar paged him, Baba dropped everything to rush to the Collectorate. It felt reassuring to have him there. Then, as if on cue, Sarat called me in. I asked Baba and Akbar to follow. Sarat looked at us quizzically. I introduced them, and said Baba had come to explain our proposal.

Sarat has a funny laugh. Only when you know him well will you understand the beauty of it. He started laughing and told the men to leave. Akbar and Baba thought they had made some great blunder and hurried out of the room.

'Sorry it took so long,' Sarat said. 'I had to send someone to the bank, and it's rather far.' He took a big wad of cash from his drawer and pushed it towards me.

Overwhelmed, my senses shut down.

'It's a personal donation. I'm sorry there aren't any schemes or funds at the moment that you can avail. I didn't want you coming another day all the way just for this, so I made you wait.' Later, it would sink in that he'd been apologising for his delay in making a Rs 50,000 donation.

In a daze, I counted the money; he insisted on it. I took my bag off my shoulder, and he promptly remarked, 'Ah! There it is, the jhola of the jholewali!' I laughed. It was our joke about the social worker stereotype and how clothes and accessories decidedly did not make the man, or woman, in my case.

Akbar and Baba were waiting outside, the picture of despondence: shoulders slumped, heads hung low. I gave them a bright, silly grin. Their eyes lit up, they stood up straight, happiness blooming on their faces. Whatever it was, I had good news!

After I told them we'd got the money and a little more, we went straight to the karkhana to pay an advance and secure our machines. But in all this, we'd overlooked the most basic thing—where were we going to set it up? This is what happens if one plans too quickly. Strategic planning should always be done in a calm environment so that one can factor in all the components.

Akbar was of the opinion we should stick to Mehendi. The area had been synonymous with prostitution for decades. The women could walk around unmolested, and the shopkeepers went about their business, unbothered by all that went on around them. We hadn't faced any problems there with our centre either. There was no fear of a Kishanbagh-like incident of an angry mob descending on us.

The logic was sound, so we went to Mehendi right away. There we met Amjad Bhai, one of the co-owners of Qamar Hotel. The rooms above the hotel had been used by the brothels, and had remained empty ever since the eviction. Amjad Bhai offered us two rooms for an exorbitant Rs 3,000, but the rooms were big and airy, could easily accommodate ten people along with the machines and had a mini storage place. The attached terrace would be great for drying stuff. We shook hands to seal the deal.

Now we really were ready.

Baba, our domain expert, set to work on the machines, which needed a lot of adjustments to set up. Though they were operated manually, they needed electricity. Akbar, a trained electrician, was instrumental in finalising the scope of operations. We had gone from zero to ready-to-start in less than ten days. There was now in place a functional plastic unit, so we procured the raw material and trained the women in their responsibilities. Baba also taught one of the women, Shanta, to operate the machines manually under the disapproving eyes of Ahmed. Over a period of time, Ahmed would learn to respect each of these women for their skills and their ability to learn everything in a male-dominated field.

I had begun sharing information very selectively with Jo. He didn't feel comfortable that I met strangers at all times, day and night. That made sense, but I could only see those people when they were available, and most karkhanas in the Old City opened only mid-afternoon and worked till late at night. If I had to meet the owners or do any kind of scouting, it had to be during the evenings.

Therefore, Jo wasn't privy to all these developments. Eventually, I updated him about them, shyly informing him that the unit was ready to function. The pride in his eyes was heart-warming. He suggested that we invite some important people for the inauguration, both for the sake of the business and to gain legitimacy.

So, I approached A. Devasena, the revenue divisional officer at the Hyderabad Collectorate, whom I knew well. As expected, she readily agreed, despite the half-day notice (I was in a hurry to start and did not want to lose much time). I also wanted someone from Boys Town to come, so that people could see what Jo and I were doing together. (The speculation about us had reduced, as I no longer visited that often. Now that I had a comfortable bathroom in my own house, I didn't need those weekly baths at his place! Moreover, my evenings were very busy with end-of-day meetings with staff at all the centres.) I invited Brother George (known as 'Uncle Brother' for his avuncular disposition), of whom I was particularly fond. Sarat, in his customary style, refused to come. He was more interested in the work than in inaugurations. I knew I had his blessings.

We were set. Devasena and Uncle Brother inaugurated the unit, and were impressed with the efficient manner in which the women and other karigars worked to start production. In preparation for the event, I had them rehearse their roles a day in advance, how they'd collect the dolls falling out of the machine, the coordinated way to cut the edges, start the painting process and then the drying.

Against Baba's advice, I wanted to sell the products directly to the market. I wanted to understand the market myself and get to know its intricacies. The first few days were adventurous. Baba and Ahmed were fast workers; their daily wages depended on the number of pieces they made. The women were getting much-needed employment, so they were also getting faster by the day.

Soon, we settled a towering bundle of a couple of thousands of balls and dolls onto a cycle rickshaw. Akbar and I would sit precariously on either side and go to Begum Bazar, which was the closest market, where I'd deal directly with the shopkeepers. They'd perhaps never seen a seller like me, preferring a middleman who could source products tailored to their requirements. Middlemen, after all, were connected to a lot of sellers and mixed and matched their wares with the requirements of the market. In spite of all this, many shopkeepers did buy from us, and most days, we sold the bulk of what we'd produced. Baba, for one, was very impressed with the high margins.

My strategy worked. The middlemen began to contact me at the centre. This way, I was in control and could negotiate with them for a rate just slightly lower than what I got directly in the market. Taking all our costs into account, including the daily rickshaw fare and the chai and samosas we had at the market, this made better business sense. Now our facility was in full swing. The middlemen collected our toys every day and paid us on a daily basis.

I had arranged to pay Baba and Ahmed weekly, because paying people daily made me feel like a feudal lord. We were making good money, covering all salaries in the unit and the centres as well as other expenses. We were on our way to becoming financially sustainable.

While the plastic toy-making unit was doing fine, and we were able to meet all our expenses and economically empower seven women, it was important that we should do something to create a nest fund or a corpus. I was keenly aware that, in case anything went wrong, I wouldn't be able to recover from the setback, given the scale of my current expenses.

I asked Jo if we could sell these toys in schools, maybe Boys Town to start with. He looked hesitant. Brother (Dr) Franky Noronha, Franky to me, and a dear friend of Jo's, was sitting with us. He said I could do it in Little Flower High School, Abids, where he was the principal. Poor Jo had no choice but to agree to let us sell in Boys Town. I organised a sale at both schools. Franky also wanted me to give a small speech to the students to explain why it was important to buy these toys, a kind of 'cause' marketing. I agreed. Many years later, Franky would join our governing body.

The sale at Boys Town was not much, even though the margins were higher than I would ever get in the market. But the sale at Little Flower was stupendous. Selling these toys at retail prices gave us a huge margin.

Buoyed by this success, I approached the principal of Rosary Convent, another reputed school located near Abids in the city. She was all for it and, like Franky, requested me to give a speech so that the parents wouldn't ask unnecessary questions when their children asked for money.

This was fantastic, but required a lot of effort from me. We had to take the toys to the school and shunt back the unsold inventory, but (and this was most taxing) I also had to give the speech and manage the counter on both days. None of my staff could speak English, and they were so embarrassed about it that they were reluctant to enter the English-medium school and manage the sale counters. Akbar would wait for me some distance from the school gate and follow close behind wherever I went. English is the language of trade and business, but also the language of privilege and acceptance. No wonder it gives so many people—me included—such a complex. So, I had to do the main selling, with Akbar handing over the required number of balls and dolls to me.

So far, the year 1998 had been kind to us. I was turning twenty-six, and my birthday also turned out to be truly special. All the mothers and the women who'd found a job with us wanted to celebrate it with me. There were at least fifty of us, so we couldn't possibly meet at any of our centres. Jo suggested Boys Town, and allowed us to use the garden outside the church in their campus. The women were excited—they would finally meet their Bada Saheb! (Akbar was the one who started calling Jo 'Bada Saheb', or big boss, and the title suited Jo's stature. I was 'Madam' to the children and staff and 'Amma' to the women.) I had never experienced such pure love in my life. For Jo, it was his first meeting with so many of our women. And this was the first time that women in prostitution had entered the Boys Town campus. Even after decades, this particular birthday I will never forget, being pampered by the women with small gifts and celebrating our togetherness, sitting on the grass lawn—these small joys have left everlasting memories.

While I was economically empowering Prajwala, my own personal finances were grim. Right from the inception of Prajwala, I had decided to be a full-time volunteer and not draw a salary from the organisation. This was ideologically driven, and no amount of counselling and advice from anyone changed my mind on this. I firmly believe that I shouldn't earn from this mission. But I had to work elsewhere to sustain myself. While my engagement with Prajwala did not allow for a full-time job, I did take up small assignments.

One of these was teaching at Jeevan Jyoti, a theological institute for nuns. I took sessions on gender sensitisation, the impact of globalisation and liberalisation, crimes against women, spirituality and development work. The sisters quickly declared me a domain expert in all of these topics. The fact that I understood religious life also acted in my favour. Their assumptions weren't off; I was a self-proclaimed Hindu nun with very strong spiritual leanings, and my long years of varied experience made me a suitable candidate to articulate my experiences from the development sector. Years later, I would meet sisters who were my former students, and learn that this course had changed their perspective and given them deeper insights. I can only say I was humbled to have got an opportunity to influence this group of people whose life's mission was to engage in god's work.

Personally, I think it was my passion that drove my ability to put together all my experiences in a pedagogic framework that made sense—that was what I brought to the table. While my fee wasn't high, it was still an income. The bigger problem was that this 'assignment' was only for a week annually.

Fortunately, I managed to get another assignment, from Nirmala Niketan, a college of social work in Mumbai. Gracy Fernandes was from the same order as Principal D'Souza of Roshni Nilaya. She had heard about my master's dissertation and wanted me to study four best practices combating sex trafficking in South Asia. They had selected the organisations and had a clearly defined framework that I had to use to report my observations. For this project, I visited Vimochana Devadasi Punarvasati Sangha in Dharwad, founded by B.L. Patil and V.S. Manwade, who were involved in the rehabilitation of devadasis; Sanlaap in Kolkata founded by Indrani Sinha, who would become one of my most trusted friends in the sector; Gudia in Varanasi, founded by Ajit Singh; and Maiti Nepal in Kathmandu founded by Anuradha Koirala. It was a six-week-long project, and I was paid Rs 10,000 for each of the four case studies on the nature of rehabilitation services that each organisation provided for women in prostitution. Additionally, my flight tickets, transport and boarding were covered.

These were heaven-sent opportunities for me. There was, of course, the money, which I desperately needed at the time. More importantly, they gave me just the right exposure after the work I'd been doing at Prajwala to prevent sex trafficking and rehabilitate the trafficked. That year and a half of intense toil, from 1996 to the end of 1998, gave me the understanding needed to appreciate efforts that were already well established and had made a mark in the anti-trafficking sector.

My first visit was to Devadasi Punarvasati Sangha at Athani, Dharwad. This was my first visit to the devadasi belt, where women and girls as young as seven or eight years were dedicated to Goddess Yellamma and then socialised to adopt prostitution. I remember travelling by train and getting down at the Kudachi railway station, where V.S. Manawade received me at the station. He was an elderly gentleman, maybe in his late fifties. We travelled by jeep as he briefed me about the devadasi system. The one-hour drive was engrossing and scenically mesmerising, with sugarcane farms on both sides of the road. The air was dry and dusty, but that did not matter to me. I was absorbing all the information that Manawade was giving me. Soon, we reached a nice building, where I met B.L Patil, the co-founder of the organisation. Patil-avare, as I started to call him, was a well-known lawyer and had a very impressive personality. He was also in his late fifties. I was a complete novice, but at no point did the two gentlemen make me feel young and inexperienced. Patil gave me a detailed insight into how they used religious leaders, the mahants, to end the devadasi system. His point was that if a regressive system was legitimised by religion, then opinion-makers and influencers from the same religion should be used to change the system. They began offering nursing courses for children of devadasis, preventing a whole generation from being dedicated to the devadasi system. The women who exited the system were also provided financial support to start an alternate livelihood.

Interacting with Patil and Manawade opened my eyes to multiple possibilities. Knowing Kannada helped, as it immediately helped forge a deep bond with the two of them, which remains strong even today. So memorable was the meeting that small details left a big impression. I can still remember our sumptuous lunch of jonna rotti (jowar roti), kaipalli jhunka (a Marathi delicacy) and anna saaru (rice and dal). It wasn't the food so much as the easy warmth of these two wonderful men that was endearing. Manawade died a few years ago, but Patil, in his late seventies now, continues the mission with the same zeal and enthusiasm that I saw in 1998.

My next stop was Gudia in Varanasi. I had taken a flight, and there was some miscommunication regarding my arrival. So, I ended up spending hours on the road in an auto, looking for the office. The anxiety that came with this did not allow me to appreciate the beautiful city of Varanasi on the banks of the Ganges.

When I reached the address, I realised it was the office-cum-home of the founder, Ajit Singh. As I hadn't made any arrangements for my stay (all part of the miscommunication), his family graciously accommodated me for two nights. Gudia worked with children of women in prostitution in those days. Here, as in Mehendi, they had the tawaif system. While Gudia did not have a specific programme for rehabilitation, they focused on education in a school very similar to our centres.

Ajit himself was only slightly older than me, and a passionate advocate for ending prostitution. Meeting a person close to my age was good for me to understand how he coped with it all.

Like Prajwala, Gudia, too, has grown over the years and has become one of the most powerful organisations in north India fighting sex trafficking. Ajit and I continue to be friends and connect whenever there is an issue that we need to tackle together.

Visiting Sanlaap in Kolkata was an emotionally satisfying moment in multiple ways. Indrani Sinha, the founder, was one of the most extraordinary, humble women I've met. She was in her late forties then. Her wisdom, her vision and the way she led her organisation, all of it impressed me, but what was inspiring was the way she listened to me.

Sanlaap, established in 1987, was ten years older than Prajwala. They had done extensive work in Sonagachi, the red-light area of Kolkata. They managed drop-in centres for education right inside the red-light area, and had already set up a safe home for the rehabilitation of young girls rescued from prostitution. The organisation was involved in prevention, protection and advocacy. While I could not see a drop-in centre or the safe home, I did end up visiting Sonagachi in the night. It was very similar to Kamatipura in Mumbai, but much more crowded, with mixed smells of mustard oil, paan and open sewage.

This trip was special for me because of Indrani-di. She carried herself with such grace and humility that I was spellbound. When I shared some of my insights from our work and some snippets about my new understanding of the porn industry, she listened with rapt interest and made me feel so important. Over the years, we became close friends, one of the best allies I have found in the sector. With her, I could share everything, including my fears and anxieties. Losing her to cancer in 2015 was one of my greatest personal losses, a void that nobody can ever fill.

I had kept my visit to Nepal for the end. For some reason, my travel plans were jinxed from the start. To begin with, I got the date of my flight to Kathmandu wrong, and realised this only after reaching Kolkata. I ended up staying with a close friend of Jo's. And then, I'd mixed up the appointment date, landing in Kathmandu a day after I had scheduled it. I had to wait half a day to meet Anuradha Koirala, the founder. Anuradha-ji is a towering personality, albeit a little aloof, but received me warmly and ensured I got a good understanding of the organisation. Maiti Nepal was the pioneering anti-trafficking organisation in the country, and had done some excellent work to prevent cross-border trafficking. They had also set up a safe home for the rehabilitation of girls, most of whom were rescued in India and repatriated to Nepal. The rehabilitation model was very interesting as they used multiple crafts for economic empowerment. Their work with HIV-positive victims was also noteworthy. Prajwala formed a collaborative relationship with Maiti Nepal over the years to safely repatriate Nepali girls who were trafficked to Hyderabad.

In time, Koirala would become a minister in the Nepalese government, and would also come to be honoured with the Padma Shri by the government of India.

During the project, I'd come and go from Hyderabad. On one such trip back home, I realised trouble was brewing. The first sign was a stranger openly stalking me. He'd come to our Mehendi centre and shout out loud that I'd promised to marry him. This had happened at least four or five times, always in my absence. Needless to say, Shweta and Vijeta were worried for my safety.

For my part, I'd felt somebody had been following me for several months in late 1997, since the time I'd gone to Begum Bazar to sell our toys. Akbar and I would part ways once the work was done, heading to our respective homes. The Old City is always crowded, so it's not unusual to feel eyes on you. And even then, I feel it's far safer for women than other parts of Hyderabad. I'd never felt the need to be alert or raise any sort of alarm. But for months, I had felt a certain set of eyes following me. Since I could not figure out who it was, I thought it was just a figment of my imagination.

One day, Shweta, Vijeta and I were at the Mehendi centre when somebody locked us in from outside. It was 2.30 p.m. and classes were still going on, so no one would come to pick up the children anytime soon. I decided that we should continue the classes, with breaks to shout for help. And that's when we realised that these rooms, which had been used as brothels, were insulated—our screams couldn't penetrate the walls! We were there for over an hour, shouting for help fruitlessly. It was now close to 4 p.m., half an hour to our closing time. The children were all visibly restless.

That's when I recalled that one of the walls had a small hole at the top. On the other side lived a group of hijras. All three of us went to that room, got onto the table next to the wall and screamed our guts out. The children were petrified—and it wasn't just our screams. I don't know if anybody heard us, but somebody finally opened the door a little after 4.30 p.m.

Something was clearly going on, but I didn't know what. The students and teachers had left, and I was by myself, completing the organisational accounts, when Amjad Bhai, the co-owner of Qamar Hotel, came over. This in itself was unusual, and so was what he told me: 'I need you to vacate the premises. I can't take the pressure anymore. They've been at it for so long to get you to leave. Now I'm sick of it.' He refused to tell me who 'they' were. 'They really don't want you here—and you've got a constant stream of media people coming here too! That hasn't helped either. God knows I've seen enough trouble in my life. Now, I just want a peaceful life, no more stress, no more jhamela,' he said, his tone both a threat and a plea. 'So, please, leave at the earliest. Anyway, with your contacts, finding another place shouldn't be a problem.' Having said his piece, he was gone.

Amjad Bhai was asking me to vacate the centre and the toy-making unit immediately. This was a blow. I had no clue what to do. I didn't want to alarm my team, and turning to Jo meant telling him about all the incidents that had happened lately. Definitely not worth it. I couldn't afford to get any more earfuls right now. However, I had no other friends, and had lost touch with most people from PIN. I also didn't want to share this with any official contacts.

Did Amjad Bhai say media? When did anybody from the media come here? I was hardly known, and I knew no media person other than Anantha Krishnan, who had initially introduced me to people at Mehendi, including Akbar. Then I remembered Lalita Iyer, chief correspondent of *The Week*.

We'd met when I was in PIN, and she was doing a story about the Nandanavanam project. We had continued to remain connected after I left PIN. When I started Prajwala, she had done an exclusive piece on my work for the Malayalam monthly *Vanitha*, and had visited me at Mehendi. It was a beautiful piece. Her photographer Vinayan had taken lovely photos. Khatoon Bi and Masoom Bi had allowed the photographs as they felt the world should know that they had changed. This was the media Amjad Bhai was referring to.

It was through that story that my relatives in Kerala and my own parents had come to know the true nature of my work. Luckily for me, the article had left a positive impression in the family. My parents did not say much directly to me, but the fact that Daddy bought many copies of *Vanitha* and distributed it to the neighbours was indication of their pride in my work.

As always, I'd been selectively sharing news about my life and work with my family. In fact, Jo was the one who was my bridge to them. My parents loved Jo and felt he was a great stabilising influence on my life. It was at his invitation that my parents visited Hyderabad. They had stayed in Boys Town and been to all the regular tourist haunts in Hyderabad, but not to any Prajwala intervention centres. I didn't want the people in Mehendi or anywhere else to know my family by sight, let alone meet them. I continue to feel that to date.

Lalita and I had struck the right chords, and after Amjad Bhai's veiled threat, I had to consult somebody. Lalita felt like the right person. I called her and shared my predicament. She was immediately concerned; as a journalist, she knew the implications. Red-light areas are invariably connected to criminal networks and can pose a real threat to life if provoked. While Mehendi was no longer a red-light area, the women were frequenting that place under the Prajwala banner. She told her husband Muralidharan, who was a great strategist. He called up one of his batchmates from IIM, Ramanamurthy, IPS, a senior police officer. The two hatched a plan.

The next day, Ramanamurthy visited us in Mehendi. Behind him trailed the entire police fleet. Ostensibly a casual visit, it was meant to warn our detractors that we had strong and influential people supporting us. He loved the plastic toy-making unit and interacted with the women—we now had eleven women working there. Ramanamurthy made sure everyone knew that this work was credible and appreciated. He then met all the children studying at the centre. The brothers who owned Qamar Hotel, Amjad Bhai and Akbar Bhai, were conspicuous by their absence. There was a significant local crowd who witnessed this visit from afar.

In his concern for us, Ramanamurthy also briefed the local police station. This backfired on two accounts. I'm not entirely sure what his instructions were, but the police were very worked up. Firstly, they were thoroughly upset that we had bypassed their authority and gone to a senior officer, especially when 'nothing had really happened'. The visibly irritated inspector actually told me, 'You could easily have come to the station and told us if something was wrong.' As if he would have believed me if I told him about being stalked, locked in or that my owner was pressured into asking me to vacate. The police, whether in India or elsewhere, are not trained in crime prevention and intelligence gathering as much as responding to a crime that's already been committed.

Then, in order to demonstrate that they were following orders from the senior officer, the local police began throwing their weight around, questioning everyone in Mehendi about who was issuing the threats and generally warning everyone with dire consequences should any of us come to harm. This further ruffled the feathers of the locals, who felt I was making false allegations. After all, they'd supported me, allowed me to run the place, and this is what they'd received for their troubles. Watching the police troop into Mehendi had already stirred up memories of the time they had come to evict the brothels. The community was understandably quite offended. I was stuck on every end, and this was just the beginning of the many other troubles that followed.

Our chief minister, Chandrababu Naidu, had started taking strong measures to prevent power pilferage. A large section in the Old City was guilty of this. Rachael Chatterjee, IAS, was tasked with recovering all the revenue lost due to power pilferage and to book cases against defaulters. In the Old City, the situation was volatile; the women were in purdah and the men were not allowing officers to check the meters inside. The Rapid Action Force (RAF) was summoned to assist the officers to execute their duties. I wasn't concerned. I'd diligently been paying the electricity bill every month and had installed a proper meter. As soon as the officials entered the area with the RAF, there would be massive power cuts. These repeated power cuts affected everybody's work drastically. Lost in worries about the growing hostility of the community, I didn't think to check the unit. The toy-making unit was running smoothly: my women and the karigars were working daily without a break. The middlemen came every day and made their full payments. This is all that mattered.

It was a Friday when I got the message on my pager. I was with Sarat at the Balajyothi office, but I dropped everything to rush to Mehendi. Our entire unit was sealed, and there was a notice on the door. Baba, Akbar, Ahmed and all the women were at the learning centre. As soon as I got there, they all fell at my feet and broke down. I couldn't understand what had happened.

And then Akbar told me. Unknown to me, he had been swayed into pilfering electricity by vested interests who had declared deep concern for the women's livelihoods. After all, these regular power cuts interfered with the output of the dolls and balls. What would these poor women do if they weren't able to keep up the numbers? Akbar had done this in his former life as a pimp, so it was an easy enough task for him. The women knew too, but nobody told me. And that's how I discovered that we'd been stealing electricity for the last ten days. The story did not end there; a case had been booked against me and there would be an arrest warrant. Not another arrest! This was the worst nightmare ever.

Eventually, I calmed down the team and asked them to go home. But they weren't willing to leave me. Their collective plea helped. Ahmed was the only one who had the presence of mind to go and get his brother-in-law's auto. I was quietly bundled in and dropped home.

I called Jo on the phone and gave him the picture quickly. There was no way that I could go to Boys Town, I definitely didn't want to be arrested there. Jo also did not insist. He couldn't think of a way to resolve this situation. Power pilferage was a big issue; hundreds of cases were being booked, the government was taking a strong stand, and as director of Boys Town, he did not want to be in their bad books. I understood. Plus, Jo was part of Prajwala at the ideological level, not at the operational level. All this time, I'd given him information only selectively. He worked for a large institution and was backed by another large institutional religious authority. His world was far from mine, and I had to deal with the consequences of my personal choices.

For the next eighteen days, I evaded arrest even as I tried to find a solution. In the meantime, I was also seeking divine intervention. Akbar took me to Yousufbaba's dargah and told me to pray at Jhatpat Bibi's mazar, or shrine. The Bibi was supposed to be great at crisis intervention. I cried my heart out at her mazar, feeling her presence. So far, the arrest warrant hadn't been executed as the officials were busy charging people with power pilferage. Fortunately for me, Lalita Iyer came to my rescue once again. She connected me to Durga Prasad, the managing director of the electricity board. I met him the same afternoon that I visited Yousufbaba's dargah. In my mind, I was surrendering. Durga Prasad was most sympathetic but clearly pointed out that pilferage was a crime and could not be condoned. His concession: he accepted my explanation that it had only gone on for ten days and directed the officials to fine me accordingly. I came home lighter by Rs 33,000, taken out of my own pocket, and free of all criminal charges.

Our case was dropped and our unit reopened, but my mind was made up. It was now clear that Mehendi was no longer a viable option. We had to pick our fights. I could not trust the people there. I informed everyone that we were closing the unit. Ahmed wanted to buy the machines, and was willing to pay Rs 20,000. I readily agreed. We sold the raw material for about Rs 3,000, and with that, we wrapped up the toy-making unit.

Over the next few months, we shifted the children from Mehendi to our other centres. Baba was a proficient karigar and found a job easily enough. I was sad to see him leave; he was somebody who understood our vision. I had to find employment for all the eleven women from the unit. Akbar, of course, stayed with me. No way was I going to let him go. That was it, the end of our story in Mehendi.

The vested interests that finally succeeded in ousting me from Mehendi must have celebrated. But I wasn't discouraged. I was already preparing my next volley: to really fight prostitution. All I knew was that now I would put myself in the direct line of fire to actively remove people from the space of exploitation, come what may.

15

Rizwana, Kajal and Some Others

Some incidents from when we were still in Mehendi deserve a mention here. I was splitting my time between Prajwala and working on my own projects. At the time, we had seven centres, and about 240 children. I'd see the mothers occasionally, at parent-teacher meetings or when they wanted to learn about their children's progress or discuss something else. Once we concluded the business of the day, we'd move on to chat about the mothers' own lives and how their work affected it. Often, I'd provoke them, ask how they felt to see children as young as their own prostituted. Most would fall silent, the conversation petering out.

One Thursday, I bumped into Sulthana at the bus stop. Three of her children—Aju (the boy who had received burns while trying to evade the police during the eviction), Jaffer and Mushtaq—were at our Mehendi centre. Sulthana was incredibly proud of Aju's prowess at studies and hoped for a bright future for him.

Those days, I was looking into whether the evicted women qualified for government housing under the weaker section housing scheme. The district collector was positive that something could be done. This would be quite helpful for her, and I'd expected more enthusiasm at the news. Sulthana's head was tilted as if to listen, nodding occasionally, but her eyes had a faraway look. Eventually, she turned towards me, inhaled, as if to muster courage, then blurted out, 'I know where a ten-year-old's being kept.'

My breathing stilled. I wanted to shake the details out of her, but was worried about spooking her. Effectively camouflaging my inner turbulence, I calmly coaxed her to give me the details. When asked about the police, she insisted that I work the rescue on my own—she trusted no one, most certainly not the police; she'd faced enough violence from lower-rung policemen. I assured Sulthana that this was not at all a problem. I had no great love for the police either after my Bangalore experience. And the Nandanavanam protests had done nothing to raise my confidence. Back then, I thought of them as colluders in prostitution rather than crusaders against it. In time, I'd come to revise this opinion, like I did with many others.

I told her that I'd rope in Akbar, Jaffer Bhai and other former pimps. She knew them all, so no problem there. The child, Rizwana, was in Talabgatta, in the heart of the Old City. Sulthana worked in that area and knew the people operating that ring. The child's mother had killed herself just after the eviction. The woman who had taken in the child after the mother's death had sold her off.

This was how I learnt that some people in Mehendi still had links in prostitution. I'd thought they'd all up and left. This must be why they wanted me gone—they feared the mothers would reveal such secrets.

I thought it over, and told her that we could do the rescue the very next day. But Sulthana didn't want it on a Friday. We settled on Saturday and agreed that Akbar would be her contact. This worked well for me as well.

As soon as I arrived at the centre, I asked Akbar to accompany me to the Collectorate. 'I want to know if our women will get houses under that scheme,' I told him. I didn't want the others sniffing out the truth.

Only after reaching the Collectorate did I tell Akbar the whole story. He was shocked; he knew the child and her mother. In fact, the mother and Akbar's wife had been in the same brothel. He'd often wondered why the child, Rizwana, hadn't enrolled in our centre. Akbar agreed that the police would only get in the way, and that it would be easier to do this ourselves. I was relieved.

We quickly sketched out a plan. Akbar felt that autos would be best for the rescue, and said that Jaffer and he would get them. I was to get the child while they kept watch outside, ready to leave as soon as I was out. Akbar would share our plans with Sulthana, and ask her to inform the child as well. I didn't want a hostile child who'd resist the rescue.

Our rescue was sorted, but then came the hurdle. What about after? We didn't have a safe home. Where would we keep her? Our centres weren't secure, nor were they equipped with cots or any other amenities required for living in. Staying with me was out of the question.

We were still mulling over this when the district collector called us in. He had great news: sixteen houses in Borabanda, where the weaker section housing colony was constructed, had been sanctioned for our women. Akbar, who had applied in his wife's name, was one of the beneficiaries. We couldn't wait to share this news with the others.

That evening, I combed through my contacts to see if I knew anyone who could house the child. I eventually contacted a former nun who ran a home in the outskirts. Sister Severine, or Amma, was ready to take in a child on Saturday. She only had one condition: the child had to be an orphan. This wasn't a problem at all. I told her I'd bring the child myself.

That night, my call to Jo was rather heavily censored. I told him about the houses. He was thrilled. His only concern: what if some of the women used those houses as brothels? I assured him I was confident about eight. Fourteen of them I knew personally, and the fifteenth was Akbar's wife. I'd done a background check on all of them before applying in their names. None but Padma worried me. We talked for a bit about making sure that she didn't get up to mischief there. Though he seemed inclined to keep chatting, I made an excuse and cut the call.

The next two days sped past. Akbar had arranged everything and confirmed the location of the house independently after checking with Sulthana.

At 4 p.m. on Saturday, I left in Akbar's auto wearing a burqa. Jaffer and others followed in two more autos for safety. Sulthana was to be in the house with the child. To avoid suspicion falling on her, Akbar had asked her to raise the alarm and scream when I left with the child.

I got out of the auto, heart thumping hard as I walked through the open door. A young girl was sitting there. She looked at me, unafraid, as if expecting me. This must be her, I thought, and signalled to her to come with me. As if on cue, Sulthana started screaming. Perhaps she thought we'd be gone before help arrived.

Just as I reached the door, two men entered the room from within. For a second, we froze, taken aback by one another. Then, as if the spell broke, we all started running. I felt the first blow as I ran towards the auto, the child clinging to my arm. He must have aimed for my shoulder, but struck my ear. Fortunately, I only stumbled. The second blow hit me on the nose, made worse by my glasses. I managed to escape, I'm convinced, only because of my height (the lack of it) and because of the burqa which covered most of my body, including my ears. The child was smart enough to keep up. Akbar had started the auto as soon as he saw us running, and we took off. By the time those two men gathered their wits, I'd already jumped into another auto that was waiting in a bylane. The Old City, with all its gullies and alleys, is a great place to lose a tail in such a chase. We had three autos, which made it even more difficult for them to track us. After crossing a few alleyways, the child and I got into Jaffer's auto, which was to take us to our final destination.

Akbar was to keep watch from a café close to that brothel. The men hadn't recognised Akbar; they'd only seen me, that too in a burqa. He was to let us know what they were up to. Sitting there with a cup of Irani chai also gave him an alibi so that nobody connected him with the rescue. This was very important for me. I had to ensure that my team had immunity and not be targeted while doing this kind of work.

As for me, I was already moving out of the city, towards Sister Severine's place, with the child. I could taste blood in my mouth. My nose was bleeding, and so was my ear. I wiped it away. None of it mattered now.

Rizwana was one of the sweetest children I had ever met. Sulthana had done a good job counselling her. I wanted to ask if she'd already been forced into prostitution, but with Jaffer in the auto, I didn't want to say much. 'I'll put you in a good school, like Aju and the others,' I told her. She was happy. '*Khala se door? Khala gandi hai.*' Away from auntie? Auntie's bad. She was referring to the woman who had sold her.

Sister Severine lovingly welcomed Rizwana, managing to communicate without knowing a word of Hindi or Urdu. I told her that I'd be back in a few days to check on the child, and left quickly before she could ask me awkward questions. Jaffer dropped me home. My first real rescue was done!

As the adrenaline began to ease out of my system, I was in serious pain, my nose and ear were throbbing. I took a painkiller and went to bed. The next morning, I briefly went to the Mehendi centre and then visited the plastic unit. The bruise on my nose was effectively covered by my spectacles. I didn't want the brothel keepers or goons to think I was scared. I suppose I was thumbing my nose at them.

Akbar told me that the men were asking around about a small woman in a burqa with a young child, but wouldn't tell him why. Selling one of their own children wasn't kosher in a red-light area, so they couldn't share their reasons. The consequences would be severe. I suppose the fact that I'd not filed a police complaint added to their confusion. Threats, intimidation and violence—their only options should they learn my identity—wouldn't work on me anyway. Akbar and Jaffer played their parts perfectly, acting as if they knew nothing.

By afternoon, I could no longer tolerate the pain. I went to St Anne's Hospital (Gudi ka Dawakhana, as it was called), and requested the sisters to admit me for a few days. The sisters were close friends of Jo, so naturally they informed him that I was in bad shape. Come evening, Jo turned up wanting answers. I had no option but to tell him what had happened. He was livid. While my pitiful condition and the hospital environment did not deter him from giving me scathing looks, it did stop him from giving me an earful. His opinion on rescues was crystal clear: it wasn't our responsibility. That was the police's job. I'd heard him say this several times over, and had still gone ahead and done things my way. It would always be a bone of contention between us.

I was in hospital for three days. My pain subsided with medication, but there was damage: my nasal septum was deviated and my hearing was affected. But I wanted to be discharged as soon as the pain reduced. Neither of the two were life-threatening conditions, and I was keen to get back to the field and reassure myself of Rizwana's well-being.

Months later, when I started getting constant infections in my right ear, I learnt that there was a huge perforation in my eardrum.

I needed surgery for my ear and my nose. I was also getting recurrent headaches. While the nasal septum was easily corrected with a micro-surgery, the ear needed two surgeries. Till this day, I am hard of hearing on my right side, and I briefly used hearing aids.

Rizwana's case taught me that I'd find support for rescuing children from prostitution from within the community itself. And that's how I embarked on a mission to remove at least the children as soon as possible. Some of my most ardent supporters were the hijras who lived next door to us in Mehendi. I truly liked them, for they were friendly, and their concern for my well-being was touching. They'd always ask, 'Madam, khaye?' Madam, did you eat? We developed an easy friendship. They would also subtly warn me about people and places who posed a threat to my life. I took those warnings seriously—they were probably the only people I listened to without any argument. I'm pretty sure I owe them my life.

One day, I was on my way to the centre when I saw Kajal, one of the youngest hijras, sitting outside with her leg stretched out. When I approached her to say hello, I realised her foot was oozing with pus and there was a deep wound around it. Alarmed, I asked her why she hadn't gone to the hospital. She shrugged nonchalantly. 'Madam, which hospital would allow us inside?' I was taken aback. How could any hospital bar people? Taking the matter into my hands like I always do, I called for an auto. Seeing Vijeta outside the centre, I told her to somehow get in touch with Akbar and ask him to come to Gudi ka Dawakhana, and then left for the hospital with Kajal.

Jo's friends, the sisters, treated Kajal free of cost, including giving her the prescribed tablets. Sister Dr Elsita, a thorough professional, just focused on examining the wound. It was badly infected and needed deep cleaning. She casually told us that if we had delayed coming, the foot may have had to be amputated. Kajal's wound needed dressing and medical care for another week. Akbar, who had arrived by then, was entrusted with ferrying her to and from the hospital. Kajal looked dazed. This was the first time she had been treated in a hospital, and with dignity.

By the week's end, Kajal's foot had completely healed. As a neighbour, it was my duty to help, just as they had helped me so many times in the past. And it is the duty of a doctor to take care of a patient, no matter who they are. But for the hijra community, it was a huge deal. I'd learn how significant it was in a few days when they invited me over.

Although we were neighbours, I had never visited them. We would meet on the street, greet each other and move on. This was the first time I was going to their house. The front door was connected to a small courtyard through a passage, and then there was a room on the far side.

There seemed to be some kind of celebration on, with flowers strewn on the floor and festooned on the door. The hijras were dressed up, and showered me with flower petals. Impressed by their hospitality, I was preparing to wait for the other guests. But they ushered me inside to a beautifully decorated chair more suited to royalty, and asked me to sit down. There was only one such chair. Next, they garlanded me and handed over a basket of fruits. Then they all danced for me! To my delight, Kajal was in the centre, dancing gracefully. Still, I wasn't sure what this was all about. It was only when the speeches started that I realised all this was to thank me for helping Kajal. Finally, the nayak, the head of these hijras, performed a nazar utaaro ceremony for me to ward off the evil eye. I felt tremors in my body during that ritual. It was a divine experience and moved me in a way that is hard to put into words.

My simple response to a neighbour's distress was for them the greatest act of inclusion. All of us, with our preconceived notions and biases, discriminate against people for no real reason. Do we even realise the trauma that it brings, the scars it leaves on their souls? We demonise those who are not like us, we perpetuate stereotypes, and we normalise and institutionalise our biases. We, who form governments, who run the schools and hospitals, are the ones who exclude them from access to basic rights. And when we realise the enormity of our crimes, we shake our heads in disapproval. But do we do anything about it? All these thoughts flashed through my mind.

I learnt my first profound lesson on gratitude from these neighbours, one that I would practise scrupulously in the years to come. I'd make sure that every act of support I received was duly acknowledged, expressing my gratitude publicly.

In the meantime, I kept rescuing children as and when I could.

One such rescue was three-year-old Viju's. Her mother Lalita suffered from AIDS, and had a lot of opportunistic infections. Perhaps that's why she was never sober, invariably found passed out at the bus platform opposite the Secunderabad railway station. Although she was young, her frail, sick body did not get her any customers. One day, Pallavi, one of the women I worked with, heard Lalita haggling for Rs 500 with a pimp in exchange for her child.

I was to meet Pallavi and some other women in Secunderabad, near Manohar Talkies, with Akbar. Pallavi pulled me aside and told me what she'd overheard. The situation was time-sensitive, but I did not want to cause unnecessary panic. I quietly told Akbar to organise an auto with a reliable driver. In the meantime, I conducted the women's meeting to brief them about the eligibility criteria for housing. Since it was a public space, the women were keen to disperse quickly and meet me at the office individually with all their documents.

Meanwhile, Akbar had found a reliable auto, the driver of which was also named Akbar. He was Sulthana's friend and knew that I'd rescued Rizwana, and he was on board with our plan for Viju. We reached Lalita's bus stop only to find her asleep or out cold—I'm not sure which—and the child playing next to her. I had met this child multiple times and had developed a friendly rapport with her in the past. Akbar carefully steered the auto to stop right next to the pavement in front of the two. I got out and waved to the child, and she happily came to me. I gave her a few biscuits and picked her up, and sat back in the auto.

Of course, you could easily call this kidnapping, and that's exactly what happened. People who had seen me pick up Viju created quite a commotion and alerted Lalita. She woke up from her stupor and, when she understood what was happening, started screaming and calling me all kinds of names. We had just boarded the auto. I alighted and offered her Rs 500, the same amount she'd demanded of the pimp for her daughter. I hoped this would settle the matter.

Unfortunately, it set her off further. Spotting the beat police passing by, she began to yell that I'd kidnapped her child. Luckily for me, Pallavi had followed us back to the bus station. She told the police about Lalita's plans. I added that we planned to put the child in the best of schools. The police were well aware of Lalita's troubles, including the fact that she was an AIDS patient with a chronic alcohol problem, so they merely made me promise to allow her to see her child occasionally. I agreed, and also gave her Rs 700 more. We were free to take Viju to Sister Severine's place.

In a few months, I enrolled Viju in one of Hyderabad's best schools with funds raised through some individual donations. I had requested the donors to pay the school directly, so that transparency is maintained. Unfortunately, I kept my promise to the police and shared this information with Lalita. This was a grave mistake, because she would turn up at the school dead drunk, shouting abuses about me, calling me a kidnapper. The school, displeased with such behaviour, would threaten to dismiss Viju. This went on for a few months until we discovered Lalita lying dead at the bus stop she frequented. Akbar, the women and I arranged for her cremation.

In another case, a seven-year-old was sold by her parents. The couple, Ashok and Madhavi, were in prostitution. They ran the business under the garb of a small water kiosk business in front of one of the bus platforms. Ashok was a pimp for his wife and some other women who operated at the huge Secunderabad bus station, which adjoins the city's railway station. Prostitution was rampant in this area, with both stations being sources of a substantial number of customers.

Every time I passed by, I kept track of the children who played around the bus platforms. One day, I couldn't spot Ashok and Madhavi's child, Durga. I caught hold of Ashok and asked him where she was, but he wouldn't give me an answer. By now, several in the area knew me and my work, including the beat constables. They took him aside and questioned him. It was then that he admitted that he'd sold her to someone in Delhi. I had heard of Ashok's chronic gambling habit.

He told the police that a relative was taking Durga to the buyer in Delhi. In all probability, this person would be the mediator for the deal. Some roughing up and intimidation by the police convinced Ashok to promise us that he'd get back the child immediately.

I picked up their other child, a three-year-old called Mary, and told the police I'd bring her back when Durga returned. Ashok and his wife had no say in the matter. I visited every day to check if Durga was back. The child returned eight days later. It was truly a timely rescue. I then went to the couple, and with the parents' consent, removed both the children and took them to Sister Severene. Three years later, both Ashok and Madhavi died from AIDS-related illnesses.

Then again, not all rescues were successful. My women and I caught a woman called Kamala selling her eleven-year-old daughter to a customer at Indira Park, where prostitution was rife, even during the day. Often, public parks and theatres are used for selling sexual services. The woman handed over the girl to us when we intervened, but later filed a kidnapping case against me. I was summoned to the police station along with the child. Unfortunately, none of my companions were ready to accompany me. I thought my word would be good enough for the police, but I was proved wrong. I told them all that had occurred, but Kamala vehemently denied it all. She beat her chest and wailed, 'Do you think I'm a demon to sell my own child?'

The police then asked the child to tell them what had happened. She gave them the most innocent look, and said that she and her mother had been walking in the park when I came and took her away!

In the face of such a testimony, the police could do nothing. I had to hand the child over to her mother. Nine years later, the same child was admitted to my shelter as an adult. She'd been rescued from a brothel in Pune, her body hacked by blades. The mother had sold the girl to a brothel in Pune, from where she was rescued by the Andhra police in an inter-state operation. She had also come to be infected with HIV. I saw her sink right before my eyes as she battled her opportunistic infections and her physical injuries. In the end, she met an early death, like many others. This child left me in a lot of pain and anguish. Should I have fought for her more aggressively that first time? Should I have organised some kind of surveillance on the mother to stop her from selling her daughter? A hundred ifs and buts cross my mind every time something like this occurs.

I had rescued two dozen children by now. Nothing monumental had been achieved, nothing that made a dent in the prostitution racket. The rescues were sporadic, and based on the information that we received. Operating in our individual capacities, we couldn't make a more tangible impact. My team consisted of Akbar, Jaffer Bhai and the other Akbar who had helped with Viju's rescue. The others did the recce, the logistical planning, all the behind-the-scenes work, while I was the face of the rescue. I didn't want anyone to recognise my team—they lived with the people we rescued the children from, and that meant their lives would be in great jeopardy should their roles be discovered.

While my intentions were good, I knew my methods were neither advisable nor sustainable. Each rescue brought with it its own share of downsides, personal injury being the most common. I would often get thoroughly beaten up or hurt in other ways and forced to convalesce, resulting in a huge gap between rescue efforts. All we ended up doing was amassing an increasing number of people who resented us and wanted us gone. Still, I did not take this seriously, because the procurers couldn't do anything legally since the child was either not theirs or they'd be proven to be unfit caretakers. It was only when an attempt was made on my life that I realised the extent of the animosity I was facing.

Mei Bibi was a chronic alcoholic and a well-known procurer of girls. While I had strong reservations about her, I tolerated her as her children were in our centre. When she invited us over for a meal, Akbar refused to go with me—he couldn't stand her. Unlike me, he wore his opinions on his sleeve. Personally, I felt that if we ended communication, we would lose a chance to change her, and I went to lunch alone. I'm a poor eater, but I am very fond of meetha paan. I eagerly accepted it at the end of the meal, but ate it only after leaving Mei Bibi's house. I walked all the way to the main road before I collapsed, losing consciousness. Luckily for me, an employee from Boys Town was passing by. Recognising me, he took me to Gudi ka Dawakhana. By then, I had regained consciousness and was vomiting profusely. The sisters put me on an IV drip and my body coped on its own. Later, Akbar found out that something had been added to the paan. Since I did not make a scene of it and never questioned Mei Bibi, she acted like nothing happened, and had the audacity to come to me multiple times to seek support for all the small and big problems she had with her children. And as they were related to her children, I mostly obliged.

It was another lesson for me: to never go around eating food with anybody and everybody, and to perhaps also anticipate the consequences of all my actions. Also, I realised, if I continued to operate this way, I would not get very far. All the same, I did not agree with Jo that we shouldn't do rescues, and strongly believed that it shouldn't be left completely to the police. Often, they were involved in the whole racket. But the way I was going about it was not sound.

Because of these past years of work, I knew the various stakeholders, the networks involved, the way the entire operation functioned, the revenue at stake. It was a well-oiled machine worked by a host of people who targeted and exploited the weakest in the community. They wouldn't change their line of work out of the goodness of their heart. This wasn't something that moral science classes or counselling could help change.

So, if we had to make an impact, we needed a different perspective. In the meantime, I needed to think about my children. I'd managed to find a few places other than Sister Severene's, but I wasn't very happy with them. I needed a long-term game plan for them.

16

A Home for the Children

I'd done quite a few rescues by now. There was Rizwana, Divya, Mary, Durga, Viju, Shabana, Sapna, Saritha and so many others. The rescues themselves had been fairly simple to execute, even if they had been dangerous. What was far more challenging was finding the children homes, charting out plans for the rest of their lives: where they'd stay, study and all those other details. This was particularly important because, while some of them had escaped before they could be abused, many others hadn't been as lucky. Some of the children had been raped and were groomed for sexual proclivity or traumatised. All of them were well aware of sex, even if they hadn't experienced it themselves.

Rizwana, for instance, was a naturally gifted dancer. Her mother had been a famous tawaif. The girl had been made to dance in a number of places, been molested by several men during the course of her 'debut' in the market and sold to the highest bidder for her initiation into the sex trade. She had some nice memories of being decked up for that first time, but had experienced only pain and discomfort thereafter. All of this had transpired by the time she was ten years old.

One night, I got a call from Sister Severine, her voice icy on the phone: 'I'd like to see you tomorrow as early as you can get here. It's best we talk face to face.' She refused to answer any of my questions, which naturally convinced me that it was clearly a very serious matter. Had any of the children run away? Had the procurers got wind of Sister Severine's establishment? Had my own contacts betrayed me?

I even began to wonder if Akbar or Jaffer Bhai had given me away. My thoughts ran riot that night. If Sister Severine refused to take the children in, what were my options? Hers had been the only place I was truly satisfied with. All the rest had lacked warmth, air or light, or needed an exhaustive background on the children.

Dread ate me up the entire way the next morning. Sister Severine was even frostier in person than over the phone. As I sat down in her private room—no offer of even water, let alone coffee or tea—she told me I'd caused her a great loss and betrayed her trust to boot. Caused her loss? Cheated her? What was she talking about?

'I can no longer keep that child with me. She will leave with you,' she told me.

'Who?' I asked. 'Why, what happened, sister?'

Now, Sister Severine's home was a busy place that got many visitors: foreigners and locals who were potential donors and sponsors. Often, the children were asked to sing and dance or perform for them. The previous day, one of those visitors had asked the children to perform, declaring that they would give a prize for the best poem or song. A three-year-old that I had rescued was greatly dismayed at not winning anything. She walked up to the male visitor, lifted up her frock, pushed down her underpants, then said, 'Can you give me the prize now?'

I'm sure you can imagine the shock all round. Sister Severine was bombarded with questions she'd never asked me herself. Her only concern when accepting the children had been whether they really were orphans—yet another reason why her home was convenient for me.

'I don't want your dirty children here spoiling the others' chances!'

That's when I realised that Sister Severine facilitated adoptions. That's why her children were well-fed and cared for. She needed them to shine, to appear pleasant and appeal to prospective parents, donors and sponsors.

Now this was news to me! I didn't have a home for the children, nor had I harboured any plans to start one. But I'd also never considered sending them to other homes permanently. I had planned to watch over them, see them grow into adults who'd successfully left behind their early lives.

My little girl's actions had lost Sister Severine a prospective home for her children, possibly even a donation. She wanted that child gone. It was unfair. None of my other children had ever caused her any distress or embarrassment. She'd only ever talked about them in glowing terms. This whole incident was just unfortunate.

I can't say I was surprised at the child's behaviour, but it did pose a challenge. I'd already got several complaints from other homes about my children's abusive and sexualised language, and their disrespect towards their elders and peers. They had been exposed to the world of flesh trade early in their lives, and it was inevitable that they had picked up adult mannerisms and language. I was used to this; many children in our learning centres behaved that way. I could see how that would stand out starkly against the behaviour of children from normal homes, and how that caused the adults around to brand my children as rotten eggs.

I soothed Sister Severine until she calmed down, then pleaded with her to keep the child for a week longer until I had made other arrangements. She grudgingly agreed. I had to do something, this much was clear. But what it was, I had no idea.

That day, I was to visit another home to check in on another of my children. I really hoped all was well with her, because I couldn't take another dose of bad news that day. As I went in, I found myself thinking what a contrast it was to Sister Severine's. The home was dingy, lacked ventilation and had twenty-odd children crammed into three rooms. I found it terribly claustrophobic. Honestly, the only thing the place had going for it was that they took in my children without any questions. I think they had some kind of government funding, and so had to constantly show the numbers.

But all my gloom dissipated when the warden told me that my child had been waiting eagerly for me. I felt a warm glow. I went to see Meena with much joy. This is what I wanted: my children loving me for what I had done for them, thinking I'm a wonderful person.

Meena pulled me to a corner of her room as soon as she saw me. She wants me all to herself, I thought giddily. In many cases, children assimilate so well with the others that they hardly remember me. This child was nine and I'd rescued her too late. She'd already been abused by a few customers. She studied my face gravely as if searching for answers, then held my gaze and asked, 'Why did you bring me from one hell to another?' It was a slap to my face.

'Wh-what?' I stammered. I couldn't be sure I'd heard right. 'What did you say?'

'*Yeh bhi to ek aur jahannum hai. Yahaan ka woh uncle bhi to ganda aadmi hai. Galat cheezein karta hai.*' This is yet another hell. The uncle here is bad. Does dirty things.

It took a while for her words to sink into my shocked brain. The 'uncle' was a male coordinator who frequently visited the home.

I didn't want to confront either the warden or the head of the organisation. There was nowhere I could take her if they threw the child out.

I stroked her head. '*Mujhe nahi pata tha.*' I didn't know. 'Give me a few days. I'll find us a place,' I promised. 'In the meantime, take care to always stay with the other children. Don't even go to the bathroom or toilet alone. Sleep in the centre of the room with the others, not alone in the corner.'

Years later, Meena would tell me that my words made her feel confident. I'd believed her without any questions or suspicions. It had told her I trusted her.

Words can have a huge impact, especially with sexually abused children. Even the most innocuous 'What happened?' asked in the wrong tone may convey a lack of trust to them. Such is the devastating impact of sexual abuse—it is the victim who shoulders stigma and ostracism instead of the victimiser.

I left the home right after that talk. As I got into the auto with Akbar who was waiting outside—I was particular never to take any male staff inside a home for girls—I told him we had to find a house for all our children without delay. He nodded silently. With him looking around for a suitable house, I was free to chew over all that I needed to set up a home. I wasn't scared or worked up even as I began to plan. It was an organic process, and this was a natural progression from rescuing the children. Utensils, mats, mattresses, provisions, clothes, the list was endless, and my mind was working overtime. Akbar had never failed me. I had to make sure I didn't fail the children.

That afternoon, I decided to visit Manish Kumar. We'd met because he'd read Lalita's article about me in *Vanitha*. He was also a Malayali and admired our work. Manish was the housekeeping manager of the Green Park Hotel located at Begumpet—and what better than a hotel to help set up our kitchen? Green Park Hotel went out of their way to support us. Manish took his team into confidence, and soon they had ideas about all the ways in which they could contribute. Not only did they help set up my entire kitchen, but we even got bedsheets and uniforms. The hotel was undergoing a makeover, and they were changing the uniforms of the female staff. We benefited from it and got black silk sarees with a silver border! Thanks to their generosity, all I needed now were provisions, mats and clothes for children. For this, getting donations wouldn't be hard.

I had a lot of donors and supporters in the city, some of whom I'd met at meetings or at Boys Town, and others had reached out to me when they'd heard of my work. I spoke about Prajwala and my rescue work at every conference or meeting I attended, and invariably, someone would reach out to donate. The fact that I never explicitly asked for money worked in my favour. This has made me believe that blatantly seeking donations is the biggest dampener for fund-raising; it makes people wary of you. Over the years, I have taken care to never fall into that trap. Also, the police knew about my work, as did the district administration and the Catholic clergy because of Jo and, most importantly, those in the childcare space. This was in addition to all my friends, connections and admirers from my time at PIN. My work had generated goodwill in many quarters.

I certainly needed all these donations—I had been paying all the organisations that were keeping my children, including Sister Severine. Even the educational institutions that our children went to charged us, and expected something extra for the incidental expenses for hostels. We even paid Boys Town when we conducted our summer camps in their auditorium. Prajwala wasn't taking free services from anyone, and both Jo and I were very clear about this right from the start.

When I reached the office, Akbar was waiting impatiently for me. At this time, our centre and office were still in Mehendi, but the plastic unit had been shut down. We were contemplating shifting the children to other centres when this happened.

Akbar had already found us a place, and wanted us to go there right away as the owner was waiting. We stopped the auto on the main road at Fateh Darwaza and walked through bylanes so narrow that only two people could walk abreast. I was worried I'd get lost on my own. It felt like some kind of maze. How do we get out? I was getting worked up.

Finally, we reached a dead end with a gate. I wasn't prepared for what was on the other side. The gate opened onto a sprawling courtyard. The building was an old devdi, a mansion of the nawabs, with an ornate front. It was a most beautiful sight. I fell in love.

It took me some time to notice the people in the courtyard. The owner, a Mr Quadri, was standing to the side. He was smiling and I instantly liked him. On a closer look, I realised that the place was shabby, and it looked as if six or seven families occupied each of the rooms. The courtyard was shared. There was a stink from the bathrooms.

I looked at Quadri. 'I like this place, bhaisaab, but I can't accept it in this condition.'

Quadri was a journalist and wrote for his own newspaper. I think his father was a Gandhian. He told me he was in the process of getting all the tenants vacated, and that he wished to let it to a single individual. Something clicked between us. I felt that he was strongly inclined to give it to us.

'I need it ready in two days. Will that be possible?' I'm not sure whether it was my desperation or my ruthlessness that made such an impossible demand.

'Make it three, and we'll shake on it,' he smiled.

I made a show of grudgingly agreeing, all the while singing in my heart!

We left after shaking hands. At Rs 2,000, the rent was quite high for me, but it was also a big place with a beautiful courtyard. The astonishing fact was he did not demand a single rupee as an advance, which is a common practice all over the city. Most owners charge two or three months' rent as advance. Come to think of it, during those days, none of the owners I rented from demanded an advance from us. Were there so many who supported us indirectly?

As Akbar and I walked back, I realised that the route wasn't that complicated after all, it's just that the place was in the interiors, slightly hard to reach. We stopped to pay our respects at a mazar on the main road to thank the gods and Allah for this wonderful turn of events. Akbar then told me that he'd been praying the whole day to find the right place. He explained, 'We've been keeping our children in different homes so that they couldn't be traced. Now that we have set up our own home, anyone can find it. So we needed somewhere that wasn't easily accessible.'

It made a lot of sense. The security of the children had never crossed my mind. For Akbar, who knew the criminal networks inside out, this had been his first thought. A place that couldn't be easily found was critical. 'Now we need to decide,' he continued, 'if we should allow anyone inside. We could go the other way too—open it up to all the influential and powerful people, so that the rest think twice before coming for us.'

We decided to consider all the angles before taking that call.

I called up Manish that evening and gave him the happy news. He promised to have everything ready in two days. He'd come personally to ensure the kitchen was set up, he told me.

Now that everything was ready, I told Jo about my plans. 'We're closing the Mehendi centre and moving to a new place. There's also space there to house our rescued children.'

Though I never told him about my rescues, he was aware of them. My occasional limping, my trips to Gudi ka Dawakhana gave it all away. He'd pretty much given up on shouting at me. I wasn't sure what his reaction would be.

He was pleasantly taken aback at our furious pace.

'The teachers at the Mehendi centre can work there. Shweta is resigning—she's getting married—but Vijeta and Rachana will continue. I still need to figure out the rest of the staff, though, and move all the stuff to the new place.'

The next three days went by in a blur. The children from Mehendi were already admitted at our Kalapather centre, the plastic unit had been closed for months now, and the meagre furniture and school materials could be easily shifted to the new place at Fateh Darwaza.

Vijeta had taken over the shifting. I must tell you that it was a great relief for me. If there is anything that I detest from the bottom of my heart, it is the unpacking of luggage or boxes.

On the third day, we all went to our new place. It looked amazing—the tenants had vacated, the place had been white-washed, the bathrooms were sparkling, the sprawling courtyard looked serene and the hand pump there was gleaming. Vijeta and Rachana had never seen anything so beautiful. It was like being transported back in time.

The very next day, Manish and his team turned up. I got them to put the boxes in their designated spaces before escaping under the pretext of showing Manish my soon-to-be-closed Mehendi office. At least someone should see that brothel room we'd used for our education centre!

Between the three of them, Vijeta, Rachana and Akbar set up the devdi in under three hours. They put up the children's art from the Mehendi centre on the walls and hung up curtains. They divided the whole building into two clear sections, the school and the living quarters. The courtyard was to be used for dining and other common activities. The kitchen sparkled with the new utensils, the bedrooms had mats, sheets and pillows arranged like in a dormitory. We were all set.

Touchingly, they had made a collective decision to allocate me a room there. It was a small room separate from the main building, so that 'Bade Madam' could meet the 'bade log', as Akbar had told them. They'd even draped a white towel over my chair, like he'd seen in government offices. The girls believed anything Akbar said. Time and again he would tell them about all the big places we went to—the police stations, the electricity board, the big educational institutions, the Collectorate and the five-star hotels. Not that he had ever entered a single place, except for the Collectorate!

I took Vijeta and Rachana aside and shared the circumstances under which some of the children had been rescued. Although they'd been working as teachers at the centre, they weren't aware of our rescue efforts, let alone met any of those children. We decided that I'd do the cooking and stay at the devdi at night until we found someone to manage the home. Vijeta and Rachana would be there during the day.

Without delay, I wanted to bring Meena, the child who had told me about the 'uncle' at the home, and the ten children under Sister Severine's care. Now that I had a home of my own, I was quite annoyed with her. I'd paid her every month for each of my children, she had done me no favours. And she collected money from the adoptive parents. So why the attitude? Of course, I could afford such ideas now. A week ago, I'd been thinking differently.

The next morning, I sat down with tea that my landlord's daughter Archana had brought me, and picked up the newspaper. 'Illegal child adoption racket busted!' the headline screamed. Some big Christian missionary institutions had been found guilty of selling children at extortionate prices to foreigners for adoption. Sister Severine's place flashed in my mind. There was no time to waste, we had to remove all our children as soon as we could.

But first, we had to buy provisions and clothes for the children. Before leaving, I informed my landlord that I would not return for a week. Our new home was in the heart of the shopping area. Charminar, great for clothes shopping, was just a kilometre away from Fateh Darwaza, and Begum Bazar, with its huge wholesale grocery stores, was less than three kilometres away. We had received around Rs 25,000 as donations in the last few days, and it was more than enough for all our needs. Vijeta and Rachana were to buy the clothes. I knew all the children's sizes, and had told them to buy two sets of clothes for each child along with underwear, toiletries and some extra amenities as well. We needed to be prepared for any new admission.

Akbar and I were to get the provisions. He was already waiting for me at the end of our street. We had hired Jaffer's auto for the day. We were the first ones in Begum Bazar, which opened only at 10.30 in the morning.

I thought Govardhan & Company looked like a big enough place. It was also the first one to open. They did not give us even a small discount. The auto was now stuffed with our purchases. We had bought enough to last us for a month, but I wasn't satisfied. I told Akbar to sit in the auto and walked around. What a delight! There were small confectionary shops full of biscuits, chocolates, wafers, murukku and other snacks, in small packets just the right size for children. I purchased enough snacks for a month.

Vijeta and Rachana reached at about the same time as us. Vijeta's mom had even sent lunch for us. Now we could work the entire day without a big break. I packed Akbar off to organise transport for the next day and to spread the word about our need for staff, and instructed Vijeta and Rachana to unpack the provisions. The logic was that they'd monitor the cook, and thus needed to know what went where to guide the new staff. Of course it also allowed me to escape the ordeal of unpacking.

I chose the easy task of organising the welcome kit. Into each kit went small packets of toiletries, two pairs of clothes, undergarments, two bedsheets and one towel. I made thirty such bags and marked the sizes on top. Apart from the first eleven whom I had to remove immediately—ten from Sister Severene and Meena from the other home—we had also admitted nineteen children in other homes, which made a total of thirty children.

Today, these welcome kits have many more things—sanitary napkins, hair remover, footwear, a water bottle—everything to make a person feel immediately welcome and not have to worry about their basic needs. I never forgot how it felt like in jail to be without a change of clothes.

When Akbar came back, he suggested that we ask some of the women from our toy unit to work in the children's home. They had been rendered jobless when it closed. I thought Shanta and Saroja fit the bill—they weren't HIV-positive and were quite hard-working. Saroja had no children of her own, but had an alcohol dependency. Shanta had a daughter, but she lived in Maharashtra, so that was also not a problem. Akbar felt nobody would dare to consume alcohol in my presence. I wasn't so sure. We called them over that evening, and found them ready to join the very next day.

That night, I stayed alone in the devdi. We were going to call it Astha Nivas, the home of trust. I don't think I cooked that night, there was food left over. What I do remember clearly is sitting on a chair with a box as my footrest in the serene courtyard, looking up at the sky and thinking about where I had reached in life. I had no regrets. Here I was, twenty-seven years old and setting up my own home for my children. I slept that night feeling content.

The next morning, I woke up to someone banging on the gate—there was no calling bell. Akbar, our resident electrician's first responsibility for the day was decided. He had to fix a calling bell. I opened the gate to see Shanta and Saroja with their bags. Now I could be a sous chef.

The idea of cooking the whole day had not appealed to me at all. I decided we'd make a large quantity of rice in the morning, then simply make a different rice dish for each meal—lemon rice, tomato rice, brinjal rice, etc. It was a trick my mother had used. The difference was that she served all of it as one meal, and I was going to serve it as three. I instructed Saroja and Shanta to cook the rice and cut the required vegetables. We were looking at eleven children that day, plus Vijeta, Rachana, Akbar, Jaffer and the three of us.

Then I proceeded to finish my morning rituals. The two women had everything ready by the time I was done. I made tomato rice and lemon rice, and instructed Saroja to make some pachadi, the Andhra version of chutney. The Telugu states of Andhra Pradesh and Telangana have some amazing pachadis. Saroja made some dosakaya (a kind of cucumber) pachadi.

The hospitality of the hijras still fresh in my mind, I told Shanta and Saroja to welcome each child with an arati and some kumkum. It was important to me that they felt welcomed as they entered their home. And this was the only sort of welcome I'd ever experienced. Vijeta and Rachana had also been briefed. If they were amused by my idea, they did not show it. My team knew I was a stickler for certain things and none dared cross me, especially when it came to treating people with dignity. One time in Mehendi, I'd asked them to give a bath to Susheela, an AIDS patient we had found abandoned on the streets. Rachana, on seeing worms on Susheela's head or perhaps because of discomfort with the disease, had shown small signs of discomfort. I didn't like that. Asking her to step aside, I bathed Susheela myself, a plastic bag covering my hand. Then I cleaned all her wounds and treated them with ointment without a word to Rachana. Susheela died the following week.

Akbar and I went to Sister Severine's place. She was jittery, the headlines had shaken her. Without a word, she handed our children back to us. She'd already received a call from the officials about an inspection, and wanted to get rid of the children. Some of them were sad to leave; she had really looked after them well.

I didn't know what to make of her. She believed her work gave the children a better life. I felt the same about my work. Both of us were doing things illegally. Did the end justify the means? This wasn't the time to dwell upon right and wrong. I had to bring my children to safety.

The next stop wasn't as simple. The warden and the head of the organisation were reluctant to release Meena into my care even after I told them that I'd started my own home. It meant a loss of income for them. Fortunately, Meena took matters into her hands and began to wail loudly and without pause. The organisation had no choice but to give up and hand her over.

On my way out, I noticed the male coordinator. I went back and told the head of the organisation that it was not good to have a male staff member in a home for girls. I'm sure my expression said it all, but I had no more time to waste. Each of us has to carry our own cross, to figure out our own problems.

We arrived with eleven children in three autos. Shanta and Saroja executed the welcome perfectly. The joy on the children's faces when they were welcomed with an arati and kumkum, their elation at their kits—I'll forever remember those. The sprawling courtyard was a hit as well.

It was two in the afternoon and the children were all settled. Vijeta and Rachana had already started taking classes. Saroja and Shanta were washing all the old clothes that the children had brought with them.

I decided to go to Boys Town. Vijeta was in charge in my absence. I briefed her on what to do for the evening snacks and left. When Jo learnt that Astha Nivas was open, he felt we should invite the brothers from Boys Town to bless the place. I had no objections, I liked them, and this place was worth it. Besides, I felt Astha Nivas had a divine magic, and I wanted them to experience it. I did not say this to Jo, of course.

When I went back, the sounds of the children felt beautiful to my ears, even with my partial hearing. The brothers would come the following day to bless the place, and I wanted us to be well prepared. Vijeta volunteered to teach the children a prayer. We made a rough plan, then created a proper schedule for the children since they would do well with a routine. And since I was sticking around until we got the right staff, I could keep an eye on things and make any necessary tweaks.

That evening, after dinner at 7.30 p.m., we all sat down in the courtyard. I asked the children to share one thing they did right that day and something that they did wrong. This was strange to them, and they didn't know how to start. Meena began. She said leaving the previous home was the right thing, but her screaming and crying was wrong. This set the ball in motion, and the others shared their day as well. I asked the children to apologise to the people they'd wronged and thank those who'd helped them. At this, they all came up to me and thanked me. I choked up. Millions of thank yous have come my way since then, but nothing has matched this.

The day of the blessing arrived. Akbar and I received Jo and the brothers on the main road. Although the brothers had been living in Boys Town for many years, none of them had ever visited this part of the Old City. It must've been a strange sight—Akbar, the brothers and I walking in single file through the narrow lanes of Fateh Darwaza. The brothers' delight at the beauty of the place was wonderful to see. I'd gone bonkers and decorated the entire building with marigold garlands. It looked very festive, and then Saroja and Shanta received them in the silk sarees that Manish had given us. It was a grand affair.

Uncle Brother, who had also inaugurated my plastic unit and was the oldest of them all, lit the lamp and cut the ribbon. Then we all sat in the veranda with the children. Jo had tears in his eyes when the children sang *Asatoma Satgamaya*—lead us from untruth to truth. Clearly, Vijeta and Rachana had worked hard the previous day. They'd also taught Rizwana and Saritha a dance, and a poem to some other children.

The brothers hadn't expected any of this, at least not such progress in one night. They thought our children would be sullen, withdrawn and traumatised. Instead, all eleven of them were running around the place, taking care of the guests, offering water and snacks. Though Jo had told me that they couldn't stay for too long, they ended up staying with us for three hours. Fortunately for them, I'd made a nice dal and tomato curry, and not one of my one-pot lunches. There was also pachadi, papad and some curd, followed by fresh watermelon. Astha Nivas, our first home, was formally inaugurated.

I felt a change in Jo when I spoke to him that weekend. Jo had never supported my rescues, but the children had transformed him. He now understood my drive. It was the first time he'd seen a child, a five-year-old at that, who'd contracted HIV through rape. For the first time ever, we agreed without argument that we had to keep going.

In that one week, I, too, had transformed. I could no longer be reckless. Not when I was responsible for these children. I would no longer voluntarily put myself in danger. From this time on, financial sustainability became a priority to ensure that my children never went hungry.

In the next few weeks, I recovered the remaining nineteen children who had been placed in different homes. We were able to recruit proper staff, including Rukmini, the residential cook. I still stayed there occasionally to make sure that the timetable was diligently implemented.

Over the next few months, I would also set up Asha Niketan, a home for adult women, in a place called Engine Bowli. But working with adult victims was a very different ballgame. They experience a whole different level of trauma that comes from years of commercial sexual exploitation.

A safe home is a necessity for any intervention that aims to end sex crimes and sex trafficking. How we manage these shelters could make or break a life. It can also become a breeding ground for unimaginable greed, for a vulnerable person is the best potential victim for an exploiter. And there's no better place than a safe home to easily access them.

17

The Daily Bread

I had started Prajwala with the money I'd saved while working with PIN. Soon, I had to take up independent projects to support myself and my centres. During this time, a number of people supported me financially. My friends Geeta and Shoba in Bangalore would send me clothes. Geeta also made some generous donations, including a gold necklace that her mother had gifted her. For years, until our financial condition improved, Lalita Iyer gave us money for fresh vegetables and fruit. As our work got wider recognition, many others reached out to donate, often in cash but occasionally in kind as well. My own personal financial situation stabilised once I got a fellowship from the Indo-German Social Service Society. The stipend was more than enough for my rent, travel and daily needs.

Ever since my PIN days, I'd been supporting Boys Town in whatever capacity I could, not because the director was my best friend, but because this institution's efforts towards nation-building through livelihood generation were extraordinary. Jo had initiated a very innovative intervention they called Appropriate Technology for Women, which trained women as masons, particularly in the use of alternative technology. Eco-friendly, low-cost housing was just becoming popular, and women were being trained in that technology as masons to lead the construction. My background in environment science and my firm faith in women's capacity to excel attracted me to this programme instantly. As Boys Town had more male staff than female, I volunteered to be the focal point for women trainees. They came from all over the country, particularly the tribal belt.

Most programmes that Boys Town conducted were in collaboration with the German Technical Cooperation (GTZ) programme, now known as German Society for International Cooperation (GIZ), of the German government. Over time, I became a trainer and facilitator for some of the GTZ sessions. Michael Zillich and a Mr Shertler were the German representatives. While Shertler was from GTZ, Zillich was an independent consultant. Working with them was immensely insightful; it broadened my vision and allowed me to review my own strategies. Shertler was highly impressed by the toy-making venture that Prajwala had started, and felt I could benefit from a workshop in Germany on micro-enterprise. And that's how my first trip to Europe happened in late 1998. The GTZ sponsorship included the entire cost of travel, training, stay and a small allowance. So far, my only international trip had been to Kathmandu for the study commissioned by Gracy Fernandes from Nirmala Niketan. Mannheim, Germany was a whole different experience.

My team, especially Tahseen, was quite concerned about the four-week trip and performed several rituals to ensure safe travels, including tying a silver amulet on my arm. Some of them came all the way to the airport to see me off. I still remember this trip: I went from Hyderabad to Delhi, then Frankfurt and on to Mannheim. I walked carefully towards my flight counter at the international airport, imitating those who were before me at the check-in counter, reading every signboard that was possible and sitting alert at the gate for hours before my flight to avoid getting lost at the airport.

The four-week training programme exposed me to the several possibilities in non-conventional trades for women and the immense scope and reach of micro-enterprises. I met some amazing people from different countries and continents—Asia, Uzbekistan and Africa—who were either involved in vocational training or were entrepreneurs. Interacting with them for a month widened my understanding and broadened the horizons of my thoughts and dreams, an invaluable gift. Iftida Yasar and Diah, two Indonesian ladies who were business entrepreneurs, not only inspired me but also became great friends. It was Diah who helped me set up my first email account on Yahoo and taught me how to use the internet. Thanks to that, Jo also set up an email account, and we were able to stay in touch on mail. International calls are costly affairs, and I could not spend my precious allowance on them. Via email, Jo ensured that I was updated on what was happening at Prajwala.

As this was my first trip to Europe, I realised that being vegetarian had its own set of challenges. Besides, I was only used to Indian food. Finding a Turkish supermarket proved to be a lifesaver since I could buy basmati rice, dal, vegetables and all the necessary Indian spices there. As there was a kitchenette in the training venue, I used that to cook my own food and also shared my meals with co-participants who loved Indian food. The training became more meaningful once my food problem was sorted.

While I gained immensely professionally, my health also saw some new turns. I discovered the hard way that sitting in the jacuzzi for long hours can trigger fungal infections. I also realised foreign climates were not good for my stomach, and I'd be constipated for days. On the positive side, I discovered that German medicines for lice infection were super-effective, resolving a problem that I'd nursed for three long years. Finally, my hair was lice-free.

Mannheim is very close to the Switzerland border. Through Brother T.A. Joseph, who was a Montfort brother like Jo, I had met Father Vincent in Hyderabad, now a parish priest in a small village in Switzerland. He had visited Prajwala, become a great supporter and had spread the word in his little parish. This is how I came to be connected to Beatrice, Franco and Marlin, his parishioners who also started supporting Prajwala. I was given my first mobile phone by Beatrice, a very precious and expensive gift that transformed the entire scope of our operations—now my team could contact me from anywhere. When Father Vincent came to know that I was in Germany, he insisted that I visit them in Switzerland. By a happy a coincidence, one of the receptionists at the training centre was travelling to the border that weekend, and dropped me off to where Father Vincent and Beatrice had come to receive me. I spent a beautiful weekend in a small parish in Switzerland, where I was well cared for. This in spite of the fact that Marlin and Franco could hardly speak a word of English, and I was staying at Marlin's house. I returned from my weekend trip with a lot of gifts for everyone back home. When I shared with Father Vincent that the training centre hosted stalls on special days to support various causes, he gave me a suitcase full of Indian art and crafts which I was to able sell in Mannheim—this ended up raising some substantial funds for Prajwala. All the trouble of lugging a huge, heavy suitcase back from Switzerland was entirely worth it.

My first overseas trip was professionally and personally gratifying, with the Mannheim training greatly influencing my economic empowerment programmes to this day.

I recollect and mention these names with deep gratitude as they were some of Prajwala's first donors and were also personally supportive of me.

My next trip was to the US a year later, in 1999. Gracy Fernandes is the one who nominated me to the US Consulate, Mumbai for an International Visitors Leadership Program. The IVLP, as it is called, is a professional exchange programme that invites current and existing leaders for a three-week sponsored stay in the US to learn from the government's public policies and interventions. The US Consulate was looking for emerging leaders from the anti-trafficking sector who could be sent for this programme. It was a great honour to be selected, and it made me believe that my work was making an impact. There were delegates from India, Bangladesh and Pakistan, but I didn't know anyone except for Indrani-di from Sanlaap. We decided to share a room to save on expenses. On that trip, we formed a respectful friendship that lasted until Indrani-di's death in 2015. There were two others from India, Priti Patkar from Prerana and Lalita from the Joint Women's Programme. Priti was very curious about me, and I, unused to such interest, was rather taken aback. It made me very conscious as a relative newcomer to the sector. The whole three weeks, I imagined a hawk-eyed Priti watching me everywhere. Now I am amused at my insecurity. And funnily enough, I find myself doing the same thing to new names in the sector, watching their interventions with sharp eyes.

This trip transformed my long-term vision for Prajwala. It gave me greater clarity on where I wanted to take the organisation and how to do it. We travelled through Washington, San Francisco, Nevada and New York, and met officials and various non-profit interventions. We were exposed to several best practices in the US through organisations doing similar work. The most valuable of these interactions were the ones I had with victims and survivors of prostitution.

One of our visits was to Mustang Ranch, a legal brothel in

Nevada, a first for me. It offered many 'services' that, in the Indian context, were further violations beyond the sexual act itself. This was an important insight for me. For example, I knew from our women and girls how customers would inflict cigarette or cigar burns on them or whip them while they were tied to a bedpost. At Mustang Ranch, you could actually buy such sexual services and all the desired equipment on site—branded cigars, a variety of blades, whips—gear which was fully sanitised. I was left wondering if the pain and humiliation of a forced sexual act was diluted by a clean environment.

The difference between an Indian brothel and a legal one like Mustang Ranch is this: in the latter, this would be an 'add-on service' and the buyer (who is called a 'john') would have to pay extra. In India, this would happen in the close confines of a room in very unsanitary conditions and maybe even with rusted blades and dirty belts and would mostly take the woman or girl by surprise. Many such reflections started consolidating my own personal position on prostitution. These visits and interactions only reinforced my deep conviction as an abolitionist.

The other insight was that the victims, whether in Hyderabad or Nevada or San Francisco, all felt pain, shame, guilt. The normalisation and experiences of exploitation were the same, even if their intensity and manifestation varied. At the end of the day, no matter the regional context, victims across the globe felt the same emotionally.

Meeting Norma Hotaling and understanding the SAGE programme in San Francisco revolutionised my understanding of the demand-reduction strategies which targeted the male sex buyers. I was particularly impressed with a 'Johns School' in San Francisco, which exclusively counselled male sex buyers who were apprehended/caught during a rescue. The men were counselled by professional counsellors and family members. A fine was also imposed and the money would be used for the exit of any woman in prostitution from the brothel where the buyer was caught. This was an eye-opening strategy.

How can there be supply when there is no demand at all? I was deeply inspired and used these learnings to design several demand-reduction strategies in Prajwala, like the Men Against Demand (MAD) movement and the Sex Buyers Change Programme, in later years. I continue to build on this model and the Nordic Model, which I had the opportunity to understand during my visit to Sweden, the first country in the world to have criminalised the buying of sexual services. The actively implemented legislation has dramatically minimised street prostitution in Sweden. Many countries thereafter have followed suit.

Perhaps the greatest takeaway from IVLP was the need to advocate for better victim-centric policies and legislations. At the time, the US was working on the Trafficking Victim Protection Act, which was finally passed in 2000. Having a legal and policy framework to fight crime ensured that the entire state machinery understood the problem and its definite structure and had a clear vision and strategy to address it. This is crucial, for an intervention by a civil society organisation can only have a limited reach, but the state has the power to change the narrative for the whole nation. The huge body of work by Prajwala in the space of legal and policy advocacy is due to the insights I gained courtesy the US's IVLP.

In 2002, I received the prestigious Ashoka Fellowship, which was a professional boost and also gave me financial security, allowing me to work without worrying about my day-to-day expenses. Vasudev Sharma—Vasu—was heading the Ashoka Fellowship in India. He was the one who spotted me, nominated me and led me through an intensive screening process. The Ashoka team is constantly on the lookout for social entrepreneurs who have a vision for long-lasting change. And somehow, he thought I would fit the bill.

Vasu, I think, took months studying my work and my personal vision before preparing my nomination. Once that was accepted, I had to go to Mumbai for a series of interviews spread over three days by panels with Indian and international experts. I had to articulate my vision, goals and strategies, and the impact these would have on the lives of the people I was serving, and also describe how they would be scalable in a sustainable way.

It was a lengthy screening and an intensely emotional one, and it helped me understand myself and my goals within a proper strategic framework. If not for the Ashoka Fellowship, I would never have been compelled to reflect on my work in this way. It forced me to ground my responses within logic, analyse the outcomes and study them within the larger context to gauge the impact. By now, I had recognised that I was fighting sex trafficking, an organised crime which was a billion-dollar industry. My visit to the US had opened my eyes to the extent and magnitude of the problem—a rapidly growing criminal enterprise.

My earlier focus had been to use our educational programme to prevent children from being inducted into prostitution, alert the community to the dangers of sex trafficking and provide care and protection to the rescued. Now, I began to concentrate my energies into bringing about larger policy changes that could benefit many more and not just the individuals I was engaging with.

I had been driven by emotion so far—what I felt and the ways in which I responded. In this new phase, I began to consider myself a social entrepreneur in the business of social change, someone whose work could have a cascading effect. After months of scrutiny, I was finally selected as a fellow.

As an Ashoka Fellow, I received learning, exposure and an expanding circle of peers, and I funnelled back into Prajwala all that invaluable knowledge and growth to build a powerful, even strident, voice against trafficking. Every day added to my learning curve. I was blessed to be learning directly on the field, facing real situations, meeting real people and solving real problems. I was also exposed to the academic side, learning about ideas and concepts that would support strategic planning.

I'd now begun to receive invitations for international conferences. The organisers invariably paid for my travel, stay and food through an allowance. Usually, breakfast would be included in the hotel stay, and if so, I'd eat that. I'd make do with the snacks at the conference instead of a lunch, and I'd either skip dinner or eat bread and fruit. In this way, I managed to save a substantial amount of per diem which became my personal nest fund. Interestingly, even today, my savings are built on such trips.

In 1999, one year after Astha Nivas was established, Jo and I registered Prajwala as a society. Jo had been an integral part of my commitment to start something for women in prostitution right from my PIN days. It is with him that I had discussed my dreams and vision. There was not a single day that I would not discuss some part of the work with him. No doubt we differed on several issues, but we also agreed upon matters such as the education of children, community awakening, non-conventional trades for women and advocacy for entitlements for victims. The name 'Prajwala' first rang in the air during my conversation with him. While we were clear about not using Boys Town connections to further Prajwala's mission, the doors of Boys Town were always open for us to conduct many of our training programmes and for holding important events. So, it was natural for me to propose that Jo would be the president of Prajwala. As the chief functionary, I would be general secretary, a position I hold till date.

Our governing body had three more members: Shoba Veigas and Anthony Reddy, friends of mine, and Bhaskar, Jo's trusted colleague. Things finally started stabilising somewhat. The registration allowed us to seek institutional funds. And once the children's home was stabilised, the United Nations Children's Fund (UNICEF) supported it for two years. Lalita's friend, Arvind Kumar, then the excise commissioner, helped us get a lot of donations in kind from traders, such as school uniforms. He introduced us to Amita Joseph, who was working at the United States Agency for International Development (USAID), who in turn helped us reach out to the United Nations Development Fund for Women (UNIFEM), which supported all our education centres for two years. She also introduced us to Sarat Dash who headed the International Organisation of Migration (IOM), India

Sarat-da was an extraordinary visionary like Jo, and believed that economic empowerment of victims could radically change the dynamics of the rehabilitation programme. He led IOM to initiate a programme on corporate social partnership with us to generate employment opportunities for survivors, the first its kind in India. Amita and Sarat-da had met Dr Verghese Kurien—also known as the Milkman of India, he was the chairman of Amul—and convinced him to consider operating Amul's pizza parlours with trafficked survivors. This would open a viable and sustainable employment avenue for them.

Minnie Mathews, principal secretary of the Women and Child Welfare Department, Andhra Pradesh, one of the most dynamic civil servants I have known, and now a great friend, was the driving force behind negotiating a spot right inside the secretariat for an Amul pizza parlour. She later got one more spot in the Commissionerate of Women Development and Child Welfare located near Sarathi Studios, Yousufguda. Mathews was also instrumental in bringing out a comprehensive policy to combat sex trafficking for undivided Andhra Pradesh in 2003. I had advocated for this policy for many years, and recommended it in a field-study report on sex trafficking from Andhra Pradesh titled 'The Shattered Innocence', which I had co-authored with Jo.

Since the beginning, Jo and I had felt that empowering trafficking survivors financially was crucial to their rehabilitation, and we continued to explore multiple economic options for the women we worked with. I started to look for financial support in the form of small loans or even grants to help them set up self-employment units, such as fast food corners, laundry and ironing stalls, vegetable vending and zari/karchob embroidery workshops. None of this directly contributed to Prajwala's finances, though. Therefore, restarting a production-cum-training facility, even if it wasn't a toy-making one, was a priority. In fact, both Jo and I felt that having such a unit visibly within Prajwala would be motivating for newcomers. We were spot-on regarding this matter. Even today, our production-cum-training centre (now called the Industrial Training Institute) offers victims exposure to a range of options that'll help them become economically empowered.

At Jo's request, Sarat-da extended all the support he could for this initiative. With IOM's help, in 2004, we set up a unique production and training centre, completely conceptualised, designed and established by Jo, that taught bookbinding, printing, welding and carpentry to survivors of prostitution and sex trafficking. We called this the Economic Rehabilitation Programme (ERP), and it continues to be a great success. Every year, ERP trains between fifty to seventy-five survivors and is completely self-sustaining. This was also the first intervention that was totally led by Jo. His rich experience managing Boys Town was the foundation for this unique programme. Boys Town had also allowed the first batch of girls to be trained in bookbinding on their campus in 2003. So, when we started the ERP in 2004, we had already trained bookbinders, which set the production unit in motion almost immediately. Jo recruited all the trainers, and streamlined both the training and the production work. IOM's financial support in procuring the machines made this unit akin to an industrial programme. Years later, in 2023, Jo's dream would come true when ERP was formally accredited as an Industrial Training Institute by the government of India—the first of its kind for survivors of sex trafficking.

The Catholic Relief Services (CRS) was another donor that supported all our shelters, both adult and children (Asha Niketan and Astha Nivas). CRS even helped us set up proper financial, warehousing and procurement systems to improve our transparency and governance, turning Prajwala into an organisation with an evolved financial accountability apparatus. It was a transformation from my bookkeeping days in those long registers one used to see in the movies of the fifties and sixties. I've still got that register with me, a memento of my days of struggle. Donors such as the CRS, which invest their time in institution-building should get huge credit, as they set up organisations for future success. It is as critical an aid as money. I met Rekha Abel at the CRS—she became a dear friend and joined Prajwala's governing body later—and Jomey Joseph, a trusted ally.

In early 2000, Germany-based Misereor funded all our prevention programmes, such as the learning centres for children, the community awakening programmes, the MAD initiatives and eventually extended their aid to fund our rescue interventions and victim assistance programmes. The transition from individual-driven intervention largely led by me to an organisation-driven mission with different layers of leadership was organic, and over time, we streamlined all our systems in terms of accountability parameters and leadership hierarchy accordingly.

While money from institutional donors was great, I was particular that we take no more than 60 per cent of the money we needed from them. I wanted us to mobilise the rest. My reasoning was this: our women and children must assimilate into the same society that failed them. And for our society to accept them, it must be sensitised to the fact that it helped their exploitation. I saw local fundraising as a way to sensitise the local community to take some ownership over their plight. If locals contributed, they would be interested and invested, and would want to take action to end the problem.

Many of these efforts at local fundraising turned out to be rather unpleasant, causing humiliation and even shaking my self-esteem. I once spent over an hour sitting with a company owner trying to explain sex crimes and trafficking. His interest lay primarily in the sexual act. I stuffed my annoyance away and answered his questions patiently. In the end, he removed his big fat wallet, considered for half a second and parted with a fifty-rupee note, saying his company wasn't doing well. I wanted to fling that note at his face, but gritted my teeth and thanked him graciously. My travel expenses and the receipt I sent him through post cost me more than his donation. Then there was the big automobile showroom that promised me Rs 10,000 for allowing them to advertise at one of our events. When I went to them after the event, they refused to pay up without a receipt for twice that amount. I walked away with nothing.

But the worst humiliation I faced was from the principals of two colleges. As a part of our local fundraising campaign, we collaborated with the Chennai-based band Sound of Music, which had visually challenged musicians. Brother Patrick from the Montfort Community Development Society (MCDS), a dear friend of Jo's, was coordinating this. The model was that we'd go to schools and colleges and talk about sex trafficking. Thereafter, the students would go on a fundraising drive and once it was done, Sound of Music would give a two-hour performance at their school or college. This turned out to be a great success, and many of the city schools raised lakhs of rupees for Prajwala and MCDS. Buoyed by this great response, we approached two major girls' colleges in the city for the same programme. Imagine our shock, when after the performance—which was a stupendous success—the nuns told us there were no funds to give, that they hadn't done any fundraising because they couldn't possibly ask grown-up girls to raise money. Why didn't they tell us this at the outset when I went to them with the plan? Since then, I have refused to go back to these two institutions, despite being invited several times after I became a known figure.

On the other hand, the most heart-warming experiences in fundraising for me have been from simple people. At Vanitha Mahavidayalaya, a government college for girls, the students walked to college for an entire month and donated their entire travel allowance to Prajwala. I have also seen very young children from schools all over the city handing in their entire piggy bank for our cause.

Then there is the most heart-warming example of all. A most inspiring and humbling source of monetary support that we've received consistently for the last twenty-one years—from a rickshaw-puller who gives us Rs 11 every day. His generosity beats the richest of the rich. From what little I know, he saw a programme on Doordarshan, I think it was called *Kranti Deep*, about me. Inspired, this gentleman started contributing daily, first by money order and now by Airtel money transfer. The first time, he sent me a post card with his information, ending the message with a simple line, '*Har din aap ke saath hoon.*' I will support your fight every day. It is individuals like these who sustain missions like ours.

18

The Power in Partnerships—and the Problems

At Fateh Darwaza my office was so tiny that there was no space for Akbar, and he would end up sitting in the courtyard where the children assembled for all their common activities. This violated a big rule for me. I didn't want any man, however trustworthy, on a campus meant for victims who were young girl children. The other problem was that I found myself constantly micromanaging Astha Nivas, never giving Vijeta or the others a chance to lead. I was sitting right there and could observe everything, so I got involved, and the staff members were also unwilling to take independent decisions so long as I was around.

By this time, we'd managed to get forty-five more houses for our women at Bora Banda and Gudi Malkapur under the weaker section housing scheme. This meant meeting the district administration as well as the women several times over. I could do this peacefully only if I was slightly cut off from Astha Nivas. We now had funding from UNICEF and UNIFEM, which required more reporting and financial management.

So, I needed an independent office where I could have meetings. I could not keep calling people to Astha Nivas or the other school centres. Equally importantly, we needed to recruit professional staff who could do proper accounting and financial management. Financial reporting was critical to all UN funding, and I could no longer manage with ad hoc financial management, no matter how diligently I did it.

We found an office space just behind the Charminar bus stand. A charming old gentleman I would soon call 'Baba' was the owner of the building. I fell in love with him right away. I had never seen either of my grandfathers, so Baba felt like one for me. He too quickly grew fond of me, always insisting that I sit with him and chat. He'd ask his daughter-in-law to feed me whatever vegetarian delicacy they had made that day. We were the only ones in this building, apart from Baba's family on the third floor. Baba had given me a small rod for my personal protection. He would do things like this without any specific explanation. This rod has saved my life several times, and I still keep it in my table drawer. From rumours that I heard and never attempted to verify, Baba was very influential and well-connected with all kinds of people. I saw every single person around Charminar bow before him with great respect. To me, he represented the right protection, both figuratively as an elder relative and as somebody who cared for my safety.

My Charminar office was accessible to everyone, and there was no way to guard ourselves from attacks other than through such self-defence tools as my rod, or having Baba sit in his plastic chair outside the building, keeping watch. One time, a trafficker from Delhi barged into my office and tried to attack me with a blade he'd hidden in his mouth. It's a technique preferred by lower-level criminals. They place the blade on the roof of the mouth, and with a deft click of the tongue, shoot the blade at the throat of the target. As soon as I understood that he wasn't a well-wisher, I reflexively bent down for the rod. This man hadn't anticipated my move, and the blade flew over my head onto the floor. I told Baba the story with much aplomb, and it resulted in him sitting longer hours at the building entrance.

Once we established ourselves at Charminar, I decided to recruit professional staff. Recently, I had met Gayatri Ramachandran, IAS, then principal secretary of the Women Development and Child Welfare Department, and she had expressed her deep discomfort with the way the government-run children's homes were managed. She was exploring the possibility of a public-private partnership to improve their management. I had come to be thoroughly frustrated that children from other backgrounds were constantly referred to Astha Nivas despite our consistent refusal to take them in. I was all for supporting any move to improve homes so that these children could be referred there.

I have said this before, and I'll probably say it until the very end: I am against the idea of child victims of sexual crimes being admitted to the same homes as children coming from other difficult circumstances. The former require special attention and specially attuned/trained adults. Efforts at rehabilitation—of both categories of children, mind you—get diluted if the two groups are integrated. For instance, children tend to compare, why are they getting special attention where I am not? And this creates resistance within the child to cooperate, breeds suspicion and distrust, severely hampering progress. Unfortunately, legal bodies do not understand this. Their priority is to quickly place the child in any safe place, no matter the kind of trauma the child has suffered.

So, to create greater awareness regarding the experiences and circumstances of women in prostitution and their children, I'd organised a two-day conference titled 'Children at Risk: Linkages and Convergence'. The idea was to sensitise government bodies so that they could be more forthcoming in their responses. We had used the Boys Town conference hall, paying for the space, and organised the event through financial support from the Indo-German Social Service Society. The first day saw child rights organisations discussing various aspects of the lives of the trafficked survivors and their kids, and the second day had the women in question themselves talking about their lives. I invited Principal Secretary Ramachandran and District Collector Bhanwarlal for the event.

Ramachandran was very impressed with Boys Town and instantly wanted to explore the possibility of a partnership to improve the conditions of boys' homes run by the government. I was interested in working with the state-run homes for girls. Running Astha Nivas and Asha Niketan had given us credibility in the management of homes.

I also needed to hire professionally qualified staff to co-manage the state-run homes and our own homes. A professional qualification in social work, especially a master's degree, equips you with a range of skills, such as strategic planning, designing a results-based programme, analysing outputs and outcomes, and the techniques to execute these skills. While our survivor caregivers had terrific skills, particularly with crisis intervention, they lacked the competence to provide structured counselling, prepare an individual care plan for each child to effect long-term change, document it or manage other data. As our financial situation improved, I started hiring post-graduates in social work. This was in 2000, when the Juvenile Justice Act, which mandated professionally trained counsellors and a more streamlined approach in admitting children to children's homes, came out.

I was looking forward to hiring well-qualified staff who would build a strong foundation for the children, and guide them gently, yet firmly, towards rehabilitation. But mixing survivors with those who had professional experience had unforeseen complications. Of the eleven who had 'womanned' our toy-making facility, two were at Astha Nivas, three at Asha Niketan and two at the office. The latter two were my primary link to all my other survivors, particularly those who had benefited from the weaker section housing scheme. The rest chose to start small businesses and sustain themselves.

Akbar continued to work with me, but I sensed that he was uncomfortable as more and more English-speaking staff joined. On their part, my professional staff found it awkward to be seen with the survivors. One resigned in the first week after being spotted by a relative with a survivor. For the first time at Prajwala, these survivors were made to feel less than their peers in the organisation. It was a great contrast to how I interacted with them. I had sat and eaten with them, even visited their homes, travelled everywhere on Akbar's cycle. I decided to give it time, hoping that things would work themselves out over the next few months.

Meanwhile, there were other crucial learnings too. And one incident in particular that brought home the importance of partnership with law enforcers, especially the police, was when one of my informers was murdered right before my eyes. That day, I had called the other Akbar Bhai to meet me at Shama Talkies. Prajwala's Akbar was not very comfortable with his namesake; he felt the man had a loose tongue and could not be trusted. By this time, we had started rescuing adult women, especially those who wanted to get out. Other Akbar was a regular informant in the Old City and had given me a lot of information, especially about women who were with the notorious brothel-keeper Reshma.

I knew Reshma personally, had seen her in Chanchalguda Jail and interacted with her multiple times. I had a soft spot for her after I found out that she was a child victim, sold when she was nine years old. As she survived in prostitution, she normalised the exploitation, began to control other women and even organised new women to join the trade. After the eviction drive at Mehendi, Reshma had moved to Gulzar House, a lane close to Charminar. She controlled all the women from Gulzar House to Madina Chowk, and had around forty women under her control. They were absolutely terrified of her. She supposedly carried blades in her mouth and was notorious for getting physically violent. With me, Reshma was always respectful, and I was the only one she stood up to greet. When I heard that she had a lot of new women in her group, I grew worried and requested a meeting with her.

But my meeting with Akbar Bhai had nothing to do with Reshma or rescues. I'd wanted to find out the number of girls who were being sold to the Middle East in the name of mutah nikah/marriage, a kind of temporary contract marriage practiced in the Muslim community. I had already seen a number of cases of 'sheikh marriages' in some areas where we worked. I knew Akbar Bhai could give me some vital information about this. Already, Tahseen, Vijaya and some of my other teachers were quietly scouting for information.

Akbar Bhai was waiting for me at Shama Talkies. I had arrived by auto, and asked the driver to wait and take me to my next meeting. While Akbar Bhai and I were speaking, I spotted Reshma and some men approaching us. I assumed she must have received my message and was coming over to greet me. Akbar had not noticed them.

In a fraction of a second, everything was over. The men with Reshma stabbed Akbar in the back with a large knife even as Reshma signalled my auto, standing in the corner, and pushed me into it as soon as it arrived. The driver didn't need anyone's encouragement to get away.

All the breath was knocked out of my body. I was in shock, and before I'd realised what was happening, the autowallah had dropped me off at the Charminar bus stand and driven off, not even waiting to take the fare. I dragged myself up the three floors to my office. I can't remember how I spent the day, but I could speak to no one about the incident. Just imagine discussing it with those who were already mortally scared to walk with our women, or telling survivors like Akbar, Laxmi and Rosy, who risked their lives daily by joining the mission. The incident was all over the news the next day: a pimp killed in a gang war in broad daylight. Reshma and her four accomplices were arrested, but I was nowhere on the scene, thanks to her.

Soon after the incident, Akbar requested me to release him from Prajwala. Our relationship was too deep for words like 'staff' or 'resignation'. The stabbing still fresh in my mind, I let him go without a word. Jaffer Bhai also stopped connecting with me.

Events like these convinced me that the rescues I had done were counter-productive, and there was a need to work towards a partnership with the police. This is what Jo had harped on for years, but I had always felt that an NGO should be a part of the rescue operation to assist the victim. I had by now met a good number of police personnel and realised that I had been prejudiced. I'd learnt that the entire department wasn't corrupt; on the contrary, some of them were great human beings. The rest were either apathetic or demotivated, although of course some were just truly bad apples. We needed to move the ones in the middle, the fence-sitters, engage with them and sensitise them. If we told them the actual stories of women and children, I hoped they would sympathise and respond appropriately.

When I proposed this to Prasad Rao, then police commissioner of Hyderabad, he organised such a session within two days of my visit. It was here that I first met A.K. Khan and Mahesh Muralidhar Bhagwat, IPS officers who would play a great role in Prajwala's work in the coming years. Bhagwat is the most dynamic police officer that I have ever met. His commitment to end sex trafficking stayed strong all through his tenure. Of all the police officers I've met, he has the most sound understanding of the role of the police force in prevention, protection and prosecution. He leveraged every existing law to fight the problem, something he continues to do.

With Khan's help, we established counselling facilities within police stations, where women in prostitution were advised on other ways to make a living. We set up these facilities at police stations in Tank Bund, Necklace Road, Gopalapuram and Afzalgunj. This was a first-of-its-kind venture, and showed a different face of policing to the public.

Partnering with the police department helped us rescue thousands of women and girls from different parts of the country. But every relationship has its difficulties. The police system is especially hierarchical, so junior officers hesitate to take initiative, preferring to follow their seniors' orders. If the superior officer was disinclined to work with us, any expectation of cooperation from the junior rungs was doomed right away.

Some of it has been my fault. My abrasive tongue has riled many people. On one occasion, a senior police officer called me to his room and accused me of getting too big for my boots, threatening me with non-cooperation from his entire team. Apparently, someone within the department had told him that I had criticised the Hyderabad police in Kerala. Frankly, I can't rule out that possibility—I most likely did so not only in Kerala but elsewhere as well. But I'd have done it in the context of a case, and if they had heard the whole speech, they would have realised that I also highlight the good work.

Some of it has been due to people's insecurities—the fear that I would hijack their efforts and walk away with the credit. I speak with a certain authority, and I don't beat about the bush. I know my work and I can back up claims with facts. My confidence is hard to digest for some, which means I'm often painted as anti-establishment, and both Prajwala and I are sidelined. For instance, Prajwala, which has earned a reputation in the anti-trafficking sphere even internationally, once failed to receive an invite to a national anti-trafficking conference organised by police in Hyderabad. This just goes to show that police officers are as susceptible to frailties as the rest of us.

Despite the bad eggs in the system and some self-sabotaging on my part, Prajwala has assisted in the removal of over 28,600 women and girls from commercial sexual exploitation in the last twenty-seven years, and the entire credit goes to the police department. Left to my own devices, I might have rescued a couple more people before getting murdered and tossed somewhere in broad daylight, much like Akbar Bhai.

Such positive experiences—the teamwork, the concerted efforts—are what have shifted my language from an egocentric 'I' to a collaborative 'we'. The power of partnership is immense, and just as the police are crucial to rescue efforts, organisations like Prajwala play a critical role in victim protection and supporting the prosecution of criminals.

We used the insights we gained from years of practical experience, studied existing legal frameworks and created manuals that codify victim-centric investigations in partnership with legal experts. Prajwala's manuals and handbooks are considered the most practical tools in sensitising personnel, and have been used in training thousands of police officers. Victims thus receive not only protection, but also humane and sensitive treatment from responding officers and others, thus greatly increasing their chances of cooperating with the police to help prosecute the culprits. That's what makes a victim-centric approach a win-win for law enforcement and the victims themselves.

Our partnership with the Women Development and Child Welfare department started much earlier, when they provided space to open pizza parlours operated by trafficking survivors. Since then, Prajwala has worked closely with the department to build community vigilance, train anganwadi workers on responding to human trafficking cases, improve the conditions of government-supported homes like Swadhar and Ujjwala and co-manage government shelters for trafficked victims.

As mentioned, our long-term collaboration with the department started with Gayatri Ramachandran, when Boys Town and Prajwala partnered with the government to co-manage state homes for children. That partnership transformed the management of those homes, ensuring that quality care reached the children while bringing transparency to the system. But this partnership was also filled with multiple setbacks: government functionaries were unused to scrutiny by civil society organisations and those that were corrupt, that pilfered provisions meant for children or mistreated them, resented our 'interference' doubly so. The challenge was to report faithfully without making it sound like a complaint against the staff.

When Minnie Mathews joined the department in 2002 as principal secretary, our working relationship deepened further. Mathews was an amazing officer who believed that the cause is bigger than the individual. She proposed that we request Home Minister Devender Goud to release the field study, 'The Shattered Innocence', that Jo and I had co-authored as it would get us greater exposure. Her strategy worked. Apart from the attention, when the time came for the political leadership to approve a comprehensive anti-trafficking policy, they did it without a second thought.

Mathews was a great stateswoman who could defuse the natural tension between the government and civil society. It was thanks to her vision that Prajwala worked seamlessly with the government to organise mass campaigns across the state to prevent human trafficking. Believe me, no single civil society organisation can achieve this without the active partnership of the government.

Chaya Ratan, who also occupied the same post, was another officer who believed in strengthening the system to ensure that even the very marginalised had access to dignity, rights and benefits. She honoured and approved every recommendation I proposed for the welfare of trafficked children and issued them as government policies. It was during her tenure that the government passed the bulk of orders that are now firm policies for the welfare of trafficked victims. We'd sit for hours over several delicious lunches, courtesy her cook Dhani, discussing the needs of our women and girls. Today, if the child victims in Andhra Pradesh and Telangana enjoy so many entitlements, it is thanks to officers like them.

In early 2000, we partnered with the Andhra Pradesh AIDS Control Society for two years to recruit, train and place 800 HIV counsellors in all hospitals in the state. This partnership was driven by the project director, K. Damayanti, IAS, whose empathy for those afflicted with HIV was unparalleled and inspiring. Through this project, I met Dr Balamba from the Government Maternity Hospital and Dr Madhubabu from Osmania General Hospital, who trained HIV counsellors for two years with me before joining Prajwala's governing body and attending to the health needs of our children. So, from having no professional staff until 1999, by late 2000, we had a little more than 850 people on our payroll for a brief period of two years, until the HIV Counselling Project ended in 2002.

Yet, as with the police, I got into trouble with civil servants too. In one instance, Prajwala was inundated with notices about defaulting on tax on our economic rehabilitation unit. We had to fight in the Income Tax Appellate Tribunal (ITAT) to prove that the income generated was funnelled back in full to the same cause and hence was not taxable. The supportive presence of Nivedita Biswas, IRS, was our greatest strength during those times. She spoke at the tribunal about our work, so that the authorities gave us a fair hearing and scrutinised our records accordingly. In the end, the ruling was in our favour. If things had gone against us, we'd never have had the courage to start another income generation unit.

In another instance, the situation turned nasty when I pushed for video conferencing in court to record the evidence of a victim. This was in the context of young girls from Andhra Pradesh who were trafficked to Delhi. The girls were in our shelter for rehabilitation and to support their social reintegration. When the trials started, they had to go to Delhi to testify. One of the girls who had gone to Delhi had turned hostile in court, and there were many theories why. The most believable one was that the traffickers had managed to get to her in some way. I felt video conferencing was the only way to prevent such a thing from happening. My suggestion, accepted by the Delhi High Court, rankled with the commissioner of the Department of Women Development and Child Welfare in Andhra Pradesh for reasons best known to him. He then launched a series of fault-finding inspections in all our shelters. That got my back up, so I went on the offensive and refused to allow any inspections after sunset. He retaliated by badmouthing me and Prajwala. The situation declined rapidly, and as collateral damage, UNICEF's funding for Astha Nivas was discontinued. Since the project period was over, this officer had to issue the renewal recommendation, and he refused to sign the file.

In my righteous arrogance—it comes when you start feeling highly accomplished—I shot off a letter to the UNICEF headquarters in Delhi about the ground staff's lack of interest, thus spoiling my relationship with its officers in Hyderabad. My myopia jeopardised an important association with a UN agency for many years to come.

This was a valuable lesson, and I took the monumental decision to never accept government funds as it could compromise our ability to advocate for the rights of the victims. There are all kinds of ways to get into trouble with the government, but a funding relationship can seriously compromise your voice. Another important lesson: to get off my high horse, and to calmly assess possible ramifications before shooting off letters to anyone, let alone top functionaries of an institution. What goes on record has long-standing implications.

Despite these hiccups, I continue to have faith in collaborative partnerships with the government. I believe this is the only way to effect lasting change. But this is not easy to do as a financial beneficiary of the government, for the balance of power remains with the donor.

Collaborations should be on a more equal footing—the only way we can negotiate on behalf of the people we serve.

Other than the police and civil services, the other significant engagment we've had is with the judiciary, which was the result of my legal advocacy. Way back in 2004, a few years after my visit to the US, I had decided to file a PIL in the Supreme Court to establish a protocol on victim protection. While looking for the right pro bono lawyer, I came across the Human Rights Law Network, where Aparna Bhat (now in the Supreme Court) was assigned to my case. Our professional relationship soon deepened into a friendship based on mutual respect. Aparna was also connected to various anti-trafficking organisations, and thus had an insight many legal luminaries lacked. She toiled for over eleven years in the Supreme Court with this 2004 PIL before the court passed a direction for enacting a comprehensive legislation to combat trafficking in 2015. Aparna was also our legal counsel in a PIL pleading for a robust reporting system to report rape videos which are circulated using technology. This PIL led to the establishment of the cyber-crime reporting portal (*cybercrime.gov.in*), and made technological firms accountable for putting in place safeguarding protocols on their platforms.

Advocate L. Ravichander, who practises in the high courts of Telangana and Andhra Pradesh, reached out to me as a concerned citizen. I now know him as a multi-faceted person who is active in the literary-cultural milieu of Hyderabad. He became a partner who mobilised funds for Prajwala, and slowly began representing us in all our cases in the high court. Ravichander also deputed two of his juniors, Deepak Mishra and Goutham, to represent our victims' cases in the lower courts. Aparna and Ravi have a very special place in my heart. They were our voices in court.

I also personally invested a lot of time and effort to sensitise the judiciary and prosecuting officers on victim-centric justice systems so that the processes were more victim-friendly. In the course of these efforts, I realised that simply sensitising officers in the criminal justice system to implement the existing law in the right spirit can sort out half the problem.

While my relationship with the police, civil servants and judiciary has mellowed and improved over time, I proceed with caution when it comes to partnering with other civil society organisations. The turf is filled with competition: we're all fish in the same pool vying for the same resources, recognition and plaudits. What's of prime importance to me is alignment regarding prostitution. I keep away from organisations that believe prostitution should be legalised and that sex work is legitimate work. I'm also wary of project-based organisations that shift their positions to echo that of their donors'. There are also vested interests that try to harm others, perhaps because they can't digest the recognition or the demonstrated impact another organisation receives. Then there are the personal vendetta missions that harm and destroy credibility through smear campaigns, attempts to block funding, etc. Prajwala has known its share of trials, and now proceeds with great caution in all partnerships.

19

A Hard Lesson to Learn

We had always needed to conceal the background of the women in our homes, particularly when we opened a centre in an area where they had formerly lived. We'd faced a mob once before in Kishanbagh—lathi-wielding protesters who'd learnt about the women's 'dirty' background. Though we'd defused the situation then, the issue flared up again. This time, the troublemakers got the neighbourhood masjid to instruct the community to boycott our centre and withdraw their children in protest. The first time that happened, I was out of town and Jo had to resolve it. Having the director of Boys Town speak to them settled things down for a while. During our investigations, we learnt that a few private schools were worried that our free education would directly hurt their revenue, and so were insecure about our centres. The next time there was a flare-up, the mothers took turns to stand vigil so that no untoward incidents occurred.

Over time, we quietly took in children from impoverished families at our other centres as well to minimise questions from local communities on why we didn't accept all children. However, we instated a (unspoken) policy not to discuss our students' families or backgrounds. We had seven such centres now and needed to exercise caution at all times. It is another matter that our website (up and running for two years by this point) and our literature elsewhere still talked about second-generation prevention of prostitution.

There was also the increasing problem of 'sheikh marriages' and 'mutah nikah', where men from Arab nations married minor girls, generally from poor families, and later trafficked them. I had asked my teachers to investigate this, and we had documented nearly fifty such cases, and made the short film *Bhagnagar* to create awareness about it in our local communities. We used an old name of Hyderabad, given the sensitivity of the issue. When we showed this film to some community elders with the support of a partner organisation, all hell broke loose. Why was an outsider interfering in our community matters, they asked.

Next, I approached the leader of the political party in power in the area. He reacted in much the same way and then proceeded to issue threats: if I insisted on stirring up trouble, I'd be in serious trouble myself.

Around this time, two things happened. Firstly, we received repeated appeals from an RTI activist to disclose our financial status. We aren't funded by the government, so we don't have to entertain such requests. Still, we gave the man our annual report, which included an audited statement. Secondly, we'd been facing some sort of vandalism at one of our centres, though none of it was serious enough to report to the police—pieces of meat had been flung into the building, and once a stone had been hurled at a window.

One day, the in-charge of that centre called me, frantic with worry. There was a group of boys protesting with posters and slogans that we were sullying the reputation of the neighbourhood by claiming there was prostitution being carried out there. The leader of this group turned out to be that self-same RTI activist. In no time, a crowd had gathered and the local member of legislative assembly (MLA) was called, in all probability by this activist himself. When the teachers explained our education programme and our connection to Brother Jose, the director of Boys Town, the MLA was pacified and left immediately.

On our part, we called the police, who then warned this RTI activist not to cause trouble. I learnt that this man's father was in the police department posted in the City Armed Reserve Police (CAR) headquarters, which is on Petla Burj just next to Mehendi. It was rumoured that the father was close to Khatoon Bi and Masoom Bi, who were both settled in the same area, and saw them regularly. These were just rumours, and I did not probe the exact nature of their relationship. But I was confused; if this man's father was in the police, that too in the Old City, then he would definitely be aware that many women who had fled Mehendi were living in Kalapather.

To prove our claims of harassment, we would have to reveal the identities of some of the women, especially those who were living in the care of Khatoon and Masoom Bi, and no way was I doing this. I had never asked the women what they had told their neighbours in the locality. It was Khatoon Bi and Masoom Bi who had identified this building for our school and all the children in their care were studying in the centre, including those who had shifted from Mehendi after we had closed operations there. As we had many children from impoverished backgrounds at this centre as well, we would not discuss any matters related to prostitution in the mothers' meetings here. That was reserved for the Charminar office.

But without proof, our claims would be called bogus and Prajwala a fraud. We really were caught between the devil and the deep sea.

Soon the Urdu dailies were full of stories of how I'd fabricated stories about the Old City and maligned it, hoodwinking donors just to receive funds for Prajwala. And in Kalapather where my centre was located, there were flyers posted all over—screenshots of those pages from our website where we discussed trafficking and prevention—and calls to boycott us were made from the masjid. I was told that they even issued a fatwa against me. As a precaution, I ended up writing a letter to the Hon'ble Chief Justice of Andhra Pradesh, Justice Madan B. Lokur, sensing a threat to our safety.

With each new development, I was more and more agitated. I had the responsibility to safeguard their identity. At the same, I had a duty to be transparent to the people from whom I sought funds. The more I thought about it, the more my anger began to mount.

Anger was to be my downfall.

Not knowing whom to direct my anger at, I directed it at the mothers. It was undoubtedly a mistake, but at that time I felt that asking them to state on record that they either prostituted or were prostituting would at least safeguard me if my donors questioned my motives. In any case, public perception was beyond me, and the way things were going, a new rumour or theory about my agendas was springing up every day. Whom all do we go to and convince? I could only do what was in my sphere of control, and at that time, it was the women whose children studied at my centres.

I asked my centres to get the mothers to attest to their background in writing. It was only for documentation, and wouldn't be used for anything else—and the heads of the centres were to assure them about this.

When the in-charges explained to the mothers (only those who were in prostitution) the rationale for such an undertaking, most grudgingly agreed. It was not comfortable for any of them. Knowing a fact and creating a permanent record on paper are two different things. For years, they had sent their children to the centre with a sense of confidence that their children were finally getting a chance to live in a stigma-free environment. Even those women who were with us from Mehendi were taken aback, for we had never taken anything in writing even way back in 1996–97 when all their lives were public news. The children were just treated as children, and their mothers' background was never discussed in the centres.

Two women from the Pahadi centre protested. This centre was located on a hillock, and comprised the most impoverished group.

Though the women had discussed this in the confines of their homes, the news immediately spread to the community. In no time, it spread like a wildfire that Prajwala was asking the women to sign on fake documents. Like rumours, misinformation spreads fast, and the situation got even more tense.

I decided it was time to personally assure the women at this centre that these papers wouldn't be disclosed to anyone anywhere. Ali, Nitin from the Charminar office and the in-charges of all the centres were already at Pahadi supporting the local teachers.

When I reached the centre, I found the locals making a royal tamasha. They were armed with lathis, chains and stones, but their voice was their weapon. Cries of 'band karo!' (close down) and 'bhaag niklo!' (leave our place) pierced the air. The mothers were also there, standing with our teachers.

I thought to pacify them, tell them that we ran an education programme for the financially distressed. But they were in no mood to listen. They were there to make their point.

'*Tukde tukde kar ke Musi me phenk denge!*' came a shout. We'll cut you to bits and toss you into the Musi. As the crowd took it up, the chant turned into a roar.

'Chhinaal, baahar aa!' they clamoured. Come out, you whore.

The lathis were in the air, as were the chains, bobbing up and down, keeping time with each slur. It was only a matter of time before they'd begin to hurl stones. This mob could not be appeased, could not be reasoned with. Some mothers came forward to defend the centre and the mob directed their fury on them, threatening to throw them out of the basti.

That's it! I'd had enough! I announced that we would close the centre.

Endangering the lives of the mothers and pushing them out of the basti was not a price I was willing to pay. The mob instantly calmed down. I assured the despairing mothers that we would find a way to educate their children, and left.

On the way back, we stopped at the local police station and informed them about the situation. They promised to keep watch. I had also been updating the deputy commissioner of police (DCP) of the area.

I'd barely moved two kilometres farther when I got a call. The mob was planning to burn down the centre. I rushed back to the police station. The police summoned the community leaders, who turned up along with a private school owner.

These parts in the heart of the Old City are communally sensitive. In the past, the smallest provocation has led to loss of life and property. It is natural that the police would first explore the possibility of a mediation and attempt to reconcile the matter amicably. In our case, I clearly did not belong to the majority community of Old City, and anybody can turn anything into a religious matter. Here, mediation was a practical solution.

When all of us sat before the inspector, I told him that we had decided to close down the centre, and I could not understand why they were still creating a problem. The group demanded that I burn all the undertakings signed by the mothers, and hand over the centre immediately to the private school owner.

My guess is that when we left the centre, many of the mothers, fearing for their lives and safety, must have told the community that they were compelled to sign the undertaking.

But where did this private school owner pop up from? How was he prepared to take over in less than twenty-four hours? What was the connection between him and these protestors? But such questions would have to wait, we needed to put out the fire first. In less than ten minutes, I had all of the undertakings brought to me, which I burnt right in front of them. That same evening, we shifted out and handed over the place to the private school owner.

In all this, the police station had been our Switzerland, a neutral area where contesting parties could negotiate. They had watched over the proceedings with keen interest—invested in the intrigue, but not a participant in or influencer of events.

The high court had taken note of my letter to the chief justice, in the meantime, and ordered an enquiry. The report was damning. The police denied that there were any attacks in any area, and the home department stated that they did not even know Prajwala. This was particularly shocking as we were closely working with the police on practically a daily basis, and were the safety net for the victims they rescued.

The enquiry report laid the entire blame on me and the fact that I had asked the women to say that they were in prostitution. It said that the women were poor, and were desperate for their children to receive an education, free of cost to boot, and so had agreed to sign those papers. That all of this had naturally created unrest in the community. And that if I had any real worries about an attack, I should have filed a complaint.

I had kept the police in the loop at every step, and not a single policeman had asked me to submit a complaint in writing at any point. In fact, even the first time, during the disturbance at Kalapather, I had been discouraged from filing a complaint. The absence of a written complaint made me look like a fool, one with a rather fertile imagination, who had fabricated those attacks.

It was a painful lesson, and came at great cost. So, I took it to heart. In the years to come, anytime we faced attacks, I would immediately file a written complaint with the police—and there have been many. Till date, other than a case of stalking, the police have been unable to solve a single case related to our safety and security, but at least they couldn't deny that it had occurred. I realised that this is how the criminal justice system functions. Oral conversations cannot be verified, after all.

For Prajwala, this incident taught me the value—and practical advantage—of transparency. We should have protected identities from the start, integrating it into our programme design.

If we selected a beneficiary based on certain criteria, they should supply verifiable indicators to prove that they qualified. We could keep such information confidential, but open it to scrutiny by any legally competent authority, and make that abundantly clear to all concerned.

It sounds basic, but it was a very valuable revelation for me, that transparency guarantees (or at least preserves) safety. For so long, the two ideas—protection and transparency—had felt incompatible. Antagonistic, even. Now, we implemented transparency across all areas of operation, and our interventions changed radically.

From then on, we only accepted children or women to our shelters on the orders of a court or a child welfare committee (CWC), which is the legally competent body in matters of children, with all the necessary proof supplied in the FIR to explicitly indicate that they were a victim of sex trafficking or sex crime. This applied to everything related to the victims, such as their release from our homes, or granting visitation rights. This meant that we would only admit or release people through a court order. Gone were the days when we would just rescue a child or woman, and admit them to our shelters without any legal document and end up being accused of kidnapping and illegal detention.

Even our rescues were led by the police, and followed the same procedure, with a proper complaint, an FIR and a court order. The court order had to clearly mandate that we had the responsibility to provide care and protection to the victim. This clearly demarcated everyone's role: the judiciary handled entry and exit, we provided holistic care and support. We fully embraced the idea that paperwork is proof and protection.

For our education centres, we formed a scrutiny committee, with mothers, community frontline workers (anganwadi workers, Asha workers, etc.) and the police, which would authorise admissions to our centres. The scrutiny committee was sensitised to our priority areas, and was told clearly that any child belonging to a family even suspected of being in prostitution would be given the highest priority.

Additionally, we created markers that could be used to identify potential victims. We knew that procurers of prostitution largely targeted single women and deprived children. So we involved the community in a survey to help identify the sections of society most vulnerable to sex traffickers, such as orphaned or abandoned children, financially distressed families and children of women in prostitution. It created awareness within the community and also became our baseline data for setting targets in each area for the centre. In fact, another thing we gained clarity on was that we had to exit an area once the vulnerable population was covered, i.e., the education centres were just learning centres that prepared children for mainstream schools and, as and when all the children were enrolled in schools, our work was completed, and it was time to move on.

Doing the right thing is necessary and important. But doing it in a way that safeguards all concerned is just as crucial. Without the latter, the former can come undone easily. And though it is time-consuming (and often dull), in the long run, the process keeps everyone safe, and you still working.

20

Palakkad Predictions

Thanks to Jo, my relationship with my family was on a somewhat even keel. I actively kept them out of my work, but we took an interest in each other's lives now. So, when I learnt from my father that Suku was struggling at school and didn't know what to study after, I helped him get a seat at St Joseph's Arts and Science in the arts section (my alma mater was happy to oblige me; I'd been adjudged Best Student once). Three years later, he still felt unclear about his future and career. My parents were unprepared; they hadn't faced anything like this with their daughters. Sumathi was a schoolteacher now, married with two daughters. Sujji had done a course in secretarial practice from the reputed Davar's College of Commerce Secretarial Studies and Service. She was now employed in a good company, and had done her bachelor's in arts through distance learning while working.

With Sujji, our love-hate sibling relationship had, in our mid-thirties, turned into a deep friendship. She has been contributing to Prajwala ever since she became financially independent, and hasn't missed a single month till date. It was different with Suku; I'd always had a soft spot for him. I found him a job in Hyderabad with Jo's help, and he stayed with me initially before moving out. Throughout that time, I made sure he was protected from my work. The move to Hyderabad gave him some clarity. He returned to Bangalore within a year, and completed a diploma in apparel design and fashion technology from a reputed institution, and now works with one of the country's biggest retail chains.

My parents were close to Jo, Shoba and Geeta, and assumed everyone else in my circle was like them. They also thought I had a stable job and income and not enough time to get into trouble. I'd never stopped sending money home, but now, I was able to shower my family with gifts every time I travelled abroad. On my first trip to the US, I discovered the Dollar Store and gleefully used $50 from my allowance for my family—ten dollars (and thus ten gifts) per person. Only Jo got a larger share of the money for his cognac and cigarettes, but far fewer items in the bargain.

As my relationship with my family became more relaxed and cordial—both sides had a landline and we spoke daily—my parents felt comfortable involving themselves with my well-being. My father was not conservative, but would occasionally consult astrologers, especially if he was visiting his hometown in Palakkad. On one such visit, he decided to show my astrological charts (which we call 'jatakam' and is usually written on a palm leaf, or ola) for a reading. That night, he told me what he'd learnt. 'Your daughter's life will be in danger, grave danger. And it'll be this very year,' the family astrologer had said. Predictably, I'd laughed it away.

But it was hard to dismiss that prediction two weeks later when there was an attempt on my life.

A few days earlier, hundreds of girls were rescued in the GB Road red-light area of Delhi. The rescue was done by the Delhi police in collaboration with STOP, a partner NGO based in that city and founded by Roma Debabrata, who was also a lecturer at Miranda College (Roma-di is one of the most daring women I know and is incredibly affectionate with me). Over 400 minors and adult women were rescued. More than 80 per cent belonged to Andhra Pradesh. And that is how we came into the picture, for the rescued victims had to be restored to their home state. The entire case was being closely monitored by Justice Usha Mehra of the Delhi High Court. Hence, the case was not only well-publicised but also held high priority in terms of all the right procedures to be followed. I went to Delhi to meet the girls who were housed in the government home, and assured them they would be safely restored to their families in Andhra Pradesh.

Lo and behold, in a few days, all the traffickers from Delhi had descended on Hyderabad to recover 'their stolen property'. I knew they were aware of my involvement in the operations as I'd met the girls in Delhi and received them in Hyderabad when Roma-di brought them to me.

Two days after the girls arrived, an auto ran into me. I was just outside Boys Town, where I had gone to brief Jo about the arrangements to send the girls to their villages. The force of the impact toppled me over. I assumed that this was careless driving or that I was standing at the wrong place, so I moved aside, but then the auto backed up, ran over my feet and sped away. That's when I realised it had been an attack.

Shaken, I decided to visit Palakkad to meet the family astrologer in person. He more or less repeated all that I'd heard from my father, but added one thing more: 'The path of sanyaasa isn't yours. It is the grihastha life that is ordained for you.'

I left the astrologer's house with that ringing in my head. My body felt strangely heavy, and I'm not sure how I managed to get back to Thamarapadam, my dad's village, from there. I was in some sort of trance. At home, I washed my feet and headed straight for the family temple. How long I sat there, I don't know. At some point, the impulse to remove my rudraksha took over. I lifted the beads off my body, twisted them over into a circle and placed them in the sanctum, all the while deeply immersed in prayer. I was no longer bound by my vow of celibacy, but there was nobody I could tell about this decision. Muthiamma was now living with Daddy's younger brother, Sundaran Cheriachan. She was in her late eighties and slowly losing her memory. Muthiamma is the only person who would be mildly interested, and she was lost in her own world.

Back in Hyderabad, things moved on as always. Work, Jo, my friends and parents kept me busy. And when it all got too much, there was my regular Friday destressing to look forward to. I am a movie buff and am partial, of course, to rom-coms. I could watch any kind of movie, but happy ones captivate me like no other. And Mills & Boons—I could lose myself in those romance books for hours, emerging with a lighter mind. I mostly preferred the classics, from a time when romance was still sacrosanct. These novels I would read with such devotion that anyone would think I was preparing for an important UPSC exam. Only Jo knew about these private passions of mine, and I'd dragged him to watch a few movies with me. His stature and his responsibilities, I think, didn't permit him to watch any more. In any case, he would much rather spend time reading his serious books.

What even Jo didn't know was that I watched movies every Friday without fail. This was my very own secret, my outlet to destress, and was deeply private to me. Watching films like *Chandni Bar* alone in a theatre with five other people gave me a sort of thrill. When the international film festival came to Hyderabad in 1997, I was one of those thousands who hung around in all the theatres. I loved movies in any form, in any language and not just the serious ones. Hindi films like *Om Shanti Om* or Malayalam films like *Manjil Virinja Pookkal,* I could see them a hundred times over. Movies with music and dance appealed to me even more. *Saagara Sangam* is my all-time favourite Telugu movie. While I like English movies, I watch them only with subtitles, for even today I am not comfortable with all the foreign accents, and I continue to believe my vocabulary in English is rather limited.

One day, I opened the newspaper to a king-sized photo of Rajesh Touchriver, an internationally reputed filmmaker whose debut film *In the Name of Buddha* had been nominated at Cannes. It was a long, flattering article describing his career and work. Rajesh had been an art director in the Telugu film industry when he won the prestigious Charles Wallace Trust Award and secured a scholarship to study visual language/scenography and direction at the Wimbledon College of Arts, London. He had also studied animation in Hyderabad and completed his bachelors in theatre and art direction from the School of Drama and Fine Arts, Thrissur. Anyway, the journalist had described him as the pride of Hyderabad, and announced his return to the city. I read the article twice, thoroughly. His photo covered the entire page and was quite impactful.

I knew this guy! The first time I'd heard of Rajesh was through my theatre friends, Jolly and Biju, who were assisting Uday Bhanu during the street theatre campaign opposing the Nandanavanam project; he was their roommate. And when I learnt he was into films, I had naturally wanted to be introduced, and had gone over to their house in the railway quarters behind Nampally railway station.

Five years later, he still had that same piercing gaze and thick beard. He now sported a hat and a large necklace.

The first time I'd met Rajesh, I'd left that meeting feeling deeply attracted to him—and also feeling terribly guilty about it. The pull had been instant and insistent. Some strange and strong emotion, some sort of prickling turbulence had made me uncomfortable. It had certainly not been his doing, he was remarkably easy to talk to. Sitting in the backyard, we had started off talking about our experience with street theatre, but had soon branched out to other topics. Biju and Jolly had left us alone, but we hadn't felt their absence. Rajesh had deep spiritual insights and appeared very knowledgeable about history and culture. I can't recall much of our conversation, but I know we spoke for over two hours. Was it that we'd been a novelty to each other? He'd never met an activist, and he was the first person from the film industry I'd even seen.

Whatever it was, that hold on me had stayed strong all the way home, while my guilt had spiralled. That night, I'd told Jo what I'd felt without sharing Rajesh's name. Jo had told me that it was normal to feel attraction, even for religious celibates, and that it was important to remind ourselves of our vows and to focus on our mission. I listened to all that he said without any argument. My mind was made up: I would not meet this man again and get distracted in that way.

That had been five years ago. But many things had changed in the interim. That year, 2002, I was able to read that article about Rajesh freely and happily, having given up my self-proclaimed vow of celibacy.

When I first met him, I don't remember if he had that English surname ... but now he had that distinctive 'Touchriver' attached to his name. Since each one of us has a right to choose our name, and the film world is filled with assumed names, I gathered it must be connected to that.

I met Rajesh soon after at a theatre performance in Ravindra Bharati one Saturday evening. My friend Ali Asghar and I were outside the main entrance when I spotted him on the stairs. We recognised each other instantly, and that connection felt fierce even though we hadn't seen each other since that evening in the railway quarters. I introduced Ali and Rajesh to each other, and then, out of the blue, asked Rajesh if he would help us with the arrangements for our fundraiser, a concert by the group Sound of Music, which we were organising at that very venue. Rajesh readily agreed, even though he was now a noted film director, and it would be unheard of for anybody else in his position to do stage work or get back to art direction.

When I told Jo about this, leaving out the other bits, I learnt that he already knew Rajesh through other sources. Coincidentally, they belonged to the same district in Kerala, and their hometowns were only ten kilometres apart. Rajesh was from Arakulam and Jo from Karimanoor! The three of us soon began to hang out together, and there was a comfort and ease between the two of them that pleased me no end.

Rajesh suggested that we should document our work—the issues we addressed, the strategies we employed, the specific hurdles we encountered—through a visual medium. In other words, that we make a documentary film. We agreed.

He refused to accept any money from Prajwala when he helped us make *Bhagnagar*, the documentary on sheikh marriages. He made a thirty-minute documentary on Boys Town—he'd fallen in love with it—highlighting the amazing efforts of the institution and its director, for which he charged only the minimum production costs.

We had come to be so comfortable with each other that we'd talk for hours on end. One time, we were so engrossed in our chat, we walked for over six kilometres, from Ramakrishna Theatre to Shah Ali Banda. I think our common connection was my deep interest in cinema and the desire to get more involved in it. For all the short films, documentaries and docufiction Rajesh made at that time, I wrote the story and worked on the commentary.

Meantime, our fundraising event was nearly upon us and we were busy with the campaign. The event at Ravindra Bharati was a success, we raised good money. But I didn't like the stage that Rajesh had made for us: it lacked the glamour of my previous fundraiser at Hari Hara Kala Bhavan. Jo, though, loved the sets and stage, and was profuse in his thanks to Rajesh and his team. I pointedly did not say a word. Jo noticed this and later commented on my lack of manners.

It was only months later that I felt like thanking Rajesh for the work he'd done for the fundraising. I was in Bangalore, visiting my family on the weekend. My father had retired from service and, from the dues received, had bought a small, ground-floor flat on the outskirts of the city. That was when the impulse overtook me. Four months later, one fine day—night, to be specific—I felt compelled to thank him.

Rajesh was rather surprised by my call; he hadn't really noticed my lack of civility (and I kept my displeasure about the stage and set to myself). He was very excited—*In the Name of Buddha* had been nominated for the 2003 International Film Festival at Thiruvananthapuram, Kerala, and he was leaving by road with a friend the very next day. I told him I was in Bangalore, which was on his route, and invited him home. He agreed, time permitting; he needed to reach before Monday when the festival started. We hung up, and I went to bed.

The shrill ring of my phone woke me up at 5.30 a.m. Par for the course, except it was Rajesh calling at a very odd hour. I couldn't hear anything at first, just someone's loud breathing. This was getting stranger by the minute. And then I heard the word 'accident'.

'Hello, hello,' I said loudly, as if to urge them to speak clearly. Suddenly there was another voice, a highway patrolman, on the phone. 'There's been a terrible accident on the Bangalore highway, close to Mahbubnagar,' he said. A lorry had run over their car. The man in the passenger seat—he had a beard—was injured badly enough to not make it. The one in the driver's seat—he had the phone in his lap—he was still breathing.

Rajesh would have been in the passenger seat. His phone must've bounced out of his pocket and into his friend Shibu's lap during the collision. The driver would've dialled the last used number on the phone: mine.

I calmly told the highway police to focus on getting them to the hospital; let the doctors declare the medical status. I hung up and then called a senior police officer from Mahbubnagar who'd insisted on sharing his official phone number—'Call me anytime you need help!'—because he'd loved the session on trafficking and prostitution that I had done for officers in the police academy barely two days back. I gave him all the information I had, requested that the victims receive immediate medical care and, if possible, moved to Hyderabad. When I updated him, Jo told me to refer them to Yashoda Hospital; Brother Franky knew the owner, Dr G.S. Rao, very well. I did that.

There was no way I could sit in Bangalore for a minute more. I borrowed some money from my father for a flight ticket. My parents did not appear perturbed about my sudden decision, or rather, I did not notice the emotions on their face. I was just glad that Daddy had enough to spare that day for my ticket. My brother dropped me off at the airport. Luckily, I caught the 8 a.m. flight, reaching Hyderabad by 9 a.m. By the time I reached Yashoda Hospital, Rajesh and Shibu had already been admitted.

I rushed to the emergency where I met Dr Aravind Rao, a senior orthopaedic specialist who told me both of them had sustained grievous injuries and required surgery immediately. Rajesh was in coma, but Shibu was vaguely conscious. Since the owner himself had referred the case, they were completing all the immediate procedures, but somebody from the family needed to sign off as these were major surgeries. I told him that I'd do it. For Rajesh, I signed as 'wife' in the relationship column; for Shibu, as 'friend'.

The two were already in the operation theatre by the time Jo and Franky got there after Sunday mass. Rajesh required thirteen surgeries from his head all the way to his thighs, and had steel inserted into his body. Shibu went through five surgeries. It would take them three months to recover and walk properly.

There was a subtle difference in the way that Rajesh and I interacted after that. We were connected in a way that is hard to articulate, but it gave us the automatic freedom to claim a strange ownership over each other. I had never felt this for anyone. With everyone else, I had always acknowledged and recognised the prior claims in their lives, family, work, or in Jo's case, religion. But with Rajesh, it was as if my soul knew that I could lay first claim on him. We didn't have to articulate or acknowledge this shift. It was what it was.

I spent most of my time in the hospital. It was only when he was out of the ICU, eight days after he was admitted, that I even left the building. After they were discharged from Yashoda Hospital, they were shifted to Vijay Mary's Hospital at Khairatabad, where they stayed for another month to recuperate and recover. The two could hardly walk and required sustained nursing care. Jo arranged for this.

Shibu's brother and father had come from Kerala, and were taking care of him. Rajesh had no family in Hyderabad, and Biju, Jolly and other friends like Sherry and Gowri were with me throughout. Two of Rajesh's brothers came from Kerala for a day to see him, but were more interested in buying pearls for their wives. They didn't even ask about the hospital bills. The only person from his family who was truly concerned was Babu Chettan, Rajesh's brother-in-law. I was not there when he visited Rajesh, but he was the only one who called me, thanked me and specifically told me to connect with him if there were any financial requirements. In later years, he would be the only person from Rajesh's family who contributed to Prajwala. We lost him to lung cancer a few years ago. He was a gentleman I deeply respected and had a great bond with.

Many months later, I learnt that Rajesh had given his family the impression that he was financially stable, bordering on prosperous, even when he was struggling. No one found it strange that I was looking after all the hospital affairs; they just did as I requested.

By now, I'd begun to address Raj as 'etta', elder one, more to show my affection than respect. He was just three months older. It was the same title I used for Jo, who was sixteen years my senior and deserved all respect accorded to an elder. Malayalam, as I mentioned earlier, is a strange language that uses the same word for husband and older brother.

The accident revealed another facet of Raj's personality. While Jo and I were big on words in our expression of gratitude, Raj was a man of actions big and small. I learnt this through a rather 'colourful' gesture: an acquaintance on their way to Shilparamam, an arts and crafts village on the outskirts of the city, had dropped by. They were carrying batik kurtas to sell there. Raj bought a dozen and just handed them over to me when I got there. I had no clue what to do with twelve batik kurtas that had the same pattern in different colours. If people thought I was promoting batik that year, I just want to tell them I had no say in the matter.

More concretely, after he recovered sufficiently, he was obsessed with making a documentary on sex trafficking for us even though he should have focused on a mainstream movie. To my mind, it appears that the movie industry is pretty dismissive of documentary filmmakers and those who make meaningful, award-winning cinema. And that attitude gets worse if the two categories intertwine. I think even the general public suffers from this bias.

Despite that, Raj convinced Jo and me that it was imperative we make a documentary on sex trafficking and prostitution. That was the only way Prajwala's work would not be questioned by anybody. He was also very clear that he did not want my involvement; he would go into the red-light areas in the country on his own. 'I want to see for myself if the stories she tells me about these places are true,' I heard him telling Jo.

His next decision shocked us even further. He wanted to fund the entire film on his own. This worried us immensely, for Raj had already spent a lot of money to give our Charminar office a makeover, one more way he had expressed his thanks for all that Jo and I had done for him during his hospital stay. My grim Charminar office was now colourfully painted, my office had a sliding door, the wall behind me was tastefully decorated and the reception space was artistically designed. All in all, it had a very fashionable yet friendly look—so different from what it was before, a nondescript place for regular operations. Now it had a distinct identity which was very becoming.

But there was no reasoning with Raj. He bought a series of decoy cameras and organised a small, trusted team. For three months, they travelled through red-light districts, massage parlours, dance bars and areas where 'record dances' were held. In many parts of Andhra Pradesh, women in scantily clad clothes were contracted to dance in public. These events, known as 'record dance', were frequented by largely drunk men. The unique selling point of the show was that it was a strip act, and as the night progressed, the women would remove all their clothes. They took candid shots of it all, no script, no rehearsals.

He returned an emotionally exhausted man. Nothing I had told him could prepare him for the reality he saw. Rajesh wanted me to connect him to survivors who would be able to validate the aftermath of prostitution. I spoke to my women and girls, assuring them that they'd remain anonymous. They readily agreed.

Even I was shocked at the footage Raj had. The way the women were treated by customers and handlers, the conditions in which they had to sell sex, the age and profile of the customers. I was well aware of this from the accounts of our girls. But what a difference between knowing and seeing! No wonder the editor at Digiquest studio was finding it hard to do his job. And then one day, the entire hard disk with the edited visuals was stolen. Three months of work, done with many risks, stolen from right inside a reputed studio in Hyderabad.

Meanwhile, I had gathered, a little bit from Raj but mostly from his team, the number of times their life had been at risk. They'd had to move several times to avoid getting caught, they'd faced attacks and even some near-death experiences when they were caught red-handed with a camera in a brothel.

I was furious, and used all my police connections to ensure a case was booked immediately at Panjagutta police station regarding the theft. The hard disk could not be traced, but thanks to the heightened police attention on the case, whoever had stolen it did not dare use it.

Raj wasn't discouraged though. He still had the raw footage, because he always saved all his work in duplicate. But now, the entire editing had to be done from scratch. This meant going over the thousands of hours of raw visuals meticulously all over again.

Despite all these setbacks, *Anamika: The Nameless* saw the light of day in 2004. It was a tribute to Jo and me. We were overwhelmed. The reactions of the 200-odd guests who attended the premiere were a testament to the power of visual language. This documentary has since sensitised millions in the community as well as countless police officers, judicial officers, prosecuting officers and stakeholders in the criminal justice system. It is also widely used in all the police and judicial academies, an invaluable gift to our mission. After *Anamika,* Raj got several offers for commercial movies. In between, when he could, he made some more documentaries for me, as I'd received many requests for them.

Jo felt that Raj and I shared a unique relationship, that we were suited to each other and should think of making it permanent. I had no such desire, being comfortable with the way things were and in no hurry to label it. Raj, on the other hand, was taken aback. He hadn't thought along those lines at all. They'd talked privately, but I was mortified when I learnt about it from Jo. More than that, how could Jo have spoken to Raj without asking me, possibly endangering our relationship, whatever it was! I was now too embarrassed to meet Raj. Fortunately, I had enough work at Prajwala to avoid him easily—and without making it look like an excuse.

Then, on 13 September 2005, Raj called Jo. He said he was open to the idea. Of course I learnt this too through Jo. I couldn't process anything—I had no clear sense of what I felt—what was I to feel? Too many things were going on, but between the two of them. Was

I even involved, except when I received information? It felt like my feelings, opinions didn't matter. I decided to keep quiet. In any case, now was not the time to disturb Raj who had been working day and night for weeks now on the pre-production for his new film, and the shoot was supposed to begin the next day.

So, when I got a call from him, after midnight at that, I didn't know how to react. Should I tell him how I resented all this? Should I be mindful of his schedule? But it wasn't him at all. A strange voice from the other end informed me that my husband had had an accident. Déjà vu! I just jumped up, noted the address and rushed to Care Hospital, where Raj was admitted.

Apparently, he'd fallen asleep at the wheel on his way back home from the producer's office, some late-night last-minute discussion. They perhaps had a peg or two, and his exhausted body could handle only that much after the weeks of relentless work pressure. The car had hit the flyover on Masab tank next to Katta Maisamma's temple. Maisamma, a mother goddess revered in the south, is a personification of Durga, one of my favourite deities, but for me, the whole experience felt very inauspicious. Just that morning, Raj had told Jo he's ready to make our friendship more permanent, and the same evening he had another accident, the second in two years. Both involved me in some way—he'd had the first one a few hours after talking to me, and the second a few hours after he consented to marry me. Was it all jinxed? I could not think straight.

21

A Funeral and a Wedding

For the last one year, my relationship with Jo had been strained. His tenure with Boys Town had ended in 2004, and he'd shifted out to an independent two-bedroom house about equidistant from Prajwala's ERP at Falaknuma, which Jo had established, and Boys Town in Jahanuma. Living independently from the congregation wasn't uncommon among the Montfort brothers, and could be done with the permission of superiors.

Jo had taken on some ambitious projects meant for the jubilee year of the Montfort congregation. He also wanted to commit full-time to Prajwala for a brief period to streamline the economic rehabilitation activities. In the wake of the tsunami in December 2004, he'd taken on a massive rehabilitation programme at Car Nicobar, and was helping build 3,000 houses there using alternate technology. Our team from Prajwala, mostly our male trainers in ERP who were recruited by Jo, led the reconstruction efforts on the ground. Essentially, the tsunami relief work was a Prajwala project that he was coordinating.

Jo wanted to complete as much work as possible for Prajwala before he dedicated his life to setting up what he hoped would be India's largest self-sustaining therapeutic community for HIV-positive people. It was to be part of a jubilee project of the Montfort brothers. In early 2000, when Prajwala had spearheaded an HIV counselling project for Andhra Pradesh, Jo had been deeply affected by the plight of HIV-positive people we had come across. He strongly felt that his congregation should take a greater role in the care and social mainstreaming of HIV-positive people, and envisioned a large therapeutic community where they could live and work together, away from social stigma and exclusion. But he wanted to do this only after he had stabilised the initiative that he started at Prajwala to train people in bookbinding, welding and carpentry.

In the eight years of Prajwala's life, this was the first time Jo had worked directly on any of its interventions. While I had managed the prevention, rescue and shelter initiatives, and even the plastic unit, when it came to ERP, Jo was the lead as it was his brainchild.

However, on some level, Jo's full-time engagement in Prajwala made me uncomfortable. I'd been absolutely fine when he'd worked behind the scenes, and left me to deal with day-to-day the operations. But now that we shared the stage, my insecurities surfaced with a vengeance.

For the first time in the eight years of Prajwala's life, I felt that my authority was being undermined. Power politics and the need to control took hold of me like I was possessed by demons.

He was the good cop, his occasional visits marked with gifts and other indulgences that everyone accepted with delight, while I was the disciplinarian, taking stock of targets to see whether they had been reached or were pending. When he came onboard full-time, Jo was openly adored by all. To the children and the girls in the shelter, he was Santa Claus personified, cheerful, fun, indulgent. To the staff, he was the elder brother and father—wise, venerated, idolised. Though he had been very popular at Boys Town as well, this outpouring of affection was new, and he greatly relished it. Many staff members visited him at home, some even shared lunch and cigarettes with him.

The more I learnt about all of this, the more insecure I got. My jealousy was a nine-hooded snake, hissing and spitting at him out of fear at every chance it got. On my best days, I maintained a frosty silence. On bad days, I was petty. I'd pick fights, find fault, act out exactly like a four-year old. At my worst, I was so worked up, I'd just get up and leave—even if we were travelling.

I *knew* I was misbehaving, but it was as if I couldn't stop myself. In the end, I decided not to interfere with the ERP. That would be Jo's independent intervention. This way, the staff members wouldn't have to answer to two people. If there was a saving grace in any of this, it was that these disgusting aspects of my personality didn't rear their heads in front of our colleagues, at least not that I knew of.

Yet, neither of us brought it up or addressed my behaviour. I think Jo was patiently trying to wait it out, giving me time to let go of my possessiveness and insecurities. And then there was that personal matter of Jo and Raj making plans for me without my involvement. It was the same animosity that had stopped me from responding positively when he'd told me of Raj's decision. All in all, I was cutting my nose to spite my face, as they say, for many, many reasons.

But when Raj was admitted to the hospital, all that antagonism cleared magically. Raj's face had hit the dashboard hard, and he needed jaw surgery and plastic surgery.

It was almost as if the past year had been a figment of our imagination. Jo and I didn't bring it up even once, though we met every day that week. We talked and talked and talked, sharing our dreams and hopes of a safe world, as if we'd been storing up all our words for such an occasion. It was like 1996, when we walked under the stars in the Boys Town playground, discussing our dreams of what Prajwala should accomplish.

I had to attend a legal advocacy meeting on a Sunday after the accident. I was slightly worried, so Jo promised to be at the hospital with Raj. He came home on Friday after a long time. We reminisced over our eight-year-long relationship over coffee. Abruptly, I told him how only he and Raj really mattered to me at my core level. If anything happened—to either of them—I'd fall apart.

He smiled at that, the charming smile of his that I'd sent into hiding. 'You're smart, you'll cope, don't worry,' he said. 'But without you, neither of us could survive.'

I began to laugh. 'In that case, you must give me the very best funeral. I need to be mourned in style. Bring in artists from the film industry if you must. Have them bemoan my demise full *Rudaali* style, wailing, beating their chests, clutching lilies. I insist on a grand affair!'

'Make sure to leave behind a funeral fund then!' Jo retorted. 'You think either of us have that kind of money?'

We hadn't laughed like this in a long time. It had that same old ease, that comfort and kinship. We sat together for over seven hours, talking about nothing and everything, at peace with the world.

Late that evening, we left for the hospital. Raj had a lot of visitors, so Jo and I sat together on a window ledge and talked into the night. The next day, I left for Delhi directly from the hospital. Prajwala was organising a conference with the Delhi-based Human Rights Law Network (HRLN) on victim protection protocols. We'd already filed a PIL on this in the Supreme Court—taking our cues largely from the US Trafficking Victim Protection Act, 2000—and it was creating a lot of flutter. HRLN wanted a wider consultation with NGOs in the field, so that everybody's collective demands could be integrated into the demands presented before the Supreme Court.

Colin Gonsalves and Aparna Bhat were representing HRLN. I had Deepa and Raja Rao from our office, who had arrived ahead of me. We spent Saturday setting up the place—the conference was on Sunday morning—and then the three of us went to Dilli Haat to relax. I didn't speak to Jo as he would have been at the hospital. Sunday morning, of course, was packed, what with supervising the conference and preparing my own presentation. Only after all this did I have the bandwidth to call Jo. He was at home. He'd gone to the hospital the previous evening, but had returned when he found many of Raj's friends willing to stay the night.

Having confirmed that Raj was okay, I told Jo all about the conference. He listened attentively, then told me that this would significantly change the landscape of anti-trafficking efforts in India, even the world.

We hung up after an hour or so. I felt he sounded tired; he was used to an afternoon siesta and he'd probably skipped it to talk to me. Before hanging up, Jo reminded me that our new driver would pick me up at the airport. I was heading back on the 6 p.m. flight. 'Don't you worry about me. You just have a peaceful nap,' I replied.

Barely an hour later, I got a call from Brother Franky. Jo is very ill, he told me. Chest pain. He'd driven himself to Gudi ka Dawakhana. But the doctors there considered it serious enough to rush him to Yashoda Hospital.

In hospital! But I'd just got off the phone with him! I couldn't process it, no matter how many questions I asked Franky. *I'd just spoken to him.* Though they were as shocked as I was, Deepa and Raja tried to calm me down.

On the way to the airport, I called up Archana and Annaiah, my landlords. I told them to rush to the temple on the street corner to pray for Jo. I told my parents, Lalita, Damayanti—anyone who was fond of Jo—to pray for him. Raj, who'd just had a surgery on his jaw, could only mumble in response as his face was all bandaged.

At 5 p.m., as I was checking in, Franky asked for the numbers of Jo's relatives. I couldn't breathe, I was choking even as I called them. He was in intensive care.

At 6.15 p.m., Sunday, 18 September 2005, as I was boarding the flight, Jo passed away.

I had lost a friend, a guide, a partner and a collaborator. Prajwala had lost one of its founders, their own Bade Saheb. I thought numbly about how he'd taken my advice to sleep rather literally. I hadn't meant forever.

My friend Ali Asghar was waiting at the airport with my colleague Reena. We reached Boys Town by 9 p.m. Jo's body lay serenely in the big conference hall.

I was numb.

But within hours, I was forced to pull myself together. We had an emergency governing body meeting on Monday morning, and Dr P. Balamba was unanimously appointed president. My next herculean task was to inform the children and staff about Jo.

Two other things that day made me deeply uncomfortable. The first was on Monday afternoon when I started getting calls from reporters. How did I feel about the conference at the Press Club, where some women had accused me of kidnapping their children? How would I like to respond to such allegations?

The other was a more serious affair: I was getting calls from many people who wanted me to return the money that Jo had taken from them to expand Prajwala's ERP. Jo had been—had been!—an efficient business entrepreneur. He knew how to get an investment, put it into business and recover it. I had never been involved in these details regarding the ERP. My own pettiness had kept me away even when Jo wanted to brief me about the business.

I knew most of the people who called me. They were very sorry for my loss. It wasn't that they didn't trust me, but they really needed that money back, they had emergencies to take care of. Over Rs 33 lakh to return—and Jo wasn't even buried yet.

I suppose the gods customise their support to each sufferer's personality. Left to myself, I would have collapsed. But now that I had to support my grieving children and colleagues, face the adverse publicity *and* figure out how to repay the loans, I had no option but to gather myself. I could do nothing to ease the pain of the children and women, but at least I broke the news to them myself. To each of them, Brother Jo, Bade Saheb, meant the world.

My father, younger brother Suku, my friends Geeta and Shoba, all came to Jo's funeral. He had thousands of mourners from far and wide. Long files of sisters and brothers followed the coffin to the church. The women Jo had worked so long for were wailing uncontrollably near the grave. There wasn't a dry eye, save mine. I watched calmly, with an endurance that would be vital in the days to come.

They kept the body for three days, with the burial planned for 21 September. He was only forty-nine years old, gone too soon because of a massive heart attack. Prajwala's collaborators from across India attended his funeral. I met Raj briefly in the hospital. He still couldn't speak, but his big piercing eyes reflected an ocean of pain.

For the first time, I truly felt—was—alone. I had to familiarise myself with the ERP, figure out the reasons and uses for the loans and his repayment plans.

Oh, how heartily I regretted my past behaviour, but I had no time to dwell on it. It took me three months to stabilise the situation, and recover money owed to us so I could repay the loans.

By then, Raj was better. He felt that we should marry. I agreed. It had been Jo's last wish; he wouldn't have asked us to consider it if he weren't convinced that it was a good idea.

On 1 January 2006, four months after Jo's death, Raj and I were married. It was an Arya Samaj wedding as per Vedic rites in the presence of family and close friends. Afterwards, we visited Jo's grave at Boys Town. We had the most beautiful wedding reception—the women, children and staff of Prajwala hosted it. I could feel Jo smiling down at us. 'Didn't I tell you you're smart? You can manage on your own!'

I straightened my spine. I would not fail Jo.

22

A Forever Home

By the time of Jo's death, our team had increased exponentially, and had around 120 staff members. We now had a good mix of survivors and the professionally trained. Over time, some amazing, committed postgraduates joined us, particularly the care-giving staff in the shelters who streamlined our operations. They eroded my initial misgivings about the professionally trained in social work. I have found that those from small towns and little-known colleges—who are less financially privileged—are far more adaptable, more willing to go that extra mile to understand the survivors and accept them as colleagues. Their salary expectations are also lower than that of people from premier institutions or middle- and upper-class backgrounds. Even if the latter's salary demands aren't high, they are hard for Prajwala to retain in the long run.

To keep Prajwala running in the long term, I felt that we should maintain a standard salary scale across projects. This would ensure parity, and chart a clear path for the staff in terms of goal-setting for financial growth. I was also very clear that all those with similar skill sets and output, whether a survivor or a professional, would get the same salary.

Survivor staff in the shelters are vital. You cannot run a good therapeutic intervention without the direct involvement of those with lived experiences. A trauma-informed approach requires an insight into pain and indignity that only a survivor can understand in its totality. No amount of passion for the cause, empathy, poring over theory for hours on end or attending countless workshops and seminars can help with that.

Our rescue team, which had professional staff and survivors, had also become stronger in numbers and skills. The members were carefully selected, and I trained them personally. I also saw them operate in the field because I led all the rescues, so I could give them feedback and improve our overall performance.

There are a number of ways in which the experience of our survivor employees have proven invaluable. For instance, in one inter-state rescue, led by an anti-human trafficking unit of the Hyderabad police and supported by us, the local police force leaked information about the attempt. The brothels were empty when we got there. What they did not anticipate was that two girls on our team were former victims of the same brothels, and knew where the traffickers hid the women during police raids.

But all in all, it was a good time for rescues. We had amazing police officers like Anjana Sinha, Umapathi Sattaru and Mahesh Bhagwat at the helm. They were sensitised officers and had participated in the nationwide training that the United Nations Office for Drugs and Crime (UNODC) had initiated. Just before this, in 2002-03, P.M. Nair, a dynamic police officer, had led a path-breaking national research on sex trafficking. The study was commissioned by the NHRC, carried out with the support of UNIFEM and conducted by the Institute of Social Science.

In the course of these collaborations with the police, I initiated rescues in places like Delhi, Mumbai, Pune, Chandrapur, Wani and Nagpur. In each rescue, there were at least forty to fifty victims, and in one place, we removed over 200 women and girls in one go.

Each of these rescues was painstakingly planned. Once we received a tip-off, usually from a former victim, we did several rounds of recce and decoy operations to confirm the facts on our own. If the information was false, we didn't need to inform the police. This was a critical step. There have been times when the information was actually meant as bait to trap us in an unsafe zone. Once I was misled by a very convincing lead. Since it was a recce to crosscheck the information, only two of us had gone to investigate. The complicated address took us through many lanes and bylanes until we arrived at a remote shed located under an overbridge. I had decided the time of the recce on my own without consulting anyone else, and had picked up my teammate on the way. So, if the perpetrators had any plans, nothing came of them, and we reached a deserted room with a few men gambling outside. What they achieved by sending us on a wild goose chase, I don't know, but if this had happened when we had the police with us, it would have meant a definite showdown. Then it would have been more difficult to secure police cooperation for our next rescue operation.

If the information held up, we would make a detailed plan with the police for the rescue. The rescue ops would be conducted by the police, assisted by a small team from Prajwala consisting of both trained professional social workers and survivor staff. Our team would be equipped with a rescue toolkit—hammers, torches, screwdrivers, etc—that was necessary during the operation. They also took aftercare bags needed for later, with a change of clothes, including undergarments, sanitary napkins, medicines, diapers for children, feeding bottles and the like. As the government had no budget or financial resources for rescue work in those times, and largely depended on civil society organisations for it, we invariably took care of the arrangements for bringing the victims back, such as organising and paying for private buses.

The risks in a rescue operation, whether privately conducted or with the police, are the same. The only difference is that, if you are hurt during a formal operation, it is recorded somewhere officially. Most rescues are done during the night so that the criminals are caught red-handed. Inevitably, the handlers and brothel keepers shut off the electricity as soon as they realise that it is a rescue effort. Since they are familiar with the layout of the buildings, they can attack, hit, stab the rescuers in the dark and then escape. It is also harder to look for the victims without light, and there is so much chaos with the customers running helter-skelter. They shove the girls and women into any space that can hide a body—basements, closets, false ceilings, water tanks, almirahs, attics, packing boxes. The hideouts are worse if children are involved. The teams have to crawl on their knees with torchlights and screwdrivers checking for crevices that could lead to openings.

In the aftermath, we usually have to deal with the media on our backs, hounding us for sound bites. There is also the risk of the traffickers stalking us while the victims resist our help. Amid this chaos, we have to escort the victims to and from our shelter for a medical examination at the hospital and their court appearances.

Once the legalities are processed, police interaction with the victims virtually ends. Only when their case goes on trial do they interact with the police again, and by this time, a few years would have passed. Sadly, trafficking cases have a long life before even reaching courts, and there's no absolute guarantee that the wrongdoers will be punished.

With all the legal paperwork done, we are usually left to fend for ourselves. It can become a circus. The attacks by the traffickers on our shelters, the hostility and aggression of the victims who feel that they are being forcibly removed, the various health complications due to withdrawal symptoms related to alcohol and substance abuse, pregnancy, sexually transmitted infections, including HIV/AIDS, and the media trying to get hold of any information on the background of the victims make things chaotic.

Unlike the West, where safe homes are maintained with absolute confidentiality and only the concerned police officers know the location and are under oath not to leak any information, in India, the government's understanding regarding such homes is rather lopsided. Certain schemes even mandate that the home should have a prominent display board on the nature of services provided. In any case, safe homes can turn into a public space, where all vested interests can cause trouble. Time and again, we have had female offenders standing outside our gate, beating their chest and wailing for their 'daughters', attracting passers-by and generally putting up a great show for the public.

By and large, victims who are rescued with police support feel that they were forcibly removed. My previous efforts, done through my own informers and contacts, had been on a small scale. I had always ensured that the victim was prepared adequately for the rescue. I couldn't forcibly remove them, since I had neither the authority nor the resources. But getting the cooperation of victims or preparing them for the rescue is impossible when the numbers are huge. And you can't rescue selectively, that gets even more complicated. How will you even know who was forced and who is doing it willingly? Besides, they're all indoctrinated to repeat the same thing—that they all ended up in the brothel of their own accord. Yes, even a fourteen-year-old child!

Commercial sexual exploitation does not only happen just in red-light areas. It can happen in houses, lodges and hotels, even fancy ones.

Sometimes there are peculiar situations that complicate a rescue. Once, on a tip-off we were able to validate, we tied up with the Special Operation Taskforce (SOT) of the Hyderabad police commissioner. After making the payment of Rs 15,000 to the pimp, the decoy customer from the police entered this three-star hotel to find a thirteen-year-old girl waiting in the room. We were shocked. The information we had was not clear on the age profile of the victim. Even worse, the victim was aggressive and hostile, and hurled the choicest abuses when we all entered the room for the rescue. The police got the brunt of it, as the child spewed venom at them, accusing them of living off her earnings. It took us three days to calm the child down. It was only when a young survivor advocate spoke to her that the actual situation was revealed. The girl's mother was her pimp, and had been prostituting her for a year. As we began to build a small thread of trust, she became increasingly agitated. She was worried that her mother would now prostitute her younger siblings who were seven and ten years old. One week later, the team rescued the girl's siblings. The mother, a burn victim, said matter-of-factly, 'What can I do? I cannot prostitute myself because of my burns, so selling my own daughters is the best way out. At least I am not selling somebody else's daughter, right?' How do you even respond to such logic?

In another rescue, the pimp herself was a child of about sixteen who was prostituting a ten-year-old in her school uniform.

Then there were other, more twisted complications. For instance, one time in Chandrapur in Maharashtra, we had clear information that there were forty-eight girls. We'd found all but one, and had already settled them in the bus. It took great effort to find the forty-eighth girl. She had been hidden under a huge pile of clothes under which were two large boxes and besides which was a wooden bed. All of it was assembled in such a way that you could not imagine a human form curled inside. The girl was all of fourteen, and refused to come with us. No amount of cajoling or threats worked. She lay on the floor, clinging to the leg of the heavy wooden bed, unwilling to budge. The situation outside was tense. The local media had got wind of the operation and turned up with cameras. A large crowd had gathered, and now the girls were turning aggressive. We needed to go, but we could not simply leave her behind.

As soon as I went in to see what was going on, I realised we needed a different strategy. I immediately asked Noorjahan to take over. Noor, a survivor on my team, had been handling the hostile women on the bus. She quickly figured it out—the problem wasn't that the girl was unwilling to leave, but that she had a child who was in the custody of the brothel keeper and didn't want to leave him behind.

A fourteen-year-old who had a three-month-old child.

We consulted the police and decided to send the others on, while a small team stayed back. After twenty nerve-wracking minutes, we finally found the baby. It had been dumped in a water tank. It was a miracle that the child was alive, even though he had turned completely blue.

We rushed with them to the nearest hospital. When I visited the next morning, the baby was recovering. I picked him and noticed there were bite marks all over his body. His mother, the fourteen-year-old girl, told me that each time she resisted a customer, the keeper would get her dog bite the child. This infant was being medically treated for the abuse inflicted on his little body.

A brothel keeper who'd get a dog to bite a baby to force a child into having sex. If rage was a physical force, she would have been incinerated. But we had done what we could.

In the early days of their rescue, many victims do not understand that we are trying to help. For them, we are another set of people who took them away from a known evil into total uncertainty. How do they know we are trustworthy, that we have no ulterior motives, unlike their perpetrators? They had their own reasons and compulsions for staying on in the brothels, including the fact that the traffickers often knew where their families lived. Exit is not so easy when the perpetrator knows and can target your family. There were also those who had normalised their experience over time and were on the verge of earning small amounts. Most often, after the initial resistance dies down, the victims adjust to the brothel's environment and cooperate with the keepers. Then they begin to receive small amounts as earnings, about 20 or 30 per cent of what the customer was charged. By the time they are rescued, these women strongly believe that they would have made big money and that we have denied them that opportunity.

Then there is the uncertainty on the length of their stay with us. This is the judiciary's call. Most often, in those days, it chose to remain silent, not passing any specific orders, at least in Hyderabad. So, escape attempts are to be expected, and have nothing to do with the quality of life in the shelters themselves.

When a victim is rescued, she is produced before the magistrate as per the Immoral Traffic (Prevention) Act, 1956. The magistrate is mandated to direct an enquiry, which has to be completed in twenty-eight days before they can take a decision on whether the victim requires a longer stay for care and protection. A longer stay could mean anything from one year to three years. Typically, custody petitions, usually funded by the traffickers, are filed immediately after the rescue. The magistrate then, as a part of the enquiry, will order a home investigation report to verify the antecedents of the custody petitioners. If the magistrate is satisfied, custody of the victim will be handed over to the petitioner. In case the report is not satisfactory or there is no petitioner, the victim has to stay in the shelter for longer periods of time. At Prajwala, we have made it a point to file self-petitions as soon as the victim completes one year. For us, she is no more a victim then, but somebody who has progressed to the survivor phase, with access to all the rehabilitation options that we provide.

I take great pride in running shelters with the highest standards of care in terms of food, clothes, access to opportunities for education, life skills, livelihood training and even entitlements from government. My jail experience had given me some sharp insights on factors detrimental to the dignity of a person in a custodial setting, and I have attempted to make sure our shelters are free of such practices.

The first shelters we set up were at Fateh Darwaza for children and at Engine Bowli for adults. As the rescues increased, the numbers grew and we had to move to a larger premises. It was then that one of Jo's business contacts came to our rescue. He had a series of buildings lying vacant near Falaknuma, right on the main road, and close to both the railway station and bus station. The landlord's rent demand was high, but at least he had been willing to let to us. We turned the first building, a vacated school with spacious, beautiful grounds in front, into our children's home, Astha Nivas. The other two buildings had been rice mills. We converted the smaller one into Asha Niketan, our women's home, and used the larger one for the economic rehabilitation unit. All three buildings were on the same main road. This was very convenient for our operations; we could now monitor things better and, if needed, support one another. The flipside: compromised security. Being on the main road greatly increased our visibility. Some of the establishments adjoining ours were less than suitable. For instance, Asha Niketan shared a wall with a wine bar. The places were not structurally safe either, as anybody could scale those low walls.

Over time, the local community began to react. Our location on the main road meant that they took note of the busloads of girls coming in and the consequent attacks by the traffickers. They would hear the girls screaming, and notice their attempts to jump the wall and escape. The wine bar next door did not help either.

Resistance from the community built up gradually. Every attack on the shelters became a reason for increased hostility. I personally suspect that the traffickers spread all kinds of rumours about our organisation. The few years that we lived there I credit to the VIP guests who came to visit our operations, including the former chief justice of India, Justice Balakrishnan; governor of Uttarakhand, Margaret Alva; chief justice of Andhra Pradesh, Justice Singhvi; the minister of social welfare in Kerala, M.K. Muneer; parliamentarians from India and UK and a horde of prominent citizens, including film actors. Such high-profile visits controlled the public to some extent, but not for too long. As our work grew from strength to strength, we added more enemies to our kitty.

At first, the locals began to accost our staff on the road, telling them that our presence was spoiling the area. Then some of them pressed the landlord to cancel our lease, and subsequently, the landlord started demanding increased rent and hinted at converting the buildings into a shopping mall. Once again, the troubles we faced in Mehendi began to haunt us. I realised I needed to act immediately, and went on an aggressive campaign to identify alternate places to rent. I guess our reputation was spreading far and wide, because none of the building owners were willing to give their place for such an intervention. In many places, even before I opened my mouth, they had already said no.

Now, with Jo gone, I began to see that so many of our relationships were transactional. Jo had earned a reputation as an extraordinary entrepreneur. Also, in all those business deals, he had represented the Catholic church, which meant the backing of powerful missionary institutions in the city. All traders understood that being on the right side of Jo made a lot of business sense.

I, on the other hand, represented only myself and my organisation. And though I was good at fighting for our children and women, I wasn't savvy about how to use my connections. I used my connections without any awkwardness for Prajwala, but beyond that, knowing me wasn't an advantage for anyone, friends, family or associates.

With our growing operations, I needed far larger premises than before, which also narrowed my options considerably. After several failed attempts to find a rented place, I decided to secure some land and construct our own place. The irony was that Jo had argued for this until he was blue in the face, but I hadn't budged. My concern had been, what would we do with all that land when no one was sold into prostitution anymore and we had to close the organisation? I can't explain why I was certain the problem would be resolved in my lifetime. In any case, I had made peace with reality and extended the deadline to a few more lifetimes, provided there was consistent, sustained action.

I decided to approach the government for some land. Dana Kishore, IAS, the district collector at the time, immediately put in a proposal for allotting us two acres of land in Mailardevapally, Rajendranagar, within ten kilometres of our current location. We were close to the final stages of approval when it fell through. Why? A top-level bureaucrat expressed grave concerns. 'How can anybody allow such a place to come up? I would personally feel very insecure for my son if any such place was close to my home.'

This was the attitude of a very senior officer! All the hard work that we had all put in was destroyed as if it were nothing because of one person's disapproval. Attitudes like these have made me feel that organisations like ours, people like us, we're the poison that can neither be swallowed nor spat out. The reason cited on paper for rejection was that the proposed location was on the masterplan for the outer ring road and hence not available. My contention is, if the government was committed, it would have definitely found an alternate site.

Faced with social pressure and harassment, my landlord decided that there was no real business sense in staying associated with me, especially since I would constantly push him to consider reducing the rents. We were more trouble than he had bargained for. He gave me an ultimatum: I had nine months to vacate all the buildings. He claimed he was planning to construct malls instead, make more money from each rental. Ironically, those places remain the same even fifteen years later.

Anyway, at this time, our existence was at stake. I had hundreds of children and women depending on me, and just nine months to figure out a solution. Though we had a lot of support from high-profile positions within the government, judiciary, UN bodies and prominent citizens, the locals thought that our work brought disrepute to the community. I did not hold out any hope from the government either after that officer's comment.

That is when Raj entered the picture. It felt like all I'd done since Jo's death was put out blazing fires. Crisis after crisis had needed managing, taking up my time and my mind space. Gradually, even though he wasn't involved in Prajwala, Raj had become my sounding board every evening to review each crisis. He came at problems from a different angle, so his inputs gave me a new perspective.

I started contacting everybody I knew to identify land for us. All our contacts across all departments, including the police, went out of their way to help. Raj insisted that we should aim for ten acres, keeping in mind future requirements and sustainability.

What Raj has brought into my life is to make me see beyond my limited vision. Unlike Jo, who was straightforward—if he disagreed, he'd let me know right away, no holds barred—Raj had a different approach. He'd support me and then slowly help me come around and see the larger picture. For example, with the rescues, he told me that if I were to be killed in a rescue, it would be an honour. At the same time, he'd point out the need to keep up rescue efforts until every victim was rescued. It'd be such a waste if I died before that happened.

A good number of our chats were conducted casually while we went about our household chores. I'd cook and mop, he'd chop vegetables, do the dishes and sweep the house, and all the while, we discussed our work problems.

Eventually, we found ten acres of land sixty-five kilometres from Hyderabad with the support our good friend K. Damayanti, IAS, whom I had met years back. I had the honour of working with her when she was the project director of Andhra Pradesh AIDS Control Society. Damayanti, now the district collector of the Mahboobnagar district, helped us identify a clear litigation-free ten-acre plot of land. She told me that having land in Prajwala's name, as opposed to a government grant, would give us autonomy in all our work. The coming years would show me how true this was.

Now all we needed was the money. Raj had seen me go from pillar to post, nearly begging for aid. When nothing worked, he felt compelled to help. This was in 2009, three years into our marriage. We didn't have much savings, but the flat we'd bought a year back had gone up in value. Raj found a way to mortgage it, so I could buy some land for Prajwala. I'm not sure whether he had any misgivings before he suggested it, but agreeing to this plan was hard for me. This was the only home we had, and I knew there'd be comments about how I had married Raj only to exploit him for his money.

It was with a heavy heart that I left to sign the mortgage papers. Not just mine, but all of Prajwala's collective efforts at fundraising had failed. Even a few board members had tried. Lalita, who was in the governing body, had got me an appointment with a major movie producer who was willing to give two acres, but wanted us to develop some portions of the land for him. The plot was 150 kilometres from Hyderabad. But that hadn't worked out as it was far off, and I needed to be closer to good healthcare facilities. I could not risk the well-being of our children by being located in some remote place with poor healthcare systems. Many of Prajwala's children needed constant medical attention as they were HIV-positive. Months passed and the pressure mounted, and still there were no viable options. Some of our board members had become rather unhappy. One had even remarked that we shouldn't stretch beyond our means, that maybe it was time to start winding up some operations. With the new airport and other significant developments in the city, land rates had been shooting up, and we couldn't even imagine buying anything within Hyderabad with the money we'd get after mortgaging the flat.

So, even though I wasn't sure it was the right thing to do, mortgaging the house was my only option. We were on our way, with still an hour to reach, when I got a call. It was an elderly gentleman who claimed to have met me. When I couldn't place him, he reminded me that we had met at the Delhi airport the previous week. We had started talking, and I'd shared all my problems about Prajwala with him. We hadn't exchanged names, but I remember giving him my card before leaving to board the plane.

Having placed him, I politely asked him why he'd called. He told me that he wanted to contribute a small amount and needed my bank account details. I was so dejected at the time that I told him it was all available on the website, and he could take it from there. Back then, we would proudly display our bank details on the website. I can't imagine doing anything like that now, with all the online scams going on. I was in no mood to talk, so I hung up as soon as I could.

Raj was driving, and I wanted to ask him one last time if he thought we were taking the right decision. After all, we had bought the flat with his money. We reached our destination soon enough, and were trying to figure out the exact location when I got another call. This time, it was my bank manager, who sounded rather frantic.

'Are you expecting any major donations?' he asked. His concern was evident: our account only had enough money to cover the running costs for two months.

'No, nothing huge.' Then, recalling my recent phone call, 'Maybe some small amount will come in the near future.'

'You've just received forty lakhs in your account from someone called Dalmia. I wanted to confirm it with you.'

Forty lakhs. I took a deep breath. Forty lakhs! It was the exact same amount that we were mortgaging our house for.

'Stop the car!' I told Raj. He shot me a look, then drove to the side and parked. I told him about the money. We were both silent for a while. Then Raj told the party that we'd changed our minds about the mortgage. We turned around and drove home.

It turned out that my benefactor was the well-known philanthropist Mridu Hari Dalmia.

Divine interventions take various forms, and I have been blessed to see several of them in my lifetime.

With that Rs 40 lakh, we purchased the ten acres of land that we had identified, and quickly set about converting the rocky land on the Deccan Plateau into a safe place for women and children.

A daunting task, but I was not alone. Raj was by my side.

23

When the Universe Conspired

We started our preparations for the new site with great enthusiasm. There was so much to do and so much paperwork. We had to get agricultural land converted for construction, get the borewell drilled and get panchayat permissions. Then there was the design. I'd told Raj all that I wanted. While security was an overarching concern on this vast ten-acre campus, turning it into a place that would contribute to the healing of a severely traumatised person was just as important.

Raj suggested Shankar, an architect from Kerala whom he held in great regard. Shankar-ji, who was later awarded the Padma Shri, turned out to be an extremely sensitive and empathetic person. He travelled to Hyderabad to inspect the site. In the meantime, my father, who was greatly impressed by the recent events, had also come to Hyderabad. He volunteered to survey the land. He was sixty-nine, but still actively working in private firms on survey assignments. It turned out that our land was much bigger than we thought. Thanks to Daddy's intervention, we understood the exact extent of land available.

Raj worked closely with Shankar's team, and the end result was an amazing design that had everything that we wanted: a children's home, an adult home, an education centre/school, a hospice, an amphitheatre, a life skills centre, a prayer hall, staff quarters, an administrative block and amenities including solar lights and biogas plants to ensure we would be a zero-waste, eco-friendly campus. A dream come true. But how would we fund it?

Bit by bit, things started moving. Amit Garg, IPS, an amazing police officer who admired our work and was in the Hyderabad police at that time, connected us to the Deccan Chargers, a cricket team based out of Hyderabad. Today, Garg is the director of the National Police Academy. As luck would have it, the Deccan Chargers had won that year's Indian Premier League (IPL) match, and decided to donate twenty-five lakhs to Prajwala from their winnings. What a start! It was 2009. Our fundraising efforts were also showing results, with small amounts trickling in and boosting our confidence.

Shankar-ji had committed to carrying out the construction through Habitat Technologies, a pioneering organisation in alternate technology that he had founded. Believers in alternate technology, Raj and I were happy to go ahead. The budgets proposed were half that of normal construction, which in itself was very appealing. But even raising that much was like climbing Mount Everest. Habitat started the work, and all of us at Prajwala ran around desperately to mobilise funds. But soon we realised that Habitat was a mistake, as the logistics of alternate construction were challenging. Being Kerala-based, they had no connections in Hyderabad, nothing was going as per plan and we were running out of time. We mutually decided to part ways, but decided to retain Shankar-ji's design.

Prajwala's financial auditor Leo suggested a civil contractor, Laxmikant, who headed the construction company Palam Nirmaan Company. They were not into alternate technology, and had to start from scratch. Our budget went overboard, doubling to Rs 10 crore! And we had to pay this over the Rs 35 lakh we'd already paid Habitat. Where would I get this kind of money? Even if I sold everything we personally possessed, it would only cover a fraction. Work had to start, but how?

Around this time, I got a call from someone called Lakshmi Pratury, who told me she was bringing TED to India, and wanted me to speak at the conference in November. Now what—*who*—is TED? All I understood from her tone was that it was an important conference, and would do me good if I used this opportunity. I agreed. Too many things were going on then, so it did not even strike me that I should check those people out, or at least google what TED was all about. Those days, I hardly had any time to google information or be part of social media. My myopic idea back then was that only jobless people were on social media. Ignorance, they say, is bliss and I was truly living a blissful existence.

The next few weeks were strange. This lady kept calling me and telling me that they would like to brief me about the speech, and that some people from the US would join in a conference call. I couldn't fathom why they were making such a fuss over a speech. I was often invited to speak at conferences, and most of the time an email or call would be enough to brief me. I'd attend the conference, give the speech and that was that.

To my credit, I did not reveal my puzzlement at this point. Usually, arrogant creature that I am, I would have refused point blank to attend. I can only put it down to Lakshmi's voice on the phone doing some sort of magic. The conference call was extremely interesting. They kept stressing that I should not pitch anything, keep strictly to eighteen minutes, and while I should talk about the cause, it should also generate hope.

Having understood that this was something really important, and that I should stick to the time (I tend to exceed the limit), I decided to prepare a presentation with only pictures. There's a selective blindness with people when it comes to the problem of sex trafficking. Most cannot fathom what it means when I say a three-year-old child was raped and trapped in a brothel. I decided, for the first time ever, to use pictures of those children of mine who had died, as a personal tribute to their lives. I prepared the presentation and, with much confidence, left for Mysore where this great TED conference was going to be held at the Infosys campus.

On the day I arrived, there was a cocktail party for the speakers and some important guests. The hall was filled with the who's who of India and the world. This was big, really big in every way. Have you noticed how most high-profile leaders are so tall, they're very nearly long? You'll hardly find anyone who is four feet six inches short. This by itself is daunting. Imagine standing in a banquet hall with the rich and mighty, all of them five feet ten inches tall at a minimum, and they literally must look down to spot you. And then you have to introduce yourself to people who already know one another. It's all quite discouraging.

I decided to keep out of the way, to stand in a corner in case someone's elbow hit my face. That's a real danger for us short people, by the way! The evening passed slowly. None of the media exposure I'd had quite prepared me for this. I turned cold with fear, my confidence vaporised.

I finally met Lakshmi in person. She was an enigmatic, charming woman, and I liked her immediately. I was also slightly awestruck—this woman had brought together all these big names.

Like me, Anupam Mishra, another speaker, was quietly standing in a corner. He told me that he didn't know much English, and I warmed up to him immediately, chatting away happily in Hindi with him. Imagine my shock when he spoke impeccable English on the stage.

That night, I called Raj. I was crying. 'This isn't my scene at all! Simply the aura of this place is killing my confidence,' I complained. Raj pacified me, and told me to look at the experience as a small break after months of stress. At least for three days, I could have good food and a nice hair bath. Stealing time to wash my knee-length hair had always been a challenge. It took forever to dry before I could tie it back in a bun because I didn't like hair dryers. Raj's logic worked, at least for that night.

I was to speak on the second day, so I had all the time to listen to the other speakers on the first day. By God, if the cocktail had been scary, this was my worst nightmare. Each speaker was exemplary. What wit, what humour, what content, what presentation! I had never in my entire life heard such speeches.

Are there degrees to nothingness? If I was at zero before, my confidence now tanked far below, dropping into an abyss that saw no sun. I was ready to pack and leave. I could not make an international spectacle of myself.

At last I had understood that this was no ordinary conference. I didn't sleep a wink that night. How I wished I could run, but I also knew that wasn't an option. The day dawned. For me, it was like the sun was behind dark clouds. Would the light ever come? I wore a red kurta and the watch necklace Jo had given me for confidence and to ensure that I would not exceed the time.

I went into the hall. These speeches are recorded, and so the organisers insisted on some make-up, again something new for me. This was also the first time that I had a mike attached to my cheek so that I could talk freely. Talk freely? They had taken away something I could have fiddled with to hide my nervousness. That irony sent me into near hysteria.

Ten minutes before showtime, my stomach reacted to the stress and I had to rush to the bathroom. I was also feeling nauseated. Two minutes before my turn, I finally stood in the wings. When I started speaking, there was an eerie silence in the hall, unlike the other speeches at the conference where the hall rang with laughter and applause. I spoke about my children and women, their sufferings within brothels and society, the trauma, stigma, censure they face, why we need to act and what it'd take to help stop it all.

I had already publicly disclosed my past in many forums. Again, this wasn't a sob story, but to convey that I have experienced stigma personally, and I mentioned that at the talk as well.

'It's very fashionable to talk about human trafficking in this fantastic AC hall. It's very nice for discussion, discourse, making films, everything. But it is not nice to bring them to our homes. It's not nice to give them employment in our factories, our companies. It's not nice for our children to study with their children. There it ends. That's my biggest challenge. When I talk to people, I keep telling them one thing: don't tell me a hundred ways how you cannot respond to this problem. Can you apply your mind for that one way that you *can* respond to the problem? That's what I'm here for, asking for your support. Demanding your support. Requesting for your support.'

At about eleven minutes, I was saturated. I could not see the audience; they were in the dark. It worked for me. I didn't want to look at anyone. What if they looked immensely bored and impatient? My speech wasn't amusing or funny. I had only pain and anguish to share. Each picture displayed on the screen a life lost too soon because of the callousness of others. These memories were too weighty for humour. That would make it disrespectful. With this running through my head, I began to get agitated. Angry for those children and with the world, disgusted by it and its wilfully averted gaze.

'I'm asking you to help them, accept them as human beings—not as philanthropy, not as charity—but as human beings who deserve all our support. I'm asking you this because no child, no human being, deserves what these children have gone through.'

That's it, I thought, I'm done. I can't give them anything more. I wound up my speech with about five minutes to spare, at twelve minutes twenty-six seconds.

'Thank you,' I said, and bowed my head in namaste.

The silence for that one second was deafening. As I turned to leave the stage, the audience gave me a standing ovation. I was choking down tears. I wanted to cry, tell the children up there in heaven, 'Look, the world is finally learning about what happened to each of you.' I fiddled with my presentation clicker, not knowing what to do, just standing there.

Fortunately for me, Lakshmi came up on the stage and gave me a hug. I was reassured. She used the five minutes I'd saved to further highlight our work. Much later, I realised that this was a deviation from the norm. Lakshmi was familiar with the crises we were going through at the time—the deadlines to vacate our current premises, the delays in construction, the money problems, etc. She casually asked me about them, and I responded briefly. I did not want to pitch anything. Just the fact that important people from all around the world had heard me, that itself was good, I needed no more.

Suddenly someone from the audience, I think her name was Rose Shuman, shouted, 'I'll commit $10,000. Can ten people match it?'

Nowhere in any TED conference had something like this unfolded.

In less than a minute, $100,000—Rs 45 lakh at the time—was raised for Prajwala. In less than a minute. Do you need any more examples of godly intervention?

It was as if the entire heavens had opened. The next two days passed in a blur. Hundreds of people expressed their solidarity and support. There were hugs and tears, promises and personal gifts.

It was also wonderful how everybody now looked down to seek me out. I had always had to look up.

Even His Holiness, the Karmapa, who was in the audience, reached out to express his solidarity for the mission.

Lakshmi Pratury turned out to be a magic-maker!

The TED conference changed my life completely. Suddenly, the world sat up and took notice of me. When I returned to Hyderabad, the first thing I did was google TED. I learnt that it is the Technology,

Entertainment and Design conference, a premiere international platform that showcased the greatest innovations and practices. I truly felt honoured to have been on this platform. And I bow my head with gratitude to Chris Anderson, whom I met briefly at the conference, for creating such a powerful space for the voices of people like me and the causes that we are fighting to amplify—for creating an opportunity to conspire for the common good of all.

I was told that everybody on social media was talking about me. For the first time, I looked at social media and opened accounts on Facebook and Twitter (now X), recognising this medium as a powerful tool to speak to the world. I was pleasantly shocked by the number of people who wanted to connect with me or follow me. I also discovered blogging, and realised that this was an opportunity to share with the world the lessons I was learning every day. Somebody out there could benefit from them.

Raj had often urged me to join social media, but when have I ever heeded sane advice? After all, I learn best, not from others' mistakes, but my own. Even now, not a day goes by when Raj does not remind me of this—not that I am reformed. I truly believe that I will learn new things when I have to, and not a day before.

In less than one month, thanks to my TED talk, and through the people I met during the conference, we mobilised around Rs 9 crore, about a crore short of our total estimate. Google donated a million dollars and became the biggest donor. With the money sorted, the construction started in earnest. We had only six months left of our deadline. But as soon as the work started, I was able to negotiate an extension. Raj decided to give his entire year to this, and took up a room near the site to monitor the construction. This was the only way we could uphold the faith and trust of all those who had believed in and given to our mission. For the first few weeks, he even slept on the rocky site.

Despite this, we were still short of a substantial sum of money. We had decided to include a biogas plant, solar lights and solar fences to address long-term sustainability. We'd come to realise that just the basic construction wouldn't work, we needed to furnish this huge place. For instance, we needed over 358 fans, and we hadn't factored in such costs earlier. What we had currently was barely enough as it was. We were learning all this on the fly.

It was around this time, in late 2010, that the Vital Voices Global Partnership honoured me with an award. Vital Voices is an American organisation that invests in women leaders who combat the world's greatest challenges. I didn't know it then, but I would gain from their committed partnership in the years to come. This extraordinary organisation led by Alyse Nelson has helped me network and learn from other women leaders across the globe.

I attended their annual event at the John F. Kennedy Centre to receive the coveted Global Leadership Award with four other women. The programme began, and eventually it was time to go on stage. I was to be introduced by Diane von Furstenberg, an extraordinary philanthropist and globally renowned fashion designer. Diane started as we'd rehearsed, and then she suddenly changed the script. She not only committed to financially support us but also requested the audience to contribute to our cause. John Grisham, one of my favourite authors who was also in the audience, made one of the largest donations.

Yet again, the universe had conspired for me!

With the donations from that event, we finally completed the construction. It had taken us fifteen months in all. When it was all ready, we shifted all of Prajwala's women and girls to a heavenly and therapeutic campus.

Raj's family and mine joined us with pride on the day—8 May 2011. The opening ceremony was a solemn occasion, with priests performing the Ganapati homam and all of Prajwala's children and women participating. The experience was divine, the place was divine, the work that we were doing was divine and, above all, a whole world of divinity stood by us to help us pull through.

I was acquiring newer ammunition in my fight against sex trafficking and sex crime. Can you believe that my TED speech has over five million views, and is now available in more than seventy-eight languages? It has also helped establish over 1,100 initiatives to fight sex crime across the world, and inspired thousands more to take up social work.

Everything is possible if you truly believe in something, and work towards your goal with absolute faith. The universe has a way to spot the truth and direct all forces to make it absolute. Your job, in the meantime, is to stay strong and persevere.

24

Giving Up My Long Tresses

Movies were always my passion. And when I saw the enormous impact that our documentary on sex trafficking, *Anamika: The Nameless*, had, I was more convinced than ever about using visual tools as a means of social change. For years this idea had been in my mind, and I would constantly tell Raj and Jo about it. Jo even felt he could become the producer if ERP worked well. After Jo's death, though, I was constantly firefighting. It was only in 2011, after the Prajwala campus was settled, that I felt the time was right for such a move.

I recalled a true incident that I had witnessed, where a father was a trafficker, and his own daughter, whom he had protected all his life, was trafficked by somebody else. I felt it was a powerful story to share with the world. My only briefing to Raj was that it should be a family thriller, which even a toddler should be able to watch. So, Raj had to tell a story about sex trafficking in a manner that was suitable for the family audience. It took him over six months to complete the script. I decided it would be better if we produced this film ourselves; it would give us autonomy in both content and treatment. Raj was prepared to use the funds from our film production house SunTouch Productions for this purpose, and I was willing to get additional resources from Prajwala's visual documentation budget. Prajwala had made a sizeable number of short films and documentaries, and our own donors were quite receptive to these visual tools. I requested Leger Foundation and Misereor for funds, and they readily agreed.

We decided to make the film in Malayalam and Telugu, which was both for our own comfort and because we thought it would work for the cause. I was an honorary advisor to the chief minister of Kerala for the Nirbhaya project, and we already had a good presence in Andhra Pradesh, so the film's reach would be good.

With funds secured, and amazing support from the Andhra police force, the production of the film was not very challenging. Barring a few minor irritations from some of the actors, we were able to wrap things up according to schedule—the advantage of having control over production.

Post-production was slightly more challenging. Shareeth, our music director, was not comfortable with Raj's treatment of a certain part of the subject and tried to change the interpretation through his background score. As he was a very senior music composer, I intervened, but found that he was not willing to change his position. As the producer of the film, I took a call and dropped him completely from the background score.

Raj and I were standing outside the Chennai studio and pondering our next move when I remembered Shantanu Moitra, the well-known music composer from Bollywood whom I had met at Lakshmi Pratury's INK conference. Lakshmi had founded INK after her TED experience. In my brief meeting with Shantanu at the conference, I had found him immensely empathetic. So, I took a chance and called him up. To my utter surprise, he promptly told me to come straight to Mumbai, and that he would do the needful.

The very next morning, we were at Shantanu's studio. He watched the movie, tears in his eyes, and told us he would do it completely free of cost. Shantanu said he would add a theme soundtrack, and that he wanted retain all of Shareeth's songs.

Within a month, he and his assistant George had woven their magic, and we had a soulful background score that echoed our vision. The signature track rendered by Shreya Ghoshal was a gamechanger.

Other than this, production was smooth—unusual for a small-budget film like ours. However, if making the film had been a breeze, getting it into theatres proved to be nearly impossible.

I personally went to all the distributors and was repeatedly rejected. A big-time Telugu producer and distributor made a great show of watching the film, a greater show of appreciating and applauding us, and finally, told us in the nastiest tone that he could not possibly distribute it as he did not want such films to enter the Telugu market.

Another big-time producer did not even watch the film but, based on his staff's assessment, asked us to change the ending of the film.

The whole process was incredibly frustrating. I had not anticipated that distributing a movie would be such uphill task. We had exhausted nearly all our options. Raj was camping in Kerala to find an opening there.

In the meantime, I was to go to Tirupati to dedicate my hair to Lord Balaji. A few months ago, someone had tried to attack me with acid, and it had shaken me completely. The man had been climbing up the stairs to throw acid on my face when, in a bizarre moment, he tripped and fell just before reaching me. The acid fell on him instead. Not knowing what the liquid was, and whom it was meant for, I rushed him to the hospital. It was when he was receiving the treatment that he held my hand and told me it had been meant for me.

I could have fainted there, such was my shock. It was the sort of attack I had only ever encountered in horrific news reports. I stood outside the hospital and pledged to offer my hair to Lord Balaji as a form of gratitude.

Back home, I told Raj and convinced him to join me. He was unhappy, and could not understand why I would chop off my hair. By this time, my hair truly was glorious, now that all the lice were permanently gone. Despite his disapproval, Raj realised I had already made up my mind and joined me with a heavy heart and a long face, which he sported throughout the train journey. It was when I sat in the train that I realised I had not made arrangements for the darshan. Making a disapproving, dissenting, and not to mention very vocal, man wait hours for a temple darshan was not ideal.

I was trying to figure out whom I could reach out to for help when I received a call from an unknown Delhi number. It was Justice Singhvi who had been the chief justice of Andhra Pradesh and was now in the Supreme Court. I knew he greatly admired our work, but we were not in regular contact. He explained it was just a casual call to learn about my well-being. I thanked him, and told him I was fine and that I was on a train, in case I lost network. When he learnt I was on my way to the temple in Tirupati, he asked me if everything had been arranged. I said no, and that I was just figuring out how to organise the trip. He immediately offered to help, saying, 'You will go there as my sister.' I was beyond grateful. He asked me for the details of the coach, which I provided. My grumpy spouse slept throughout the call.

At midnight, when we reached Tirupati, Raj despondently moved our luggage to the door of the compartment. I had said nothing about Justice Singhvi's call as I had no idea how things would pan out. My phone had lost network at some point, and thereafter the charge ran out, so there was no way to contact me.

I intended to call Justice Singhvi the next morning for details on how to go about the arrangements. We were the last ones to alight from the coach, and I was surprised to see a number of police personnel escorting a serious-looking gentleman. They approached me. It turned out that Justice Singhvi had specially requested the district judge to take care of me, and he decided to turn up in person to receive me.

From the corner of my eyes, I looked at the spouse, who now wore a dazed look. Not even in his wildest imagination would he have visualised this. Neither had I, of course, and was now on cloud nine.

We got the kind of darshan one can only dream of. For over five minutes, we stood in Balaji's resplendent presence. I had dedicated my knee-length hair to the lord to thank him for the gift of my life, and he made sure that I was accorded this most divine reception to express my gratitude.

As we left the temple, I got back my phone from the police escort and switched it on. Lakshmi had been calling me. She wanted me to come to Pune immediately. In any other circumstances, I would have said a flat no. Other than medical emergencies, funerals and rescues, I never go anywhere at a few hours' notice. Maybe it was because I was in Balaji's abode that I mellowed and acquiesced, but I said I could only make it the next day.

Raj was overwhelmed by the divine experience, so his pleasant self was back. He also found my new shorn look quite interesting, and took some good pictures.

I reached Pune around 3 p.m. the next day. Only when I reached the Marriott Hotel did I realise that I had not even asked Lakshmi why she needed me so urgently. That was the last day of the second INK conference, I knew.

As I wandered about, I looked for familiar faces, knowing I would find many. I had already attended a TED and an INK talk, so some people at least would recognise me—perhaps a little slowly because of my new look.

As I entered the foyer, I spotted Lakshmi and asked her what she wanted me to do.

'Speak,' she said, looking at me rather quizzically.

I looked at her blankly. 'About what?'

'Anything. Your life in the last one year.'

'When?'

She looked at her watch. 'Right after the break. You're the first speaker. And you have exactly five minutes.'

I don't remember what I said, except that it was about the movie and my struggle to find a distributor. My speech received a thunderous applause and a standing ovation. Maybe these places practice standing ovations as a standard protocol? As I was walking down the ramp, a voice whispered, 'How much do you require to distribute this film yourself?'

This was a question Raj and I had discussed that very morning on the way home from the railway station. In case we did not find a distributor, I wanted to know if we could hire a theatre ourselves and release the film. Raj had given me a figure, and I had gulped. No wonder the distributors were thinking so hard—if they took the film up, they would have to at least recover their cost, and it was not a small amount.

The voice in my ear was a woman's, but I could not see her face. It was very dark in the hall, and the next speaker was already on the stage. I said Rs 50 lakh, and she just squeezed my hand.

That evening, I met a lot of our friends, including Shantanu Moitra, Javed Jaffrey, Joi Barua—the usual suspects at an INK conference. I was desperately looking for a face to put to that voice, but could not find anyone.

I returned to Hyderabad the next day. The very same afternoon, the same voice called me on the phone, and now I had a name. She introduced herself as Anu Aga. Of course I knew who she was: businesswoman, philanthropist, member of parliament. She wanted to know how she could wire the money to us, and wished us the very best for our efforts.

In the next fifteen days, the entire amount reached us. We were able to distribute the film independently in Kerala. Chief Minister

Oommen Chandy watched the film with his entire legislative assembly members and had tears in his eyes. We were told that ours was the first film he had seen in forty-five years.

In Malayalam, the film was called *Ente*, which means 'mine', and in Telugu, *Naa Bangaaru Talli*, which means 'my dearest daughter'.

For the Telugu film, I had to crowd-fund the distribution. Many people reached out, but still we were short by Rs 13 lakh, which a simple gentleman by the name of Kannan Subramanian covered.

Naa Bangaaru Talli won three national awards, four state awards and nine international awards. The last scene, which the major producer wanted us to change, fetched the lead actress, Anjali Patil, a national award. Shantanu Moitra won his first national award for the background score of this film. The movie ran in theatres for forty-five days. I got calls from hundreds of young men who were sex buyers, but had given up on paid sex after watching the movie. The movie was then acquired by an OTT platform, and is currently streaming on Disney Hotstar. Raj donated the entire proceeds of the satellite rights of the film to Prajwala.

I thus not only became a film producer, but also a one-time distributor. This last feat I have no wish to repeat. Lord Balaji made sure that I reached my destination safely. But I have become addicted to the movie business, and consider it a good way to bring about social transformation. I have already produced five movies on human rights concerns, including one on witch-hunting.

Movies are no more a hobby for destressing on a Friday morning. They have become a powerful weapon for me to accelerate social change, something that I happily partner on with my soulmate Raj.

But I began this chapter to tell the story of shearing my hair at Tirupati. It is only fit that I end it with an affirmation of devotion to god. Whenever the going has got tough and I could only think, 'Enough! No more!', someone somewhere would whisper into my ear and the silver thread of hope would return to my hand, and aspiration and action would reunite.

My favourite deities, Kollur Mookambika, Tirupati Balaji, Maa Katyayani and all my family deities have reached out to me in different ways. I have felt their presence in my life throughout, on happy occasions and sad ones, difficult times and easy phases. The way I feel about it is this: I am cocooned in a web of divine powers.

25

Why Do Rapists Thrive with Impunity?

After fourteen years, Prajwala finally had a place of our own. No more extortionate rents, zero chances of eviction, no one to harangue or harass us and no mobs or vandals that we had to bow down to.

We had tried our best to make the campus welcoming. Raj's vision ensured that our new campus looked more like an ashram than a shelter, and locals had mistaken it for one. Passers-by even thought it was a resort. We had envisioned it as a place for rest and restoration, and public opinion seemed to be on our side on this. Our hope was that the women we'd built it for would find it so, and largely, it felt like we had succeeded. Of course, there would always be some women who preferred to return to their previous lives, or who have not had enough time with the trauma care, so escape attempts were to be expected.

Finally, both Astha Nivas and Asha Niketan were in one place, and only the ERP programme was housed in a rented building, since it didn't make sense to move it out of the city. Not only would that damage the business, it would considerably increase production costs. The only cost we had then was to ferry the women from Prajwala to the ERP unit. We found a multi-purpose solution by purchasing a delivery truck, which could not only transport the trainees but also deliver the goods made at the ERP unit to customers, heavily reducing our cost of transportation. By now, the production unit was manufacturing a wide range of products, including notebooks, registers, wooden and steel furniture. Over ninety small government-aided schools were our customers. We supplied them with school notebooks, registers, benches and almirahs every year. The business was good, covering the cost of training, salaries for the staff, stipends for the trainees and the rent of the building. The landlord must have found it worthwhile to accept flak from the community for that one building. He had evicted two-thirds of our operations there, and was charging an astronomical rent of Rs 1,00,000 per month.

My own office was still at Charminar. All our advocacy work was in the city, where the secretariat and the district administration were located. The new facility was in a village too far away from any government administrative set-up, and proximity is crucial for any advocacy work. Though my friend, the original owner, Baba, had died in his early nineties, his children continued to support us.

One of the parties inconvenienced by our move was the police. Earlier, we accepted rescued women any time of day or night, as per the directions of the court. Now, the police had to drop off the girls at the Charminar office or the ERP unit before 6 p.m., after which we shut for the day. But as most rescues happen at night, the police had to accommodate the rescued in a women's police station until our offices opened again the following day.

This had been a calculated move on our part. We wanted to avoid security breaches, and didn't want our new shelter to be identified. There are bad apples everywhere, and we knew a fair number of those in the system would be happy to sell us out for a little money.

There was another fallout, one that we should have anticipated. Along with the space, our team had expanded as well, and it was tough to assess in depth the character of each person. And soon enough, trouble began.

It started with small transgressions, reports of manipulated vouchers. Someone who travelled by bus submitted vouchers for autos. Though the amounts were negligible, it reflected that person's integrity. I've always been clear that I need to fully trust everyone on the team. I can't go about cleaning up outside and inside the house, so to speak. So, when anyone was found guilty after a formal and fair enquiry, they were summarily dismissed.

There was one serious incident of cash missing from our office. Our daily expenditure had increased greatly, digital payments were still uncommon and none of the vendors was interested in cheques.

The shelters had to return any balance cash at the end of every month. They delivered the amount in a sealed envelope to the head office through the driver of the truck, who commuted every day to and from the shelter. The driver swore that he had not opened the sealed cover, and yet, when the amounts were calculated, a small but significant amount was missing. While the shelter team took accountability for the missing amount and replaced it, something was definitely amiss.

Then the most embarrassing incident happened: cash was missing from the personal belongings of a victim. When we take a person into our shelter, we document and store all their personal items until their release, at which point we hand them back. I immediately initiated an enquiry to check if this was a one-off case. To my utter shock, we had cash missing from almost each bag. Clearly, someone in the frisking and storage department was responsible. Around the same time, there had been an incident when some women in the shelter had gone on a rampage, damaging property and hurting the staff. We had lodged a police complaint against them, and they had been remanded to sub-jail. This employee must have known that there was a chance that those women may not return to claim their belongings, and felt free to walk off with their money.

I lodged another police complaint, this time against my own employees. Needless to say, they were all outraged. The police aggravated the situation by limiting their search to the houses of survivor staff members. They got nowhere with the investigation. I was frustrated, disappointed—and now worried. One of the remanded women was about to collect her belongings, and hers was the largest amount missing. In desperation, I requested the police to conduct a narco-analysis, or lie detection, test. The police agreed, and that was when the team leader—the team leader!—came forward and handed over the entire amount. This person was a professionally qualified member whom the police had not even bothered to interview.

This incident occurred at a time when there was already discord over my inclusion of survivors as staff members in all departments. The 'professionals'—though I believe they are all professionals—felt that my trust in the survivors and the value I placed on their inputs undermined their own authority and learning. This was a clear case of maladjustment, and clearly they didn't understand our survivor-centric approach.

Another cause for dissatisfaction was the new grievance mechanism I had instituted. I encouraged all the residents in both our shelters and all the education centres to write to me confidentially about any problems they had with the staff and management. I once terminated a teacher after the children in the education centre complained of abusive language—only post due enquiry, of course. So, of course, children in the shelter would threaten strict teachers: 'You're just a paid employee; wait till we file a complaint against you.'

I was aware of these dangers and the emotional condition of our children and women due to the sustained trauma they had been subjected to. We had, therefore, devised a strong enquiry protocol to arrive at the truth, and this worked most of the time. But it was also true that a small number of employees in the shelter would have to play nice to the residents to avoid confrontations.

These conflicts were tiring me out. They were unpleasant, exhausting, demotivating.

Then came another shock. This one was external, and it forced me to initiate a radical measure that would have a longstanding impact both for the organisation and the country.

It was 4 February 2015. I had just returned home and was getting ready for my evening prayers when I received a frantic call from Vamshi, a male volunteer from MAD, a community sensitisation programme that engaged with men and boys regarding the role they played in increasing the demand for prostitution, encouraging them to become a part of the solution. Vamshi was an active member who had given us useful information in the past.

He was very upset and wanted me to see some videos that his cousin had received on WhatsApp. Vamshi didn't know how long they'd been circulating. Unable to pacify him and concerned by his tone, I told him to forward those videos to me.

An hour later, I watched them.

It wasn't what they did, but *how*—that's what got me. It was a show, that was what it was. An invitation to the viewer. Come! Enjoy with us. Look, we'll share it all with you! Won't you join us? We're having so much fun.

They masturbated for the camera. Told the recorder where to focus. They really put on a show. It was eight-minute-long exhibition of five men violating a child, a twelve-year-old. Her cries and shrieks spurring them to greater atrocities. At all times, there were at least four men savaging her.

The recorder. Was he less of a participant? All those viewers who'd got off on the whole video, who'd passed it on to others like them, what about them?

The second video was no better. It took me hours to recover. Would it never end? *Could* it ever end? It happened to me three decades ago. It has been happening for centuries.

It happens to four women every hour here in India.

Across the city, the state, the country, across countries and continents.

Different perpetrators. Different victims. Same crime, on repeat.

With one big difference: now, with the internet and social media at their disposal, so many others can delight in this—this disgrace, this absolute abomination.

This was humanity at its worst. We all had a hand in it, allowed it, enabled it to thrive with impunity.

Me too, when I didn't report my own experience of sexual assault to the police. But now, what was my excuse for failing to act?

I took a deep breath. This would be do or die.

Some of the evening's trauma must've still lingered on my face when Raj got back. He took one look at me, then asked, 'What can I do to help?'

I handed over my phone. 'I want this modified with a few changes.'

Reduce the video length, blur the victim's face, focus on the rapists, their faces highlighted in circles.

I'd use their weapon against them, I decided.

That was a strange night, the calm before the storm.

Raj went to office the next day, edited the video, posted it on our YouTube channel and sent me the link.

That afternoon, I initiated the #ShameTheRapist campaign. I posted the video on my Facebook page and my Twitter account, and requested my followers to identify the faces so that they could be reported.

The post went viral. There was huge turbulence online. Whether media outlets saw it and kept quiet, I don't know, but only Uma

Sudhir from NDTV came forward to report on the campaign. An online paper criticised it: 'Shame Sunitha Krishnan: 5 reasons why sharing the WhatsApp rape video is wrong'.

My plan was to use the video and confront the world on its silence, then remove it and take legal action by reporting it to the Home Ministry. As per the plan, I erased the video the next day.

So angry was I about all this that I could've spontaneously combusted. But at least this time, I wasn't responding emotionally. I was planning, strategically even, and was clear about my long-term goal. I even had a Plan B chalked out.

But in none of that planning had I anticipated the backlash. In less than an hour after the NDTV live interview, my vehicle was vandalised in broad daylight. Journalists from every TV channel descended on my office. While I had not planned it this way, it did bring my campaign into focus. I reported the vandalism to the police and they booked a case. By afternoon, my mail was filled with pornography of all kinds, some with threats added: 'This is what we'll do to you!'

I filed a case with the cyber cell. In the meantime, Raj's Facebook account was blocked.

NDTV adopted #ShameTheRapist as a national campaign. Their support was much needed and timely.

I certainly seemed to have rattled these kinds of video-makers, even those who shared them. Perhaps rapists who recorded and circulated those gruesome acts were worried I was planning to target them next. I don't think any of them had even in their wildest dreams imagined that a woman would start a campaign of this nature.

Those videos in my inbox were slowly turning into something like a national database for rape videos. And I watched each and every one of them. Some were in Telugu, but many others were not, like those initial videos I'd seen.

Having closely worked with the police, I was familiar with the federal jurisdictional concerns of the state police. The Telangana and Andhra police could do nothing about these videos. They were in the jurisdiction of other states.

Thanks to all the media coverage, within three days of the campaign, I was able to meet the Union home secretary and then all the concerned officers in North Block. I handed over a letter, along with all the videos on a pen drive.

Then I waited impatiently for a response. Five days passed, and I heard nothing from them. Why had there been no action? I hadn't handed them suggestive videos. The men in the videos were undeniably rapists who were glorying in their criminal acts. What were they waiting for? What would it take for them to institute an all-India team to look into them?

The lack of timely action—it got to me. It felt like I needed to spur and prod them, coerce them, if need be, into action. It was time for Plan B. On 18 February, ten days after submitting my letter to the home secretary, I sent a detailed letter to the chief justice of India. On 27 February, less than ten days later, my letter was taken up suo motu, and accepted as a PIL in the Supreme Court. It came up before a two-member social justice bench, comprising Justice Madan B. Lokur and Justice U.U. Lalit.

My requests in my letter were simple: one, I wanted all the videos to be immediately investigated by the Central Bureau of Investigation (CBI), since it had pan-India jurisdiction; two, a mechanism for citizens to anonymously report such videos without becoming a complainant; three, a directory of convicted sex offenders that would be available to everyone and, four, engagement with technological firms to make online spaces safe.

The bench passed orders with immediate effect. The CBI was to investigate the videos, and the home ministry was directed to consider the other recommendations. Concerned about my safety, the bench also questioned the Telangana police on what was happening on the case.

Anil Sinha, director of CBI, and Raja Balaji, the officer-in-charge of investigating the videos, investigated the videos on a war footing. They made a status update in the first week of March on the possible states those videos were from, and the Supreme Court immediately ordered those states to cooperate and nab the culprits.

The fact that the government of Odisha, one of the states from where a video had purportedly originated, had not even deputed a lawyer to the Supreme Court angered the judges so much that they immediately ordered a fine of Rs 50,000, which was to be handed over to us. The judges felt that we should receive it as we had initiated this campaign and were fighting in court for it.

The Supreme Court heard the case every week, demonstrating all the seriousness that the government had lacked. The judges were also dissatisfied with the government of Telangana for not doing enough to nab the culprits who had vandalised my vehicle, and imposed a Rs 25,000 fine on it. The Telangana government was fuming—it had no intentions of paying the fine, and was set on proving that it had done the needful.

This was the beginning of another chapter in my life. The Telangana police had already diligently recorded my complaint and started the investigation. In the Old City of Hyderabad, if the public decides to be hostile, it is very difficult for any information to leak out. Just imagine: a vehicle was vandalised in broad daylight in a private parking area with direct public access, surrounded by shops, but there were no witnesses.

The commissioner offered me personal security, which I politely turned down. Why should I accept safety when women and children in this country were not safe; their dignity and bodies shredded and exhibited for mass public consumption?

All suspects from around our office were picked up and detained for hours for questioning. Public resentment among families living around our office began to grow. They began complaining that their children were being picked up by the police and detained for long hours. People from the neighbourhood were barging into my office and threatening our staff.

I was mostly absent as all this played out. The case was heard weekly, and I had decided to be a 'party in person', which essentially meant I was arguing my own case with Aparna Bhat beside me. It was my team back home that was bearing the brunt of the community's hostility. For eighteen years, we had been a peaceful presence in that area, and now people working in Prajwala could hardly walk on the road without somebody passing a snide remark against me.

Over twenty-one staff members resigned because of the daily harassment, and because their personal safety was at stake.

On one of my trips back to Hyderabad, I found that even my landlords had become uncomfortable. It was time to move. This time,

I did not have to struggle to purchase land: we had built a small corpus in the last five years. I was looking for a two-acre spread that would allow me to shift my office as well as the ERP unit.

We began to mobilise resources for the new campus. Unlike in 2009, I now had worldwide visibility thanks to TED and social media. There were committed and dedicated people all over the world who wanted to back us. Folks like Lavanya Ravulapally, Lalita Gollamudi, Padma Cherukapally, Sumana Rao, Aparna Ganti and others were willing to go to any extent to mobilise the funds. There were also friends within the country who reached out.

We used our corpus to buy two and a half acres of land. The fundraising by our friends ensured there was enough money not only for construction but also to refurbish our corpus. It took time and effort, but in the end, we found something suitable. The area was on the outskirts, ten kilometres from Hyderabad, just next to the airport. It was far enough from the bustle of the city, but close enough to connect with it, and it was just forty-five minutes from our shelter (we were now calling it a 'therapeutic community').

Raj decided to design the campus himself, and got technical support to complete the structural bit. Along with Prajwala's headquarters (which we referred to as 'Base Camp') and the ERP unit, we wanted a few more facilities—a fifty-bed emergency shelter to accept a new victim at any time of day or night. This would ensure that the police could confidently bring a victim to us at any time. They would receive appropriate first-response support and be shifted to the larger campus after a few weeks. Besides, there would be a small housing unit for the founder and board members. Raj thought it would offer a conducive environment in case we needed to work late into the night. The structure would of course be self-sustaining, zero-waste and eco-friendly.

And thus began the construction of the new campus, one that would finally give us a permanent address in every way. The entire design was inspired by mandala architecture, or the architecture of enlightenment, widely used in Kerala and Tulu Nadu, with elements of healing and calming aesthetics as the primary concerns.

Big changes were in the offing for Prajwala.

As for me, I found it a novel experience to argue my own case in the Supreme Court. Though I found giving speeches a simple enough affair by now, understanding the legal framework and preparing arguments were rather tough. And we were up against the big guns—all the major technological firms—to make online platforms safer and more accountable. The CBI investigation validated my fears. The online space was swarming with such videos, and it pushed the court to take up my demand for a mechanism for anonymous reporting by citizens.

As a direct result, the home ministry established the cybercrime portal in 2018, which had a provision for anonymous reporting. This was a landmark interim judgement, one that has changed the course of dealing with cybercrimes in the country. Any citizen who sees any rape video of a child or an adult on any social media platform or messaging application can report it anonymously, without becoming a complainant on the record.

The final judgement in this case had a cascading effect on the intermediary guidelines, assigning more accountability to technological firms to take up the onus to make their platforms safer and mandated the establishment of an Indian Cyber-Crime Coordination Centre (I4C), which would become an important body in combating cybercrimes in India

Another outcome in court: eleven years after we filed a PIL in 2004 demanding a victim-protection protocol, the Supreme Court passed an order in 2015 directing the Indian government to develop comprehensive legislation to combat human trafficking.

We had struggled for years, fighting against nameless, faceless entities, forces far bigger and more powerful than ourselves. We had our wins, sure, but they had not been at the pace we wanted, nor at the scale we desired. Now, we had effected changes that would have a sweeping impact, changes that would protect victims, changes that would safeguard potential victims. The satisfaction was immense.

26

Thamarapadam and the Civilian Honour

It was 2016.

Twenty years after I founded Prajwala with Jo in 1996, some of our important operations were now in safe and permanent locations, especially the shelter homes and the organisation's headquarters. The learning centres continued to be operated from rented premises. Prajwala's interventions were streamlined and demonstrating considerable impact. We were now partnering with civil society partners across the country, and also had a collaborative relationship with state and central government branches. We also partnered with various international agencies such as UNODC and the US Consulate of Hyderabad for very many campaigns. Thanks to the controversial #ShameTheRapist campaign that I had spearheaded, I was a more visible figure in the country, a visibility that greatly supported our mission.

On the personal front, it was already our tenth wedding anniversary. How fast time flies! It was exactly a decade since Jo had passed away. I wanted to visited Tirupati Balaji for our wedding anniversary. As our anniversary falls on 1 January, we decided to start for Tirupati on 31 December, right after the annual new year celebrations at Prajwala. This year's celebration was special, as the employees at Prajwala and I had choreographed a fashion show, and all the children were desperately waiting to watch this surprise act. Unfortunately, perhaps due to the excitement or my unfamiliarity with wearing heels, I tripped while climbing the stage. A sharp pain pierced through my ankle, although I managed to walk the ramp through that pain! But once I was off the stage, I knew something was critically wrong. A quick x-ray on my way to the airport revealed that I'd sustained a painful hairline fracture. I hobbled to Tirupati the following day with Raj, and from there on, for the next six weeks, I was limping and walking with the support of a crutch.

This injury came at a time when my schedule was packed with high-profile events that we were planning for months. We were launching the Swaraksha Caravan in the first week on January. This was our largest and most ambitious community-sensitising anti-trafficking campaign in partnership with the governments of Odisha, Andhra Pradesh and Telangana. It was organised in collaboration with the US Consulate of Hyderabad. Thirty civil society organisations were partnering with us in the execution of this campaign, bringing together state governments, the district legal services authority, police and civil society organisations as one team.

The caravan was flagged off on 9 January 2016 at Ravindra Bharati. It was a grand occasion, and we had to take the support of an event-management company to execute it. For weeks, I had been personally involved in supervising a musical titled 'Still I Rise', which was a fusion of the classical dances of Bharatanatyam, Kuchipudi and Odissi by a professional troupe led by Nayantara Nandakumar. Nayantara, who had founded 'Our Sacred Space', a happening cultural venture in Hyderabad, had choreographed this beautiful piece with sex trafficking as the main theme. For months, we had slogged to organise not just the opening but also the entire caravan that would travel for 165 days across the three states, encompassing fifty-three districts.

Representatives from the central government of India, the US embassy and other important dignitaries were gracing the opening. Justice S.V. Bhatti from the High Court of Telangana was the chief guest. The colourful and glittering function was a first in Hyderabad for this cause, and the 'flagging off' of the caravan was witnessed by hundreds of policymakers and influencers. I was perhaps the centre of attraction, hobbling around on my crutches, blowing on the conch to symbolically inaugurate the caravan.

Our team, with several survivor leaders, were going to be travelling in a customised bus for 15,600 kilometres, stopping at every district en route and conducting massive sensitisation programmes organised by our state and non-state partners in the district. In the weeks preceding this, principal secretaries from various ministries across the states carried out exercises and briefed all district officials on the smooth passage of the caravan in their regions with a view to maintaining law and order. The last three months of 2015, I was juggling the Supreme Court case while also visiting all three states—no easy task, I assure you.

As the campaign was conceptualised and executed by me directly through our team, I was the focal point of contact for all the three state governments. Partnership has an extraordinary power in bringing social change, but it also requires the investment of significant tracts of time, energy and skills. It requires mindful engagement and sustained effort to make it real.

This was perhaps the busiest beginning of a year in my life. I was coordinating the caravan as it moved from district to district, addressing thousands of people, all while recovering from a painful fracture. Days and nights would blur together, especially as the caravan picked momentum.

In spite of this tight schedule, there was a personal commitment that I felt compelled to honour. It was our temple festival at my father's village Thamarapadam on 26 January, which would mean two days of my time. I would have to rush to Delhi right after the pooja for the inter-ministerial committee meeting mandated to draft the anti-trafficking legislation that I had been advocating for over the last twelve years as a part of the final Supreme Court directive in the 2004 case that I had filed. This meant extensive travelling with my injured leg. But to understand my reasons for travelling to Thamarapadam, you need to also understand my connection to my family deities.

For me, Thamarapadam and Muthiamma, my grandmother, were one and the same—they meant home, a sort of peace that no storm could shake. As children, we'd go there once every three years, when my father claimed his leaves. And each of those visits felt, still feels, like a dream.

Thamarapadam was right out of a fairy-tale. True to its name, this kugramam, or remote village, was full of lotuses. Palm trees stood sentinel at the borders of paddy farms, a natural fence that separated them from the roads beyond. The houses were a picture too: their stark white walls sandwiched between the red-tiled roofs and the red-oxide floors, their thinnas—porches—often built with seating, offering respite from the sun to visitors.

There were less than a hundred families, most of them related, here. Practically everyone, including us, was from the Ezhava caste. At the edges of the village were those from other communities and denominations. On one end lived a Moplah Muslim family and on the other end, a Cherumakkal (Dalit) family. But none of the caste dynamics or other sociological patterns disturbed us then. As children, we hardly understood any of it, living in a central government colony with employees from all over the country.

While our family wasn't rich, it was the most privileged one. The eldest son, my father, worked in the central government, and two of my uncles were in government services, including the army. My father, known as Krishnan Kutty (kutty is a term of endearment which means son) to everybody in the village, had four sisters, and all of them were married by the time we were born. I remember the weddings of my uncles, my cheriachans, which happened later. My aunts were scattered across various parts of Kerala and would come to Thamarapadam to meet their eldest brother and his family. We were mini-celebrities there, with our alien language (though we were Malayalis, my siblings and I spoke only Hindi), city clothes that were stylish for the village and the talent show we'd put up every evening. The entire village was in awe of Krishnan Kutty's children.

Our house was the classic ottu veedu, an old-style tiled-roof building. It had a temple and a sarpa kaavu that housed all our kula devatas, family deities and ancestors, so we often had relatives coming over to commune with them. I have a deep connection with the deities there, and the sarpa kaavu has a special place in my heart. The annual temple festival, highlighted by the Kalamezhuthu pattu, or what I call kalam pooja, always coincided with our visits, and gave us a chance to meet our relatives, who'd travelled from near and far to invoke the gods. The pooja connected my soul to a higher power well beyond my reckoning, and I'd float around in a daze for days. Even the memories of it can send me into a powerful mental space.

The kalam pooja was typically conducted by people from Pulluvan caste. They ready the space, then create an image of the deity—the kalam, or art, that gives the pooja its name—in the consecrated area. Drawing the kalam as per the rituals takes several hours and is done to music performed with instruments such as the pulluvan veena, pulluvan kutam, thaalam and more to invoke the gods. The closing rituals include more music and dance, and in the end, the painstakingly made kalam is finally erased. Devotees take the powdered colours home as a blessing or prasadam.

Muthiamma, the matriarch, would preside over our family pooja, a queen and an amazing organiser, graciously welcoming guests and carefully taking note of the absentees. Occasionally, her eyes would wander over to me, my immersion in the pooja drawing a smile. My relatives had always supported my devotion to the family gods. With Muthiamma, it went further; she'd carry me all the way from the foothills of Palani to the temple on top of the hillock, climbing 689 steps. Palani, over 110 kilometres away from Palakkad, is home to Subramanya Swamy, the son of Shiva, and one of my favourite gods.

Muthiamma and I had a special bond. After all, she'd looked out for me since before my birth! She would indulge me in all kinds of ways. Only I had the privilege of tasting her chammanti directly from the ammikal. It was a sort of game she let me play, letting me quickly swipe that coarse coconut chutney from the edges of the flat mortar before she rolled the pestle back. Muthiamma's chutney was out of the world, as also was her kadala muttai, a condiment made with peanut and jaggery. For some reason, her coarse kadala muttai tastes far better than any sophisticated chikki, a similar item available in the market.

She always declared to everyone she met that I was a rare child, a special creation of the gods meant for great things. She'd constantly tell my father to let me do as I pleased, and not be a thadasam, or obstacle, to my desires. I'd initially put her partiality down to my religiosity. Only later did I realise that she saw much more in me than I—or anyone else—did.

Our connection had stayed strong over the years. She never knew—nor did any other relative—of any of the events that befell us. Distance helped, perhaps, and the fact that we met only once in three years. So when we met, it was only those now-and-then matters that got covered, such as marriage, educational status or employment.

When I told Muthiamma about my decision to stay unmarried, though she had seen it coming, it had taken her a bit by surprise.

She was still that small, wiry woman from my childhood, skin soft and smooth, stance stiff and straight, hair in that uncompromising bun. She had cocked her head, chin jutting out, eyebrows furrowed, fingers resting on her hips. Still as a statue but for her earlobes, weighed down by her dangling earrings that swayed gently, and her eyes, which searched mine intently.

We stood like that for a minute in a gentle standoff, then the tension broke. Her forehead had smoothened, her eyes crinkled and her lips relaxed into a smile. She'd given me a knowing look, one that said she knew better, gently patted my shoulder, then walked away. That was Muthiamma for you. Prescient!

Over the years, as all my uncles moved out of the village and the older generation left for their heavenly abode, the temple began to get neglected and the kalam pooja took a backseat. My family, too caught up in our own world of struggles, really did not give any serious thought to this dereliction of duty.

I knew Muthiamma was unhappy with the way things were, but she had no way of pushing people to do anything. All of her sons were working in far-off places. My deep connection with the temple, the kaavu and my bond with Muthiamma was perhaps why I got recurrent uneasy dreams.

It was 1997 and I was already in Hyderabad. On one of my solo visits to Kerala, I expressed to Sundaran Cheriachan—my father's younger brother, now retired from the army and in Thamarapadam with me that day—that I wanted the temple to be revived. There was a strange rightness and authority in the way I expressed it. My uncle immediately agreed, and said he would consult with the astrologers on how to go about it.

Perhaps the fact that Sundaran Cheriachan and his wife Laxmi Cheriamma had always deeply loved and respected me also helped. They were the only ones among my relatives who sought me out. When I was younger, Laxmi Cheriamma, who was a teacher, would take me to her school and introduce me to all her colleagues with great pride. That I took this momentous decision to revive a temple when I was only twenty-five was not a small thing for any of my relatives.

The consulted tantri told us to conduct a massive homam (a fire ritual) after which the deities would be addressed to learn about their willingness to remain in the temple, even though the required poojas had not been conducted for many years now.

Since it was my idea, I decided to take care of all the expenses. My IGSSS fellowship had just come through, and I had some savings. I decided to use all of it for the three-day homam.

Daddy, Mummy, Sujji and Suku came from Bangalore. The two people who were most moved by, and proud of, these proceedings were Muthiamma and Daddy. Something extraordinary was happening: a girl in the family had taken the decision to revive the gods.

The ninety-eight-year-old tantri from Thatamangalam performed the ceremony. He was a grand old man with bright shining eyes which seemed to assess you right away. Thamarapadam reverberated with his chants for three days. Relatives from all over visited. Both the homam and the reason for the homam intrigued everyone.

After three days of the homam, the twelve deities in the temple were questioned about their willingness to stay in the temple. Most of them refused, but Loka Parameshwari, Kaliath Bhagawathi, Subramaniam Swamy, Ayyappa Swamy and our ancestor Muthappan were willing to stay. While these five were consecrated, the rest were taken to the Bharata Puzha and immersed.

Daddy, who was the eldest brother of the family, decided not to allow the temple to be neglected anymore, and declared that every year on 26 January the entire family would meet for the annual temple pooja. It was also felt that the kalam puja was no longer required, as the homam had clearly shown which gods were there and so no further invocation was required. The entire family agreed.

We sorted out the question of the daily pooja when I offered to pay a nominal amount of Rs 1,000 per month to anybody willing to light the lamp every morning and evening and clean the place. Babu, a hearing-and-speech impaired distant relative living in Thamarapadam, agreed. He was a toddy-tapper and was happy to do this every morning before he left for his work and every evening when he came back.

Muthiamma was on top of the world, and would repeat this story over and over for the next three years until she started losing her memory in 2000. In 2002, she left the world to join the deities. Suku, who was visiting me in Hyderabad, and I rushed to Thamarapadam to pay our last homage and participated in the rites performed. Daddy had already reached there a day before.

Muthiamma was physically no more in Thamarapadam, but I went to Kerala for our temple and sarpa kaavu. I knew she was there for me in those little walls, awaiting my arrival every year. Not even my crutches would deter me from getting there. I reached Thamarapadam on 25 January. Very rarely did Raj join me on this trip, and this year was no exception.

I'd already reached the village at about 10.30 a.m., having taken the flight from Hyderabad to Coimbatore earlier. Daddy was supposed to reach by 2 p.m. Sundaran Cheriachan and I had spent a pleasant hour reminiscing when I got a call from my assistant, Nitin. He told me that someone from the home ministry was trying to contact me. Could he give them my number? This was as per our established protocol. I didn't want people to have my number without my authorisation.

The Supreme Court case is still going on, it must be about that, I surmised. Go ahead, I told Nitin. A few minutes later, I got a call, this time from an unknown number from Delhi. The person at the other end identified himself as someone from the home ministry.

'Sunitha-ji, you've been selected for the Padma Shri in social work. Would you be willing to accept the award?'

My first reaction was that this was a prank call.

'Sorry,' I stammered. '*Phir se bolenge*, please? Reception *kharaab hai*.' The line's not clear, could you please repeat what you said?

He did, and it sounded exactly like it had earlier. I was being honoured with the Padma Shri.

Who could have recommended me? Not the states that I worked with, I'd have known about it otherwise.

What an honour! And that too when I was in my hometown waiting for Daddy to join me.

'Ji, thank you,' was all I could manage, my disbelief not letting me express my elation.

By the evening, it had sunk in a bit. And when hordes of media persons tracked me down to our remote village, it definitely began to feel more real.

Suddenly, Thamarapadam was famous. A place that had given me so many beautiful memories with my wonderful Muthiamma who had seen something great in my future way back then. I knew she was smiling up there.

When 26 January dawned, the day of the pooja, Thamarapadam had thousands of visitors waiting to meet me. During the pooja, I do not get up to meet anybody. Students from adjoining schools, political leaders, influencers—they had arrived to meet and greet Sunitha Krishnan, daughter of Raju Krishnan, soon to be a Padma Shri awardee!

27

Protectors, Predators, Prey

What do my everyday battles look like? To understand this, you need to know a little bit more about the world that I am battling. Let me start this way: it is a common belief that habits take twenty-one days to form. Stick it out for three weeks, do that thing religiously, and voila, your life's changed for good.

Every crime against a woman has a specific impact on the mind of the victim. But in sex trafficking, you see something really strange play out. In about three days (sometimes a little longer), new victims generally undergo a deep psychological shift. They stop feeling like victims. First, they start surviving, then they start normalising and then they become habituated to their circumstances. Such is the devastating impact of the ordeal. Perhaps in the initial few days of being trafficked, the person still relates to being a victim—feeling caught, helpless, weak, the very bottom of the power ladder and at the mercy of people they (most likely) trusted. But gradually, this changes.

To understand this better, one needs to know what really happens behind the closed doors of a brothel. People are sold into prostitution for the purpose of selling sexual services. Traffickers, in the form of spotters, transporters and others in the chain, make efforts to identify vulnerable persons who can be lured or cheated by fraudulent means and brought to a brothel for the specific purpose of selling sexual services. Let's say three months from the time a person was coerced into selling sexual services, and calculating only one customer a day, they would have been raped by ninety men. But that doesn't make financial sense for the keepers. They need the women to entertain at least five customers a day to make any real money. Five multiplied by ninety is 450. In three months or ninety days, a woman would have been raped 450 times. That's 1,825 instances of sexual violations against one woman in one year. I have had harrowing accounts from some of girls we rescued who were forced to entertain up to fifteen men a day.

If one instance of sexual violence alters the emotional well-being of the affected person, just imagine what becomes of this victim's psychological status?

But why coerce at all? Why the trafficking? Why not encourage willing persons to voluntarily sell sex? The answer is the same as it is for any other labour-market practice—for cheap labour. Willing people can negotiate, for they come with free will and can leave whenever it pleases them. A coerced person loses their ability to negotiate and falls under the complete control of the trafficker. This is also why younger children are preferred, both for the demand in the market and for their compliance. Demand for sex with virgin children, perversions, fetishes and unconventional sexual habits are multiple reasons why a coerced person is preferred. But the overarching reason is the gain in revenue. The UN says sex trafficking is one of the fastest growing criminal enterprises. With the lowest amount of investment—at best, the cost of transport and the sale—the sex trafficker and the brothel keepers gain a lot more every day. For example, it hardly takes a few thousand rupees to trap a girl in the name of love and lure her to elope. The amount invested in transporting and buying the girl would be recovered on the very day she is sold, for there is a high demand for a virgin girl in flesh trade. After investing less than Rs 5,000 in buying a girl, a procurer could sell her for anything between Rs 20,000 and Rs 1,00,000, depending on her age, for the first encounter itself.

There are men willing to pay a very high price to have sex with virgins. Even by modest standards, the amount invested can be recovered in less than a week. Thereafter, every trafficker is just building the profit. Most coerced persons, be it a child or woman, are not paid for months together under the guise of recovering the brothel keeper's investments. In fact, they are told, 'You can leave after you can pay back what we have invested and all the debts we have incurred because of you.'

And what are the debts? If there is a police raid, the money paid as bribe or for the legal process; if there is pregnancy, the money paid for the illegal abortion; if there is sickness, the money paid to the doctor; and then, of course, for the clothes, cosmetics, alcohol and all the paraphernalia required to sell sexual services.

For how much can you buy sexual services in India? It depends on the location. If it is on the street, you can get a blowjob for less than Rs 100. Practically all sexual services on the street will range from Rs 100 to Rs 1,000. The issue is that the sale of sexual services on the street has a locational crisis as it must be done quickly, for instance, in a movie theatre or behind a bush in a public park.

Now move a little higher to lodges or houses, which are considered brothels. We do not need a red-light area for a brothel. As per the law, any place of sexual exploitation, including a vehicle, is a brothel. In a lodge or a house, there is the availability of a room, and thus the time and scope for many more services. Hence, the cost is higher, ranging from Rs 1,000 to Rs 10,000, and the figure keeps moving up as the setting becomes more elite, such as a resort or a five-star hotel.

The chances of victims being rescued within the first few hours after being trafficked are minuscule. Most are lured in the name of love or marriage, so when the family realises someone is missing, the possibility of their being trafficked is the last thing on their minds.

Why should anybody be shocked by this? It is called the flesh trade for a reason. These business enterprises have invested extensive amounts of time, money and effort into it—spotting, grooming, procuring, transporting and paying for the victims' living costs. After all that effort, shouldn't they be entitled to a payback and a profit? Interestingly, as per a UNODC report and our own observations, across the globe, this criminal enterprise is largely dominated by women.

Never mind that their victims don't enter that life willingly, that they are systematically groomed and/or cheated, blackmailed, threatened, intimidated and coerced in several ways before they eventually 'consent'. By the time the three months pass, the victims are forced to become complicit in their own dehumanisation, viewing their bodies as receptacles for others' pleasure, while their minds, in survival mode, trick them into accepting their circumstances.

It's not the brothel keepers alone who are to blame. Across the world, a woman's honour is believed to reside in her vagina, in its purity. The victims of sex slavery, whether woman or child, are also a product of that society and this kind of regressive narrative is usually ingrained in their thinking too. After experiencing such severe trauma, the victim ends up believing that hogwash, even if she doesn't agree with it. What does her opinion matter anyway? It's about how others will treat her. And in most cases, the stigma and ostracisation starts at home.

The very fact that it happened—even if the girl or woman was raped—makes her unworthy, undeserving of acceptance, kindness or dignity. It makes her a party to the crime. And in most cases, the social stigma and isolation that she fears starts at home.

It should hardly be surprising that victims, largely for the purposes of self-preservation, end up normalising their exploitation. And a few weeks into the experience, they start supporting and cooperating with the perpetrators. What other option even exists for them? This dependence on their abusers creates some sort of fellow feeling, an attachment, some kind of bond, much like Stockholm Syndrome. As such, when we rescue them, we make all parties, victims included, unhappy. And some of them make it their daily business to make life miserable for us.

Sex trafficking is an organised crime, and one that is hurt in various degrees by our interventions. Each time a girl is rescued, somebody's revenue is hurt. It shouldn't be a surprise that those of us in the rescue missions end up making enemies, a lot of them.

The damage only increases as we gain the trust of a victim, who then chooses to disclose information about her traffickers—their places of operation, their accomplices, their hideouts and plans in case of police raids, etc. Eventually, if justice prevails, it ends in a prison sentence for them.

The backlash from traffickers has ranged from attacks on our shelters to physical assaults on me and my staff. I have personally been attacked some eighteen times. Over the years, the nature of attacks have changed, but not their regularity.

Invariably, when the police initiate the rescue, the victims would have been in that situation for at least two or three months. By this time, they're extremely distrustful of all the stakeholders, and hostile to the idea of being admitted to a shelter. This hostility to a shelter home is also a cultivated one. Many of our survivors have reported that brothel keepers have told them countless tales of the horrors that constitute life in a shelter, how they will languish there without seeing daylight for years to come. They encourage the victims to identify their brothel keepers as close relatives in court and make all attempts to escape from the shelter to get back to them.

Essentially, this means that the victims we rescue often don't always see it as an escape. They've been so thoroughly indoctrinated that nothing we do or say helps. It's like arguing with a flat-earther or an anti-vaxxer.

It takes months—long-term trauma care and individual and group sessions of counselling, peer interactions and art therapy—before they even acknowledge their victimhood. All our protocols have to factor in this resistance while dealing with victims.

What we didn't have in our protocols back in 2011 were plans for two possible situations: when traffickers pose as victims and infiltrate our shelters and when victims have special needs.

Let me start with victims who have special needs.

Dealing with special needs requires different skills, which neither my team nor I possessed. Initially, we hadn't come across any such victims. It was only in 2011, after we moved to the larger shelters that we rescued our first special child from a brothel. With no training in that field, we weren't capable of helping a victim who could not share her trauma in any way other than through self-harm or violent attacks on others. Traffickers, we learnt, tend to like mildly or moderately intellectually challenged persons. They are easier to deal with, more easily persuaded with tricks and bribes. They can be dressed up properly, and may not appear to be different from the others. A severely challenged person is of no use.

In 2011, the CWC started referring to us children with special needs who had been raped or found in a brothel. Right after a rescue, all stakeholders are preoccupied with completing the legal formalities and referring the victim to a safe home at the earliest. It gets rather difficult at that stage to convince the CWC to refer the victim elsewhere. Refusing to admit such a child feels inhuman, which is how twelve-year-old Amina, found in a brothel, came to our shelter.

Amina was moderately intellectually challenged, and I knew keeping her with us wasn't going to help her. Her needs were different, and we didn't have the training to handle her. We had to designate two staff members to keep an eye on her. Though she was a sweet and loving child, she had recurrent episodes of violent behaviour. I told my team to look for a specialised institution suited to Amina's needs, and request the CWC to transfer her there.

My counsellors Sujatha and Kranti searched in earnest, and found a place that worked with special children. During their field visit, they found the staff to be competent, handling around ten to twelve children. The place looked good, and we felt it was in Amina's best interests to shift her to a place with appropriate holistic support provided by a trained team.

We decided to do a trial run for three months before a formal transfer, closely following up on her well-being in the interim. She'd been with us for one year now, and I didn't want her to feel abandoned. We settled on conducting periodic checks every fortnight to assess the suitability of the institution.

After two months of regular visits, my team started to feel slightly uneasy. With each visit, they found one or two children missing from the home. Further, the staff looked visibly harried if my people casually enquired about their whereabouts. They would snap at us and ask us to mind our own business.

My team flagged these concerns to me. Perhaps we might also react in the same way if someone else made unnecessary comments or asked intrusive questions about our home, I said to them.

A series of crises at our own shelters meant that that our team couldn't manage visits for the next three weeks. When we finally made that visit, Amina wasn't around. Upon inquiry, we learnt that she'd been taken to the hospital and would be back soon. This time, my team found that the inhabitants were all new faces and none of the older children were present.

Feeling worried, Sujatha and Kranti decided to wait until Amina returned. After three hours had passed, my team began to truly fret, especially as the institute's staff began to get agitated and downright hostile to our presence. Finally, unable to take it anymore, Sujatha called me. Alarmed, I told her it was best to leave without making any fuss—there was no point in jumping the gun—and instructed them to visit early in the morning the following day.

The next day, at 8.30 a.m., Kranti and Sujatha found the entire place shut, with only an employee and a caretaker who were getting ready to leave.

Kranti alerted me right away. I asked her to hand over the phone to the employee. I told the woman that if Amina wasn't handed back to me in the next two hours, I would lodge a police complaint. In fact, I'd send the local police right away, and named a few big names in the department, including the police commissioner.

Maybe it was my tone that did the trick, but that woman started to cry. Sujatha and Kranti told her that they'd go with her to get Amina back, and bundled her into our vehicle. The lady was extremely stressed. She called someone up, but couldn't speak freely. They went on a long drive to a god-forsaken slum in the industrial part of the city.

The woman led Sujatha and Kranti to Amina, who was in a small shanty with lots of coins scattered around her. There was no trace of anyone else, but there was enough evidence to indicate that many people either frequented it or lived there. Obviously, they'd all cleared out, leaving Amina behind.

To be frank, we were broken. A trafficked child had been re-trafficked by traffickers posing as an NGO, and we were in some way responsible for it.

Amina couldn't tell us what had happened, but the various marks on her body certainly told a story. My formal police complaint against the organisation did not yield any results, except adding one more name to my long list of enemies.

It took months for Amina to return to some semblance of her normal self, and it took us another year to find a competent organisation. The Mallikamba Manovikasa Kendram now provides support for all the special children referred to us by the CWC.

What do you do when protectors are the predators? There are many instances across the country when criminals operate shelter homes for the nefarious purposes of selling sexual exploitation, begging, adoption, organ trade and sex tourism. The infamous Muzaffarpur shelter home rape case is one of many examples. I have had the unfortunate experience of confronting many of them in the last many years.

The other complicated scenario we were unprepared for was when the predator masquerades as a victim. As I've said earlier, victims can move up the pecking ladder as organisers and brothel keepers. It's perhaps a most natural progression. After all, when you believe there's no way out, you have no other option but to find a way to survive there. Many older women cannot even get enough customers to contribute to the revenue model; the demand is always for younger girls and newer faces. So, they have to start working in support of the trade, and the best option then is to become a procurer or brothel keeper.

We once had a nineteen-year-old Bangladeshi trafficker infiltrate our shelter. She was with us for two years—and why? Solely to ensure that none of the Bangladeshi girls testified in court. Before being admitted to our shelter as a victim, she had already trafficked ninety girls from Bangladesh, managing the border, transporting them via West Bengal and supplying them to various brothels across Hyderabad.

We had no idea. She was among the most well-behaved residents. I even cited her as an example in one of my talks as a case study of a recovered person. It was only when an international agency alerted us that we discovered her true intentions.

Another trafficker stayed in our shelter for three years. She had multiple cases pending against her, and was using our shelter to hide. And we've had yet others who became inmates to wreak havoc, hurt our reputation and force us to shut down. I'd been in the rescue-and-shelter business for eighteen years before I realised that a trafficker can engineer attacks from within. It was a rude shock.

It was the end of September 2014, and Sujatha, the team leader of our shelter was going on maternity leave. At the time, I was busy promoting our movie *Naa Bangaaru Talli*, and was to be in Delhi on Vijaya Dashami, the last day of Dasara. For some reason, my flight was cancelled, but I hadn't yet informed my team about it. It was a Friday.

That was when it happened. Nearly fifty women went on a rampage in Asha Niketan. They assaulted the employees and vandalised the campus, attacking anything and everything they could lay their hands on. There was utter chaos. The other girls were huddled in fear.

Nobody could understand what the matter was. An administrative staff member called me in total panic, apologising profusely since he thought I was in Delhi. I told him to calm down, that I'd dial the authorities and asked him to hold fort until they arrived. I hung up, then requested the local police for immediate support before setting off for the campus.

The inspector sent a small team to assess the situation. When they arrived, they were unprepared for the scale of the attack. They asked the inspector for backup right away.

It took us some time to reach the campus. The sight that greeted us was frightening. Our truck, our jeep and the entire building—windows, doors, offices—were ransacked and damaged. Over fifty police personnel, men and women, were attempting to control the mob.

When they spotted me, the rioters froze, dropped their sticks and stones and sat down without a word. I asked the police to take a step back. It was a strange scene. The rioters were sitting on open ground, while the others watched the drama unfold, fear and disbelief in their eyes.

I approached the women and asked them to go inside. They just sat there, avoiding eye contact. I told them I'd speak to each one of them personally to understand their grievance, and that I wouldn't leave the campus until I had done so. This convinced them. One by one, they got up and went inside.

The police were surprised; they'd had a tough time controlling the mob. A sub-inspector, with great confidence, told me that I shouldn't be leaving everything to my staff, that I should monitor the centres regularly, as the girls were making grievous allegations. Many of the girls had complained to the police that life at the shelter was horrible, the food inedible, their basic needs were not being met, and that, worst of all, my staff sent them out for prostitution. He said, with some hesitation in his voice, that some of them even alleged that they had been subjected to sexual abuse by lesbians.

This was neither the time nor place to defend our work nor the standards of care we maintained, so I just told him that I would look into it and stay there until everything was settled.

It was my worst nightmare become real. Just the thought of even 0.1 per cent of any of the allegations being true was nauseating.

The next eighteen hours were the longest of my life. I spoke to each and every girl in Asha Niketan; there were around 200. Most of them said the same thing: they were concerned about when they will be released from the shelters and what life options they'll have. Not a single person mentioned any other complaints. I brought up the allegations that the sub-inspector had shared. They all denied that such a thing had happened.

But my mind in a turmoil, I asked each of the girls over and over whether anything untoward had taken place. Around 150 women were only witnesses to the events that unfolded, and they insisted that nothing had happened. They were trying to figure out why the riots had occurred.

We had a sound safeguard mechanism in place as well as a confidential grievance management system. In the past, some residents had used it to inform me about staff they considered negligent. The problems had ranged from not being given medication on time to the staff being too strict. We had taken appropriate measures in every instance. That night, none of the residents slept in their rooms, fearing for their lives, apprehensive about the residents who had gone on a rampage that morning. They slept in the corridor where I was.

I then focused on the rioting residents. These fifty women were hostile, sullen and silent. It was a while before I could get them to speak, which surprised me since they had been quite vocal that morning—I could hear them over the phone when my staff members had called. Why did they go silent when they saw me? Was my presence not part of the plan?

When they finally did speak, all they wanted to know was when would they be released from the home. My explanation, that it was the court's decision, found them disbelieving. They insinuated that we needed to keep them in the shelter and the court just followed what we said. After questioning them intensively, I noticed a pattern: thirteen women were genuinely hostile, while the other thirty-seven appeared to be parroting lines they had been taught. Each time I probed these women, they got flustered. Some also said that I was never around and always in Delhi.

There was clearly something going on, but what it was, I couldn't tell. This rebellion had been timed to coincide with Sujatha's and my absence. I decided to discuss this with the director-general of police (DGP) and the district judge, and sought an appointment for Monday.

I wrote a comprehensive letter to the DGP, requesting increased protection, with a police outpost on campus along with a brief on the allegations made by the fifty women. It is another matter that not a single girl repeated the horrible allegations the police had reported to me.

On Monday morning, I returned to the city to meet Anurag Sharma, IPS, the first DGP of the newly formed state of Telangana. He received my complaint with great alarm, and immediately ensured that a police outpost was set up within the campus. I requested for continued police protection, to which he readily agreed.

Next, I met with District Judge T. Rajani. She looked grave, and informed me that a group of advocates had submitted a petition requesting legal action against us. They demanded that no girl should be admitted to our campus as there were grave violations going on, including girls being sent for prostitution. I was shaken and silently handed over my letter. When she read through it, she looked even more disturbed. The letter from the group of advocates carried the exact same allegations that the girls had made—and which I'd put in my letter. Even the wording was similar. This proved beyond a doubt that a larger conspiracy was at play.

I decided to stay on campus until Sujatha returned. She had been watching all this from her staff quarters on campus, and was anxious to get back to work. Within a week of giving birth, she was back, such was her dedication to our mission.

We decided to monitor the situation. The counsellors were instructed to work closely with all the girls, especially those who were part of the violence. The police were also constantly on campus. It was just a matter of time before another incident occurred—the infiltrators wouldn't keep quiet for too long. It was clear that they were here on a mission that needed to be speedily completed.

On the eighteenth day, they made a move. Just like before, they attacked two staff members, attempting to throttle them. This time there were only thirteen women, the ones that I had identified as the prime instigators. The other women were nowhere near the crime scene. Since the police were on campus, these women were arrested and remanded. A large group of lawyers arrived instantly to appeal for bail. Six of the troublemakers were out on bail in less than a week, and the remaining seven were stuck in jail for a little longer.

It was only after these women left the shelter that the remaining thirty-seven women opened up. They had been threatened into joining the riots. When we checked their files, it was clear that the troublemakers knew them from before and, in all possibility, also knew about their families' whereabouts.

Many years later, in 2021, one of the thirteen women—let me call her Radhika—was once again admitted to our shelter. She told us that her twelve co-conspirators were young brothel keepers whose sole agenda had been to defame the shelter and have it shut down. They had wilfully created a situation that would force us to file a police complaint against them, for it was better to go to jail, where they could then immediately seek bail. She had been included as she knew most of their secrets, and told us that these women were in touch with a lot of lawyers and some 'big people'. Radhika languished in jail for more than six years, and was released only after legal aid authorities intervened.

Interestingly, a few months after the disturbance, I saw an article in *Economic and Political Weekly* by Kimberly Walters. She had cited these women in her piece. Walters had researched women who were rescued under the Immoral Traffic Act, 1956, and had met some of these women in a 'reputed' sex workers' collective, and they had given their first-person account anonymously, of course, on how horrifying these shelters were and the flaws in the 'protectionist' approach. The article discussed bits and pieces from my blog without actually mentioning me. It posited me as fundamentally opposed to the agency of a person and their right to self-determination, to choose what they want to do.

Many in the development sector based in India from the sex workers' lobby would, in the coming years, oppose our model of work, especially our safe shelters, which is another issue that we face today. Misinformation would be spread, accusing us without bothering to verify any allegations. Complaints would be lodged with statutory bodies, press meets would be held criticising us and I would be painted as somebody who had the ability to wipe out people.

The sex workers' lobby, which has many international sympathisers, and organisations like ours subscribe to fundamentally conflicting ideologies. The lobby is opposed to our anti-prostitution stand, asserting that all adult women are in prostitution by choice. They view the selling of sexual services as 'normal work' and call for the legalisation of the flesh trade. Thus, they are 'sex workers' and should be accorded all rights as a labour force.

Since the lobby believes that adult women are in the business willingly, they are opposed to safe homes like ours, calling them 'detention centres', places of incarceration rather than rehabilitation, places that impinge on the liberty of these women. They also argue that none of the adult women rescued were trafficked, and that organisations like ours are a serious threat to the rights of women who choose to work in the flesh trade. This lobby had a stronghold on the HIV/AIDS groups that implemented targeted intervention programmes to promote condom usage as a means of safety and harm reduction among women in prostitution.

Over the years, the rancour from our differing ideologies has become personalised, and I have often had reports of the nasty rumours spread by this group about me. I'm branded as 'protectionist', someone with regressive and moralistic beliefs who will not accept the agency of women to decide for themselves.

I have considered these ideas, and my own position has only gained more clarity. Prostitution is the oldest form of sex slavery. How can self-determination and agency exist when women are faced with societal constraint, toxic patriarchal norms (in placing the blame on the woman, in locating honour, purity in the woman's chastity, in commodifying women in so many ways), grooming and coercion? These multi-pronged attacks leave women bereft of options, and so emotionally coerced that working in the sex trade becomes the only choice available.

Our own experiences have shown us that thousands of women are lured in the name of jobs, love, marriage and film roles, and then forced into prostitution. Even those rare few who had chosen to work in the flesh trade of their own accord had done so because of a lack of options. I have not met a single adult woman in prostitution till date—and I've been in this line of work for thirty years—who chose to continue in the flesh trade because she felt fulfilled and considered it a good career decision. How can something so fundamentally exploitative, something that batters your body, mind and soul and bars you from society, be a vocation, a voluntary choice?

The sex workers' lobby, backed by high-profile lawyers and progressive intellectuals, waited to pounce on us the moment something went wrong. It was a great disappointment for them that our shelters demonstrated impact, that we were aggressively lobbying to replicate our model in the states we worked in and, most importantly, that even under terrible duress, we refused to shut down.

Our shelters have become centres for learning for officials and stakeholders from the state administration, the judiciary and the police. The Lal Bahadur Shastri National Academy of Administration, the premier training institution for civil services, has made it mandatory for new recruits to visit Prajwala as a part of 'Bharat Darshan'. The National Police Academy has mandated the same for probationers. Our four shelters, including the one we managed with the government, had an increasing number of survivor-advocates who represented the impact of rehabilitation, and have been studied for replication across the country.

Notwithstanding all the positive recognition, the onslaught on our efforts (where not even the pain and trauma of victims is kept in mind) is a painful reality that we face every day of our work.

One such incident was the suicide of a resident. This was an Uzbekistan national who was both a victim and an accused in two separate cases. In one case, she was cited as a victim and was admitted to our shelter, and in another case, she was accused of making fake Indian documents. The judge, in her wisdom, felt that it was better for the woman to stay in our shelter than be remanded to jail. It is not difficult to understand the frustration of an individual who feels trapped in confinement and unable to break free. More so if she is a foreign national from a faraway country and faces language barriers in the shelter. Even though interpreters were brought in for limited purposes, day-to-day communication continued to be a challenge. On our part, we would assure her practically every day that we would find a way out. On the face of it, she seemed to be adjusting.

What triggered the suicide is hard to say. Her death was shocking for the entire shelter, and extremely challenging for us to handle. We were swamped by enquiries and had to arrange for her body to reach

Uzbekistan. Her own embassy took no interest in supporting us by either tracing the family in Tashkent or financially supporting the cost of sending the body home. We had to use our resources and contacts in UNODC to organise that.

Representatives from the sex workers' lobby and human rights groups pounced on us. A series of enquiries from human rights commissions flooded us for months to come, and we spent a significant amount of time addressing them. Even years later, I find references to this suicide whenever the sex workers' lobby wants to target us.

Suicide is a mental health concern, and Prajwala has helped thousands of individuals it serves to overcome their trauma and get past suicidal ideation to consider a future for themselves. This, beyond all else, shows the quality of care that the organisation offers. While depression and self-harm are common among our residents, Prajwala has been successful in providing immediate psycho-social support to prevent them from harming themselves or others.

In the coming years, we faced various kinds of attack. One took place on our emergency shelter, again something that was triggered from inside, where the women damaged our property and even set fire to the building. At the time, I was attending a conference in Houston, so Raj and the police intervened. This led to a damning WhatsApp message sent by a feminist lobbyist to all the feminist leaders in the city, attacking not only me but also Raj. There was also a widely circulated article in an international daily by a freelance British journalist who vilified our work. This gentleman had not even seen our office, let alone our operations and had written a piece directly attacking me. The article, of course, had statements by anonymous activists from the sex workers' lobby in the city.

We responded as we could, within the framework of the law, filing a case against the girls who tried to burn down the shelter. The case still continues and may go on for many more years to come. The police have been unable to trace any of the women, most of whom were from various states in the north. We also filed a defamation suit against the publication, which was then forced to not only remove the article in its entirety and offer an apology but also pay our legal costs. I felt it was beneath my dignity to demand compensation for the pain and trauma they caused not only me but the mission and the organisation. No amount of money can offset that. In any case, this is also an ideological war, for both the incidents had strong connections with those who opposed us from the development sector.

When there was any unrest in Prajwala, a pattern would emerge: the same people picked up these stories, widely circulated them in WhatsApp groups and wrote articles or filed affidavits in the Supreme Court citing these incidents. It was as if we had a small but significant group constantly watching us.

What did all this do for us? It gave us clarity on the names and faces of those who opposed our ideologies, and even greater clarity regarding those who supported us and believed in our efforts. More importantly, it allowed us to review and reflect on our strategies, strengthening and streamlining them in such a way that the impact is visible and easily understood. I suppose this was the silver lining, though I didn't view it like that at the time.

But there were also instances that boosted our morale and gave us the strength to persist even when we felt attacked from all sides. One such incident occurred just a few days after the damning international article was republished in a local English daily (which has also since been scrubbed). I was feeling extremely low and disheartened, wondering what to do to counter this attack on our work. My team knew not to disturb me when I was in this mood. But then Nitin, my assistant, came in and told me that an old gentleman wanted to meet me. I looked up and silently mouthed, 'Can it be avoided?' Nitin shook his head, kept his gaze steady and asked, 'Shall I send him in?' That was an answer in itself. I gave in.

This gentleman was in his early seventies, and something about him reminded me of Daddy, perhaps the way he wore his shirt or the kind of spectacles he had on. I greeted him and offered him a seat. He sat down somewhat reluctantly and said, 'I don't want to take too much of your time, I only came to give you this.'

'This' turned out to be a cheque for Rs 11 lakh. I was stunned. It must have shown on my face, because he continued, 'I read a bad article about your work, and I thought this is the time you should know how many people support you. This is my gratuity amount and I want to donate it to Prajwala.'

I managed to get a grip on myself, and called Mallesh, our head of finance, to take the cheque and issue a receipt. All I could do was to get up and touch his feet.

He only had one parting comment, 'Kindly keep my name confidential!' I won't reveal your name, sir, but know that your actions that day were a balm on our souls. It lifted our spirits at a time when we most needed it. Your visit gave us strength—it reminded us of the worth of our work and told us we had allies even if we had enemies.

Every adversity in our life has made us stronger. The survivors in the organisation decided that they wanted to be the public face of Prajwala, and took over the entire responsibility of internal hospitality when we had visitors. They also proposed that we should have a monthly opportunity for outsiders to come and see our work. So, Parivartan Yatra, which means a journey of change, was introduced. Now, every third Saturday, outsiders could visit us for a curated tour and lunch if they registered in advance for it.

Another major position that the survivors took was that they should be given an opportunity to defend the organisation, that I should not be the only one bearing the brunt. So the survivor advocates became champions for Prajwala's beliefs.

But the most important development was streamlining our safeguard mechanisms from a trauma-informed approach and ensuring objective verifiable indicators for them. For example, we set up a protocol to address grievances, with time frames to resolve them and responsibilities assigned. This ensured that my involvement was minimal, and the entire team took the initiative to look for a solution. A monitoring mechanism tracked the timelines and connected it to monthly performance appraisals to ensure that all concerns were addressed immediately.

I have spent so much time dwelling on those who opposed us, perhaps I should also talk about those who supported us.

During the pandemic, the National Human Rights Commission brought out an advisory indicating that 'sex workers' were unorganised labour. It later pulled back the advisory based on our counter-argument.

Similarly, when the chief justice of India issued a handbook on *Gender Sensitisation for Judicial Officers* and offered 'sex worker' as a substitute for many words, including 'hooker', many of us wrote a dissenting letter. It was on the basis of that letter that the chief justice introduced the term 'trafficked victim' in the handbook.

Despite the best efforts of the sex workers' lobby and their nationwide protests, the Trafficking in Human Beings or Person Bill, 2021, which was the outcome of our 2004 PIL, argued by Aparna Bhat for eleven long years, was passed in the Lok Sabha. This bill is meant to ensure that all the victims of commercial sexual exploitation are entitled to rehabilitation. It is another matter that it did not get tabled in the Rajya Sabha and lapsed. This does not mean that it will not be passed in the coming years. Now the new Bhartiya Nyaya Sanhita (BNS), which replaces the Indian Penal Code (IPC), recognises trafficking for prostitution as an organised crime. Need I state how big a win this is?

But the best update is about Radhika. She took it upon herself to rescue all the girls enslaved by the twelve brothel keepers who had engineered the riots at our shelter. This resulted in the rescue of fifteen more girls and the arrest of more than twenty traffickers (including the original twelve). Radhika herself filed a case against all her traffickers and testified against them. The court gave the traffickers twenty years of rigorous imprisonment and awarded Rs 7 lakh to Radhika as compensation. While there is no way to compensate her for what she has endured, taking great liberties with that famous Neil Armstrong quote, I'd say that it was a great victory for her and a small blow to all sex traffickers!

Reader, you now have a glimpse into how absorbing each day of my life is, and the constant battles we fight against a vast and faceless enterprise. Every moment offers a new challenge, but the universe also reassures us in new ways that we are on the right track and what we are doing matters.

28

From Warrior to Conqueror

Like all other events in my life, cancer also came without any warning. It was 2022. I was in Delhi, addressing judicial officers at Vigyan Bhavan in a programme organised by the National Commission for the Protection of Child Rights (NCPCR). It was a marathon session. Keeping in mind COVID-19 protocols, the organisers had divided the large number of participants into two groups, and I was to talk to them both. At the end of the session, I felt a slight discomfort in my throat. I'd felt it a few days prior as well, and had attributed it to my lengthy speaking engagements.

There was also the blood in my sputum, but I ignored that too, putting that down to some abrasion in my throat or nose. When I saw it for the third time, I wasn't so sure anymore.

I decided to check with Dr Balamba, a dear friend and the president of Prajwala. She was alarmed and suggested that I immediately consult a pulmonologist. I couldn't do that right away since I was travelling, and by the time I got back to Hyderabad three days later, it had slipped my mind. I didn't find any more blood in my spit—out of sight, out of mind.

Fortunately for me, the good doctor did not forget, and that's how I ended up with a consultation at Apollo Hospital. I told Raj, although he wasn't greatly worried, since I was so casual about it. For my part, I was mildly annoyed that this had put all my work plans on hold, but I didn't say anything out of respect for Dr Balamba's concern for me.

I met the pulmonologist on Monday morning, a highly qualified young doctor who was also a great admirer of our work. We chatted about everything under the sun, and discussed the reasons for the blood in the sputum. He suggested a few tests, including a CT scan.

The scan report showed a lesion in the lungs. I was slightly taken aback, what did that mean? Googling never helps in such cases, but when I met the doctor the next day with all my results, he did not sound unduly alarmed, merely noting that we'd need even more tests to examine the lesion further.

This time, Raj was suitably alarmed but covered it up well, merely stating that he'd accompany me to all the appointments. I was rather worked up myself. This had taken up a large part of my time when I had a lot on my plate—the financial year had just concluded, the annual audit had commenced and funding for interventions such as Asha Niketan was coming to an end. The tests were also quite expensive. After two days of tests, the doctor wanted to conduct a PET scan. The scan clearly showed that the lesion was located on the left posterior lobe of the lung, and had not spread anywhere else. My doctor was quite happy with this finding, but recommended a bronchoscopy to tell them what sort of lesion it was. I had to be admitted to the hospital for this procedure, which was done under general anaesthesia.

I'd shared this news with my brother, a few close friends and two senior staff members. Obviously, they were all concerned, but I wasn't in any discomfort at all. It all just felt like too much to do when what I really wanted was to buckle down and get on with my work.

The bronchoscopy did not help matters. Uncomfortable from beginning to end—it gave me a cough, a pain in the chest and more blood in the sputum. It was as if I had become sick after coming to the hospital. After my family's nasty experience with COVID-19, I had taken medical insurance. It was a cashless card, and I was very confident it would take care of my hospital stay. But my insurance was rejected, and we had to pay by cash. This compounded my general unease and disgruntlement. All my symptoms now felt acute, and when I was discharged, I felt sick.

Then came the kicker. We had thought the bronchoscopy would end the suspense and allow us to move on to other things, but the report was inconclusive. My pulmonologist's take was that it was either a benign tumour or tuberculosis. In case it was a tumour, a thoracic surgeon could do a sectional surgery to remove it. I decided to tell everyone that it was just a tumour. The option of it being tuberculosis really did not make sense. I'd taken care of enough TB patients among our residents, and had generally observed a steep weight loss. Here I was, quite chubby, not even a few grams lighter after all those blood tests!

Only Raj, Dr Balamba and my friend Bhuwan Ribhu knew about the inconclusive bronchoscopy reports. Bhuwan, Nobel Laureate Kailash Satyarthi's son, had over the last ten years become a close friend and confidante.

Bhuwan and his wife Priyanka Barik were quite concerned and asked me to share my reports with them. As a surgery was inevitable, I requested for an emergency governing body meeting, so that the board could depute somebody to look after Prajwala's affairs if I needed a break for recuperation. In any case, it was April 2022, and the annual governing body meeting to pass the annual financials was pending.

Something told me that this was not going to be a small break. I was restless. Uncertainty bothers me. I can deal with the worst of realities if I know what it is, but all these speculations and hypothetical diagnoses played havoc with my equilibrium.

Bhuwan, meanwhile, had taken my reports to Dr G.K. Rath, the famous oncologist from the All-India Institute of Medical Sciences, New Delhi, and was taken aback when the doctor asked him why a bronchoscopy had been done when the location of the lesion was clearly evident from the PET scan. Apparently, no bronchoscopic needle could possibly reach that area. Dr Rath immediately called up Dr Vijayanand Reddy, director of oncology at Apollo Hospital, requesting him to review the reports. Dr Balamba, who checked in daily, told me she personally knew Dr Reddy, and promptly called him.

This poor gentleman, attending a conference in Prague, was bombarded with calls from India, requesting him to review my reports at the earliest. He asked to meet me at the hospital the coming Tuesday at 11.30 a.m.

That day, when Raj and I went to meet Dr Reddy, I had a lot of bodily pain. The doctor asked for the PET scan report. After one look at the report, he gave Raj and me a piercing look and stated matter-of-factly that it was lung cancer. He wanted a biopsy done immediately. I looked at Raj with much relief and a smile on my face. Finally we knew the problem. Maybe Raj found the relief in my eyes and my smile reassuring, because he looked peaceful as well.

The biopsy report confirmed the presence of a malignant cancer or adenocarcinoma. Unlike bronchoscopy, it did not require hospital admission, and the procedure was done in less than two hours.

I had no problem with the idea of cancer, but when I shared the final diagnosis with my family and colleagues, they expressed pain, shock and disbelief, all of which I found quite touching but slightly misplaced. The problem was clear to me and solutions even clearer, I was fine.

In the coming days, I knew that I'd be preoccupied with tying up loose ends at work and with the medical formalities, so I posted about my diagnosis on Facebook. The idea was that it would prevent invitations for speeches or alerts about cases. I'm not sure if I did the right thing, for the very next moment, I started getting obituary-like messages from all over the world, unsolicited advice about alternate therapy and other cancer survivors talking at length about the painful road ahead. Suddenly, the world was filled with cancer, practically everybody knew someone who either died or survived cancer and, of course, they also knew what worked best.

I had had a taste of this in 2020 too when I became one of the first COVID-19 suspects in Telangana. It was in early March 2020, I had just come back from Bangkok and had some peculiar cough symptoms. Dutifully, I declared my symptoms and was promptly isolated in a government hospital for two days, with the doctors and hospital staff treating me like I had the plague. I got a lot of media traction, and with it came a series of obituary-like messages extolling my virtues and how I had achieved so much at such a young age. This time was no different, and came with the added baggage of unasked-for advice.

Everybody except my mother knew about my condition. Daddy had passed away a few months ago, and she was coping with the deep vacuum in her life. I did not want to add this extra burden, but she needed to be told something because my brother and sister-in law, Jisha, were to come for the surgery, and Jisha was planning to stay with me at the hospital.

I gave my mum a diluted version ('Some lesion in the lungs needs to be removed!') without using the 'C' word. By now, I could see how the word 'cancer' causes panic. I must have been convincing enough—she didn't probe. As for my brother and his wife coming to Hyderabad, she probably thought the sibling bonding was good and encouraged it.

Raj was worried, I could see. He was spending more and more time on household chores. We did not have domestic help, and Raj was slowly taking over my share of tasks. Coming home early now became the norm for him. I sensed his worry, but was not in the mood to talk about it. I was raging inside.

The costs of all the diagnostic tests, now mounting to a couple of lakhs, made me realise that this is not a medical condition for the poor. My health insurance hadn't been honoured, and with the hospital admission looming, I was considering moving to a government hospital for treatment. I called my friend Dr N. Jayalatha, who was the superintendent of MNJ Cancer Hospital, a government hospital, to explore the possibility of treatment there. She assured me of all support, but warned me that they could only do a normal surgery. The government hospital wasn't equipped to offer the minimally invasive robotic surgery that would curtail the pain and facilitate quick recovery. So, the poor not only had to contend with huge costs for diagnostic tests, their treatment also involved more pain. There was clearly work to be done to make healthcare affordable, but that would have to wait.

It was back to the private hospital for me. In any case, Raj had felt reassured by Dr Reddy's competence as well as the onco-surgeon who specialised in robotic surgeries that he had recommended, Dr Chinnappa Sunkavalli.

We had bonded very well with this surgeon, Chinna as we had come to call him, who had been candid while talking about my condition and the treatment. I was greatly assured by the way he was planning my surgery, considering various contingencies. While I could not understand all the plans he'd chalked out, it made me feel that he was deeply concerned, and this was more than enough for me.

In the meantime, I had been in touch with the insurance company and been assured that I would face no problems this time. They had also started to process my previous request on a reimbursement basis.

Prajwala's group insurance for its 200-strong staff was with the same company, and my hope was that it would not make business sense for them to reject my claim once again.

Still, Raj and I dipped into our resources and arranged all that we could. My brother had already transferred some money to my account.

During this time, cancer was the least of my worries. I was preoccupied with wrapping up all that I needed to, so that Prajwala could run smoothly in my absence. Rekha and Lalita from our board were going to be responsible for administration and monitoring the programmes during my sabbatical.

Everyone there—the staff, children, women—were now aware of my condition, but didn't know how to react. I was working as if nothing was wrong. The Prajwala staff wanted to conduct a prayer meeting for my well-being. Since there was no getting out of it, I requested them to do it in smaller groups. The tears and pain, especially of my survivor staff members during these prayers, revealed the insecurity they were all going through. I was symbolic of a safe life for them. If I were gone, what would happen to them? I had personally rescued many of them, so there was also that bond. My brother and his wife, who were around, got a clearer picture of the big family I am part of that would stand by me in all crises.

On 25 April 2022, I was admitted to Apollo Hospital in the late afternoon, and the following morning, Dr Chinna and his team performed the surgery. It's good he had a Plan B. The robots were programmed for adult bodies, and could not work on my four-foot-six-inch frame. His friend, Dr Hemanth Vuduyaraju, a surgeon at Yashoda Hospital had joined this operation as Chinna's Plan B. He completed the surgery manually, sorting out the complications. The cancer was removed, with 40 per cent of my lung as well.

Dr Chinna was confident that I would not require further treatment, such as radiotherapy or chemotherapy, and that proved to be the case when the biopsy reports of the surgery came back. While the operation was a success, I was very unhappy. The health insurance had been rejected once again, and the hospital bills were mounting. With our funds and my brother's pooled in, we were still short by Rs 7 lakh. I was on oxygen full-time, and could barely speak a few sentences. Although worry consumed me, I couldn't voice it. I had worked for three decades and had no financial security. Had I made the right choices?

Then I received a visit from the hospital management. They told me that the hospital would take care of my entire medical expenses as a tribute to my work. I realised immediately that my friend Upasana Kamineni, whose family had founded Apollo Hospitals, was behind this decision. It had not occurred to me to reach out to her for help, but that she had supported me at this crucial point hugely reaffirmed my faith in my mission and my implicit trust that the powers above very taking care of me at all times.

For the next two months, I coped with a compromised lung, recovering from a major, life-altering surgery. For the first time, I understood what breath meant. We take our breathing so much for granted—what happens when you can't, even for a few seconds? I went through all this, and the transformation that comes from realising your own mortality.

But the most important question I contended with was this: all my life, I had spoken about kindness and its importance to people who sorely need it. But had I ever been kind to my own self? For two months, my emotional, physical and mental stamina wavered. This was the first time I'd ever been away from my work. Perhaps it was godly intent that I experience a complete break from everything for at least a few weeks. And it was truly a break, my first ever! A rest from talking, I'd gasp if I spoke more than a few lines. A rest from thinking, I got fuzzy and my head would ache if I concentrated. I couldn't read more than two to three pages without getting tired, I couldn't even watch a movie!

For two months, I isolated myself and chose silence. As I coped with all my discomfort, I tried to see where I could be kind to my own self. A part of me had been removed, and I needed time to recover and start functioning again.

I was looking forward to my new self, my second innings. By a happy coincidence, this took place before I turned fifty, on 22 May 2022.

There is no question that I was genuinely blessed: the cancer was diagnosed in the first stage, the right doctors saw me and the safe cocoon of my biological and extended family encompassed me. I am grateful that I am healing and am being able to write this book.

One year has gone by, and I like to be identified as 'cancer conqueror' more than a 'cancer survivor'. In fact, I sometimes forget that something like this ever happened to me. If not for the call from Chinna for my fortnightly review, I might not even remember. There is too much to do. Like Robert Frost said, 'The woods are lovely, dark and deep, But I have promises to keep, And miles to go before I sleep.'

There is one absolute truth in the world, and that is death. I do not fear it, but I definitely want to make sure that I do all that is possible to the best of my ability before my end. And for the rest, like they say, leave it up to god.

29

Why Positions Matter

From the age of fifteen, for thirty-six years now, I have been filled with an ever-increasing anger about how unjustly society treats victims of sexual violence. Anger was my constant companion when I met people, faced new situations, did what I could to help and demonstrated results.

It took some time before I realised that the world is not a homogenous unit. There are all kinds of people here. Those so lost in themselves that they do not care what happens to others, people that are affected only when their near and dear ones are and those who want to reach out but don't know how to go about it. The last two kinds of people fill me with hope, for they are the ones who can engineer change.

As a society, we accept sexual violence. We find it inevitable. And we know who is to blame. It is always the woman. The way she dresses, talks, walks, does things. Or what she didn't do. Literally anything and everything about her can be weaponised against her, used to justify the sexual violence she suffered. For the fault always, *always* lies in her. She is to blame. Who told her to go there? At that time! What was she thinking?!

Our attitude changes when it is a child, however. Thankfully, we're outraged—at least the vast majority of us. A few years ago, the head of a child welfare funding foundation asked for my thoughts on condoms for children. His organisation's position was that children in prostitution are a reality that we need to face. And since they cannot be all rescued, one should consider the possibility of 'harm reduction'. Imagine if more join this brigade and they all start looking at harm-reduction techniques in a context when younger and younger children are being sold both for online and offline sexual exploitation. There is only so much we should tolerate, and the child for me is the zero-tolerance zone. Children are easy targets, and it is imperative that every human society ensures that all our resources are directed towards prevention and protection. There is no time to waste on devising harm-reduction strategies.

Another more commonly accepted idea is that of the male libido and its vast, unquenchable ocean of desire. We need to cater to it, sate it, keep it in check or all hell will break loose. All the protocols for social control will be violently destroyed. Women and girls brutally raped in the streets. And because the expectation of chastity is only from one gender—boys, of course, will be boys—we buy into this idea and add it to the reasons to legitimise prostitution.

I remember attending an elite conference in Kolkata of women business leaders. While I received a standing ovation for my speech, there was this accomplished person who started shouting at me. Her concern: 'If you rehabilitate all these girls, what about the safety of my daughters?' It took time for the idea to sink into my thick skull that this woman *actually* believed that somebody else's daughters should be raped in a brothel so that hers could walk safely on the street.

But I can't blame her when we all internalise these patriarchal norms. My experience has been that education, wealth and accomplishments have nothing to do with kindness or concern, or even being human.

In fact, with advanced language skills and better jargon, there are those who legitimise prostitution as women's agency. This emerging way of thinking does not engage with how something that can harm your body, mind and soul can be a 'voluntary' decision, free of constraints. Such a position has huge support in terms of power and funding, for it can be used to peddle the idea of 'harm reduction'.

If even one-tenth of the health ministry's resources that focus on harm reduction are directed towards rescue and rehabilitation efforts, a huge world of change will be seen. Look at the way the Swadhar and Ujjwala homes are managed. These homes, supported by the Ministry of Women and Child Welfare, are meant for the rehabilitation of women removed from difficult circumstances, sex-trafficked victims being one of them. I was once requested by government of Andhra Pradesh to visit all the Swadhar and Ujjwala homes in the state and submit a report. Most of the homes reported that they had not received funding for three or four years in a row. My interactions with homes across the country have revealed the same neglect. Schemes such as Swadhar are so badly designed that there is not even provision for a cook, and they allocate a pitiful Rs 250 per month for the healthcare needs of a traumatised woman.

The disproportionate investment of government and international resources towards harm-reduction programmes as opposed to prevention, rescue or rehabilitation truly bothers me. Any stakeholder from the criminal justice system across the country, be it the police or the judiciary, will tell you about the huge gap in the availability of specialised homes for the care and protection of victims rescued from commercial sexual exploitation. In fact, the police confirm that there are not enough resources to conduct inter-state rescues. There have been several occasions when we had to cover the costs of bringing back the girls from another state. On one occasion, a police team from another state even requested support for their stay in Hyderabad as they were not given money for accommodation.

Any intervention that is aimed at combating commercial sexual exploitation is accorded the lowest priority in the system. If all the community-based organisations (CBO) supported by the National AIDS Control Project became part of the rescue and rehabilitation operations for at least minors—they know exactly what and where it goes on—I believe that child trafficking for prostitution in India will be reduced by half.

Traffickers co-opt the idea of women's agency into their agenda. Over time and with systematic brainwashing, they can easily ensure that a victim begins to believe it is her choice to sell sexual services—even if they got into the 'business' as a child or through coercion. Years of training and indoctrination went into making her believe those lies. Yes, she's an adult now. But does that wipe out all that she suffered as a child?

Can these devotees of self-determination declare that a significant number among these pro-choice women in prostitution were not trafficked in the past? And that the present 'willing choice' does them no harm? What angers me so much is that they do not even address these facts when they build their pro-choice narrative. In fact, I am told that some of them even state that our focus on trafficking of women in India is so that we can gather funds.

Perhaps they will respond with, 'Sorry, my liberal thinking ends with the right to self-determination. I'm not concerned about suicidal or self-harming behaviour, for that is also their choice. I am no saviour!' The way they say it, 'saviour' sounds like a crime against humanity.

This narrative, packaged in a rights-based framework, is difficult to disentangle. The language and discourse around it has become more and more liberal, leaving people like me looking more and more regressive and rigid. The result is that very many now believe that legalisation of prostitution will ensure more safety for the women in prostitution.

It is in human nature to look for easy answers, and equally to adopt a position that assures acceptance into the elite, intellectually progressive world. Take the usage 'sex worker'. A huge section of society actually thinks that it is just a more dignified word for 'prostitute', the politically correct word. Even judges in the Supreme Court have fallen to this misconception. In fact, the word 'sex worker' comes from a long labour movement that aims to legitimise the sale of sexual services. It is part of global efforts by activists who believe in the labour rights of adult women to sell sexual services willingly. In short, 'sex worker' is not a term of political correctness, but of ideological positioning.

Some former associates from my PIN days now take this position. When I ask them their view on these issues, they fumble in their explanations, but want to be on the progressive side. One of them, a man who has known me for over twenty-five years, couldn't bring himself to introduce me to the new, progressive group he's with, and kept saying that I worked with sex workers' children. I had to gently correct him: 'children of women in prostitution'.

We need more people who can advocate the right kind of thinking. The focus, in my opinion, is to first acknowledge that there could be a significant number of women who are coerced into prostitution or had to take it up due to constrained choices. The words 'sex worker' is not a replacement for the term 'woman in prostitution'. The word 'prostitution' is clearly defined in the law as 'commercial sexual exploitation', and till date, there is no legal definition adopted in India that explains the word 'sex worker'. Understanding this will ease the multiple layers of tension between the two groups, and perhaps even pave the way for a dialogue to see what exit strategies are possible for those who want to move out of sexual exploitation.

There might be also someone like Radhika who would want to fight against the injustice meted out to her, provided she got the right kind of support. Then maybe there won't be situations such as the one I faced when I filed a criminal complaint against the trafficker of a thirteen-year-old girl. The entire group of a sex workers' collective, joined by some functionaries from an international organisation, landed up at my office, demanding that I withdraw the case as the person I accused is HIV-positive and from their CBO.

A crime is a crime, no matter who commits it. In 2018, thirty-six children, the youngest being three and the oldest eleven, were rescued from the small pilgrim town Yadadrigutta and admitted to Astha Nivas. These children had been kidnapped when they were very young, and were now being groomed for prostitution by a group of women from the Dommara community who practice prostitution as a way of life. Many of the children were given hormonal injections and had been sexually abused. Practically all of them had witnessed sexual acts as part of the grooming and training. The massive rescue operation was led by the dynamic police officer Mahesh Bhagwat, and the high court had taken suo motu notice of the case. Court-ordered DNA tests were done, and none of the women claiming to be the mothers had any biological connections to the child. A high-profile human rights lawyer was representing the alleged kidnappers in court. Thanks to her legal acumen, the case has been dragging on for years now. Even though chargesheets were filed years back, the trial has not started. Do keep in mind that we are talking about children here, and the law mandates speedy trial within a year. In the interim, a few organisations held a press conference accusing us of separating mother and child. For the last five years, not a day has gone by without some talk about this or that organisation planning to submit complaints against us to statutory bodies regarding these children.

Where is the hope even to build dialogue in such a situation?

I firmly believe that approaches such as self-regulation, as advocated by sex workers' lobby, are unworkable from the criminal justice point of view. The model offered is this: when they know a woman is coerced into sexual exploitation, they will make all efforts to restore that person back to their family. So, here's my simple question: how many criminal cases have they filed against those involved in coercion? Surely the woman did not coerce herself? Are there no other players involved? The abettors? To my knowledge, no such case has been filed anywhere in the country.

Proactive interventions such as these would definitely raise the bar of trust between the two groups, and perhaps initiate a dialogue to figure out the markers or indicators to identify trafficked or coerced persons in a given brothel, whether offline or online. This would truly be of great help to all those involved in rescue efforts. Consider a website that sells adult sexual services. Is there a way that the law enforcer can identify those who have been forced into selling sex and made to pose as willing women?

Let the women in prostitution who are reconciled to their fate continue in that line, but they ought to know—and have the choice—that, if they want to exit, support is well within their reach. I will do everything in my power to help women exit prostitution, not just in the first instance, but practically, by providing them with the capacity for alternate livelihood means.

There is a practical approach to the exit strategy. Resource investment in helplines and support systems for women in prostitution are concrete places to begin. Additionally, mainstreaming prevention campaigns in existing government programmes is perhaps the most cost-effective approach to addressing this problem.

If the government, international agencies and other groups can take up the fight against HIV/AIDS on a war footing and invest all that they have in it, why can the same not be done to combat commercial sexual exploitation, which contributes to the problem?

Maybe—and just maybe—if this prioritisation comes about, more NGOs will also join the brigade to fight sex trafficking from an actual intervention perspective.

While Prajwala has evolved into a powerful force to advocate for prevention and rehabilitation, it has been in the face of a persistent onslaught. We survived the attacks and vilification campaigns only because there are people out there—donors, supporters, thought leaders, influencers, policymakers and a range of well-wishers—who stood by us.

The fight for change is a tough one and sure to continue beyond our lifetimes, perhaps why so few remain on this side. And perhaps also why many organisations limit themselves to working with children—there's some kind of universal common consensus about them. I continue to hold out hope that the few harm reductionists in our midst do not take over that space as well, and so-called progressive lawyers do not become the voice for alleged offenders of child rights.

At some level, despite my dedicated and professional colleagues, and in spite of the vast network of well-wishers, it continues to be a lonely battle. Ultimately, it is the survivors themselves who give me true hope. When provided with access to opportunities and an enabling space to discover their strengths, they are able to voice their position. I have had several occasions to witness this. During the pandemic, my friend Salil Kader and I had started a virtual discussion series called #RealityCheck to initiate a dialogue around anti-human-trafficking interventions. Reshma, a survivor advocate and a vocal leader, was to be part of an episode. She immediately put her foot down, insisting that the language of communication—including that of the experts—should be one they all understood, not English. If it was to be an episode meant to understand the needs of the survivors, then it should be conducted accordingly. She would not be 'used' as nominal presence for anybody. We conducted that episode in Hindi, which most girls understood, and they spoke with great confidence, while the experts, who spoke Hindi well enough, but had not really used the language on formal platforms, were fumbling for words.

In another virtual interaction with an international agency, I had two survivors sitting with me in the background as I wanted them to understand what was spoken at such international forums. One organisation meant to be a federation of, by and for survivors was represented by a professional communications specialist. After the interaction was over, the only thing my girls asked was this: why is a non-survivor representing a survivor federation? Are these federations so well-funded that they can hire very articulate communications specialists? A point to ponder.

In an informal debate with my girls, I was playing the devil's advocate, and asked them what was wrong if women and girls chose sex work? It could be informal work, like many people are claiming. Iti Mirza, a soft-spoken girl, asked me quietly, 'If your own daughter chose it, will you allow her to go?' Another robust voice, Shravanthi, jumped in and said, 'Like school of social work, maybe it is better to also establish a school of sex work! After all, now there are more and more courses for informal work.'

Survivor engagement and bringing survivors' voices to the mainstream is the most 'in' thing now. Like so many other things that can be misused, this space could also be at risk. Many organisations publish opinions under the banner of survivors while peddling their own position.

Survivors and survivor articulation are the only real forces that can defeat those who legitimise sex slavery. But it must be an organic evolution.

My role in all this is to build an enabling environment for that to happen. It is an uphill battle. Most child survivors, once they grow up and pursue professional careers, want to leave their past behind and move on with their lives. They do not want to be repeatedly reminded of past trauma. Many do not even like to keep in touch with us, for our very name signifies what they have left behind as a closed chapter in their life. Once, a donor who had supported our community-based economic empowerment programme wanted to meet at least one girl in action at work. Without really thinking about it, I took them to an auto stand in the city outskirts, where one of our women was driving an auto. The woman saw me from afar with my two guests, and quickly left that place. Later, she called me and requested me to never come to the auto stand directly. If anything was required, she would come to the office. She was apologetic, but firm. 'I already face so many problems working in a male-dominated space. If they learn that I was trafficked, they'll make my life miserable.' I was truly ashamed of my short-sightedness.

A child survivor who got placed in a prominent hotel explicitly requested our team to never come anywhere near the hotel for any kind of follow-up. She fervently requested the team to convey to me that, if I visited the hotel, to never refer to her as 'my child'. We've had problems in schools where the older children have been subjected to probing questions by curious teachers who might have read a positive article about us. Many refused to attend school after that. Those who are married and socially reintegrated also feel the same. Once they are settled with their families, they do not want unnecessary reminders of their old lives.

Survivor engagement can be done only with a select group of survivors who choose to come back to the organisation to join the mission. Mindful programming to build such an option is critical in facilitating this outcome. We have been successful in building, slowly but systematically, a group of such powerful voices to lead our community-sensitisation programmes.

This group, if truly empowered, cannot be tutored by anybody. That has been my experience. If a survivor joins us when she needs temporary financial relief, she might just say whatever we are advocating. But if anybody probes further, she may end up saying, 'I don't know, this is what these people asked me to say.' The key to building survivor leadership is to create as many avenues as possible for this person to reflect on her life journey, to understand the larger picture, explore her convictions and figure out what her true opinion or stance is. Every survivor is not a leader.

There are survivors who join Prajwala with the sole intention of serving, and are not interested in advocacy efforts—just as there are social workers who are willing to dedicate themselves to welfare programmes, but do not feel comfortable taking up a rights-based fight. A good set of such survivors are now part of our caregiving team. I guess each one of us finds our own space of comfort from where we can contribute, and every contribution has its own relevance and importance.

The forces working towards legitimising prostitution might face similar challenges. This will be an ongoing struggle for all of us, and we must each figure out our own way forward.

After our Swaraksha Caravan, which had travelled over 15,600 kilometres, and interacted with more than a million people across dozens of districts in three states, the government of Telangana declared every third Saturday as Swaraksha Day. Survivor leaders join government functionaries on this day in their respective districts to sensitise adolescent girls. The inclusion of survivor leaders in a state programme is highly significant. The government is directly listening to them.

Within Prajwala as well, I see more and more survivor advocates being mentored by senior survivor leaders. They have become a force to reckon with, challenging us every day to review and reflect on our existing programmes.

I started my life by connecting with women on the ground, learning from them, observing the world around them, listening to their pleas, witnessing their strength, admiring their resilience and bowing before their generosity of spirit. I do the same today, as I watch thousands of child and adult survivors emerging gracefully from the fire of their trauma, recovering their life, rebuilding their dignity and courageously leading others. My political positions have evolved over the course of living, interacting and deeply engaging with thousands of undefeatable women and girls—my Aparajitas. I do not think it happened in a day. I made mistakes, blundered and floundered, but I had the courage of conviction to acknowledge my myopia and review my approach. Today, I am still a work in progress, and I have been for the last thirty years.

30

The Long Game

The last year of my father's life, and especially the last six months, were a critical period in my own life, forcing me to assess and review the choices I'd made.

During the second wave of the pandemic, my family—my dad, mom and younger brother—were admitted to hospital with coronavirus, with my mom and brother in the ICU for a couple of days. That month-long situation was emotionally draining, unpredictable and scary, as more and more deaths were being reported everywhere. Through my contacts, my family managed to get beds and good care in the hospital, but when the final bill came, despite my brother's health insurance, there was a significant amount left to be paid. I felt helpless when faced with that sum. But as a family, we pulled all our resources together and managed.

As with the cancer, it was a time that I had to reflect on my life choices. Was it a sensible choice to be a permanent volunteer in a mission that does not allow me to take even a day off, where I only earn enough to keep me afloat from day to day? What sense does it make when you can help thousands of children, but are unable to support your own family financially?

It is not that I have not tried to contribute. On my behalf, Raj designed and oversaw the construction of my parents' house, financing a major part of it. They have a small but nice place to stay. Raj and I have tried to fulfil all of my dad's wishes, including going on an international holiday—his eightieth birthday was celebrated in Bangkok.

It was also my dad's wish to write about his adventures while working with the Survey of India. I worked with him to finish his biography and we released it on 21 August 2021 on Onam, the biggest festival for Malayalis. His biography, titled *Ormakal/Memories*, is a bilingual book, a rich collection of anecdotes from his life that features select pictures. He passed away three months later, at the age of eighty, on 29 November 2021, content. From the time he turned seventy-three, my father kept declaring that he will only die after seventy-five, so that he can claim his full pension. Daddy was greatly concerned about any news related to salaries, pension, dearness allowance, insisting on updating the bank passbook every month, just in case the government decided to give him a bonus. Online banking was not an option, he had to physically meet his dear bank manager every month.

Daddy's death was a blow for me. I had lost a friend and an unconditional supporter. During the memorial services ceremony, we distributed his autobiography to all those who attended. Everyone remarked that they had no clue he had accomplished so much, or that he was the one who had surveyed the northeast frontiers and received the governor's medal for the same. They also did not know that he had survived a forest fire and an avalanche. He was an unsung hero as a person and as a father, never getting the credit for his largeness of spirit.

His death made me question many things, including taking stock of where I have reached, and whether I have upheld his simple, unconditional faith in my choices.

So where have we reached as an organisation?

Prajwala is one of the largest anti-sex trafficking organisations in the world. We have demonstrated that rehabilitation is an achievable reality, not a myth. As a unique intervention that has shown considerable success in all its verticals—prevention, rescue, rehabilitation, social reintegration and advocacy—it is a model for governments to learn from and replicate. Prajwala is also a powerful statement of what can be achieved through partnership, be it with survivors or with officials from the government (state and national) and international bodies, and has proved beyond doubt that state and non-state partners can work together for the common good. Equally, we have shown that, in the fight to end human trafficking, listening to the voices of survivors is central to building initiatives and approaches.

Our engagement with victims and survivors is now at a stage where we can see tangible outcomes: our survivors are professionals, some are even survivor advocates who lead Prajwala, many are married, with families of their own, and we've had hundreds of convictions as well. Our prevention intervention has cleaned some areas of street prostitution completely, and one intervention with sex buyers has had zero recidivism. We are perhaps the only organisation other than the UNODC that has designed a number of training manuals and handbooks to train officials on human trafficking. Our education programme now includes the vulnerable urban poor, and has been integrated with vocational skills, ensuring that thousands of youths are employable. With all this, our financial needs have increased, and the struggle to make the organisation financially sustainable is a never-ending challenge.

Prajwala has evolved over the last twenty-seven years. We now have a robust governing body, with committed individuals concerned about the cause. The team has different programmes, with competent leaders for each intervention. Today, my role has shrunk to mostly mentoring, administration, advocacy and fund-raising. During my break, while I recuperated, not a single intervention suffered. Perhaps the next step is to set up teams dedicated to fund-raising and for advocacy.

While reflecting over these past decades, I have come to realise that change comes from within. You need to articulate and acknowledge the transformation within you to make it visible. If you cannot see what you have done, how do you expect anybody else to acknowledge it? This articulation of the years gone by is important. It helps you understand your past, and shows the world the struggle, pain and sacrifice it extorted from you to achieve your current reality.

This reflection has also made me realise something so basic, it ought not need articulation—intention needs to be followed up by action. If you really want to end trafficking, you need to get into the field, get your hands dirty and start evolving responses. Sitting in the comfort of your study or living room, and making strong presentations on human trafficking does not change the world. Go out there and start hitting at the organised crime from all possible ends—do the work, and in the real world.

I want to end sexual violence in its entirety, but I also want to be acknowledged for this. I want to be known as somebody who did not accept the wisdom of the ages of it being an inevitability. I want to demonstrate to the world it *is* possible to change—if all of us work towards this, it *will* change. I do not want to be another face in the crowd, I want to be known as the one that tried to correct a fundamental wrong. And I want this recognition not just in public life, but even in my personal life.

There is enormous damage to not being recognised for your efforts: it is the easiest way to kill an idea, a practice, a position, an ideology and even perhaps a truth. Articulating your choices and making them understood to the world around you is a big part of bringing about that transformation. When your efforts are understood, other similar-minded people will join the effort, perpetuating a cycle that will finally achieve the goal.

Recognition is a sign of progress, that's what makes it so important. If I believe in changing the world of sexual violence, then I have to keep talking about what can change that situation, about newer interventions to accelerate that change, about the results of those interventions, and I have make sure that everybody acknowledges it. If Prajwala or its work is ignored, it means rehabilitation as a model has been bypassed, and people can conveniently continue to say prostitution is a necessary evil and that it cannot be changed.

My anger has helped me build concrete responses and driven me to take up bigger challenges. Today, I am no longer driven by my own individual response. As part of Prajwala, I represent a large family with extraordinary, committed individuals from all over the globe who also believe in the change I envision. Prajwala is not only the name of our organisation, it also signifies a movement to end sex trafficking and sex crime. Anybody who believes in that mission is Prajwala too.

I am Prajwala and, like millions of other Prajwalas, I believe in a world free of sex slavery. I do not know what lies ahead, and have no regrets. Every day of my life has gone into making me a billionaire of moments. Today I know that there is no such thing as 'no option'—everything is possible if we work towards it.

As an individual, I am learning to be more kind to myself, ensuring that I slowly build some level of financial security for myself and my family. Now I take time off and nurture every relationship that nourishes my soul. I will continue my mission with renewed force, but perhaps be more mindful and strategic, without allowing the toxicity of my adversaries to touch me. At the same time, I hope to have the openness to build better bridges for a dialogue to defuse this vitriol. After all, there is space for all of us in this universe. And hopefully, with my positivity, I will bring about more transformation in mindsets all around me.

31

I Am What I Am

Today, I am supposed to testify. This is a case that I had filed in 2014. Two traffickers were found extorting families of victims by falsely claiming to be Prajwala staff. The case is finally coming up for trial eight years after the original complaint was filed.

As I walk through the crowded corridors of Nampally court, escorted by two team members and a court constable, I am reminded of that day many years back when I was attacked in the same corridors. Back then, sex trafficking cases were heard in the excise court (why these cases were given to the excise court is a mystery to me till date) located in the cellar. The corridor used to be dark and dingy. Back then, I had come alone for the hearing in a case that I'd filed against a trafficker (a member of one of the CBOs) who had trafficked a thirteen-year-old girl. As I headed down the corridor, a group of lawyers crashed into me. I felt an elbow being shoved right into my stomach, and doubled over in agony. The apology came after a pause—I could not see the face, but the voice was crystal clear in my ears. It was the voice of the defence lawyer who was cross-examining me, accusing me of fabricating the case and falsely implicating his client. Somehow, I walked through the pain, sat at the witness stand and completed my cross-examination. The trafficker was convicted for seven years and fined Rs 50,000. It was the first conviction we had achieved.

Today, when I walk down these same corridors, I am secure in the knowledge that my team is closely ensuring my safety and security with the support of a court constable. The public prosecutor has made sure that I am seated in a secure place till our case is called. It's been a long journey to this time.

After my court appearance, I had to go to the Protection of Children from Sexual Offences (POCSO) court. An eight-year-old from our home was testifying against her father. This man had not only sexually assaulted her but also sold her to his friends. I wanted to be there for her. As a person of support for the child, authorised by the CWC, I was allowed to sit inside the court where the in-camera trial was going on. I watched my little angel testify in a clear voice against her father and his friends. The defence lawyer tried his best to confuse and rattle her, but the child looked steadfastly only at the compassionate magistrate and spoke with such clarity that even the defence was at a loss for words. Finally, the judge asked the child what should be the punishment given. In her high, clear voice, she said, 'Capital punishment, so that no father does this to any child.'

I could see the judge's face; the colour had changed. She kept her professional calm, but it was clear that she was as affected as I was, tears pouring from my eyes, blurring my vision. Only a few years ago, a different child had accused me of kidnapping her before the police in the presence of her criminal mother, was re-trafficked to Pune and admitted to our shelter years later, where I had to cremate her after she died of AIDS. This little one represents the confidence victims gain in our therapeutic community, gaining the strength of conviction to testify against perpetrators, even when they are parents.

We are not always successful. The other day, I was reading the daily report of Astha Nivas sent by the coordinator. She was describing a fight that had happened in the home with some new children. One child, just about twelve years old, was shouting that she would kill one of the children, and then 'Big Madam' (which is me) will be sent to jail and the shelter will be closed. How deeply traumatised and indoctrinated this child must be to make the connection between murder and shutting down the home. This is why I feel so strongly about a zero-tolerance approach regarding children and sex trafficking. The damage to the child, to the future person they will be, to society, to the nation is far-reaching.

Over the years, there has been a small but significant number of victims, both women and children, whom I have failed. No matter how much we tried, in how many ways we tried, we could not get through to them. The victim remained a victim, hostile and aggressive, and I would give up and request the court or the CWC to shift the person to some other facility as the toxicity of the hostility was affecting other survivors. In one instance, we came to know an adult victim who had seemingly been on the road to recovery after ten months of stay with us, and had been pursuing training in carpentry. It turned out that she had remained in touch with her trafficker throughout the stay using the weekly phone call option. She had even asked him to pose as her brother in court.

Every such instance leaves behind pain and guilt in my heart, exactly like how I feel when we enter a red-light area to rescue some victims and leave behind hundreds as we do not have the logistical ability to handle greater numbers. Then again, you might not be able to change the whole world, but you can change the world of individuals whom you care for and nurture.

After my brush with cancer, I felt strongly compelled to meet all my children. Our team organised a nice reunion. Most of our children were now grown-up women who had become doctors, engineers, graphic designers, camerawomen, gym trainers, social workers, lawyers or were married with kids. My team had placed a comfortable chair for me in a position from where I could see the gate clearly. I saw a smart young woman in police uniform entering the campus, and wondered why she had come. There had been no rescue the previous night. Was she here for any of the victims in our shelter or had she come to deliver some message from one of the police stations we worked with? I was just going to call out for Ali to take care of her as hundreds had come for the reunion, and I did not want the police officer to feel unattended. Then I saw the her smile at me, and did a double take.

Surely it was not Rizwana! Was this my first rescued child from Mehendi whose little fingers I had held as we ran from one auto to another, my nose and ears bleeding, before we reached Sister Severine's place? Images of Sultana, Akbar, Jaffer flashed through my mind. I have no idea where or how they are now. We'd fallen out of touch with each other as life took us our different ways. Do they even know that the little one they had risked their lives to rescue was now a head constable in the police force?

I had lost in touch with Rizwana after her junior college. We supported her education and hostel fees when she was doing her graduation, and once she found a private job, she had slowly stopped communicating. I thought, like so many children who prefer not to be reminded of their past, she too wanted her space, so we let her go.

But now she was back, smiling ear to ear, smart in her uniform, carrying a beautiful memento of a mother and child in her hand. For once, I was speechless.

My children hugged me, cried their hearts out, danced for me, submerged me with hundreds of gifts and reminisced over stories that I had forgotten, stories of the times I had cooked for them, danced with them, sat next to them in the hospital bed, shouted at them. For the first time, we expressed what they were to me and what I was to them.

I felt like the queen of the universe.

That's when I realised I had always been the queen ... whether I'd been staying in the filthy slums of Chaderghat, sharing a bathroom with many families in a shanty, or at Shalibanda in my two-room house, or now, in a nice small flat. When had I ever lacked anything? I'd been pampered. Unconditional love, devotion and generous display of gratitude and gifts had always followed me everywhere I went. So lost and consumed was I in my journey that I had not paused to relish them.

I do not think I was a great strategist or a planner. I simply took things one day at a time. For the better part of three decades, I never gave a thought to the consequences of the choices I made in my personal life. To my mind, I am only an instrument in the hands of higher powers. Never had my choices felt like a burden or a sacrifice. It was just my way of living. And no harm came of it. On the contrary, I only gained every minute. My soul is contented, my heart full of joy and my mind is filled with renewed purpose.

Aren't these the reasons why people work hard to further their careers, amass wealth and acquire properties? I know I have got more than what I have given. I also know I cannot take credit for what I am doing, as some unknown power has always guided me quietly.

Does that mean I have no unfulfilled wishes, that I am above earthly desires? Absolutely not. All my life I have wished to own a small villa or cottage with a garden and a beautiful swing. My fantasy includes a cook who can whip up delicious vegetarian food from both north Indian and south Indian cuisine. I should be able to invite guests and feed them to their heart's content. Just the idea of asking my guests what they're craving and softly instructing my cook leaves me with a nice feeling. Another fantasy is to walk up the stage to receive an Oscar, although I'm not sure in which category. I have even visualised my dress and my speech! But not all fantasies will come true. I am good with that too. No tax on dreaming, right?

That day, after the reunion, I walked down to my chambers, and on my table was a beautiful letter from Bhavani. This is the child whose mother had sold her, and who had been instrumental in rescuing her younger siblings from the clutches of her mother. Bhavani is now a chartered accountant, and she had written to thank me for all the support she had received from the organisation. She now wished to financially support her siblings still under our care—one is pursuing a degree in nursing and the other a degree in arts. Bhavani wanted to reduce the financial burden of the organisation by taking care of her siblings, and promised that she would take care of more children as and when her finances improved. Here is a child whose sheer perseverance is remarkable. Against all odds, she completed her board exams through open school, competed with regular students in her junior college, topped the district, self-coached to qualify as a chartered accountant and pursued her education without any tutors. Now she wants to take care of more children like her. Is there anything more inspiring?

Happily, yes. There are even more inspiring stories to share. Seema, the child-mother who was coerced to entertain customers to protect her little son from being bitten by a dog, leads our rescue missions today. She and Noorjahan are daunting figures in any operation. I do not think they have failed in a single rescue assignment. Seema is filled with an energy that is never sated. She is constantly on the lookout for information and ready any time, day or night, to plunge into a rescue. Her goal—to end trafficking!

Life has come to a full circle. The challenges and struggles of the initial years have been replaced by newer trials. The geographical area of twenty kilometres that we operated within in the Old City of Hyderabad has now expanded across eleven countries. From four in the team, we have over 200 spread across India. But what remains the same, then to now, are our indicators of success. The smiles and restored dignity of survivors, the only markers of our impact, have remained unchanged from 1996 to today.

EPILOGUE

Acknowledging My Debts

I am given to strange likes and dislikes. Likes are fine, but disliking people—that creates trouble for me and the other party. And once I get it in my head that I dislike them, I start looking for more and more reasons to justify that feeling. I can also be very nasty to the media. I snub people with a single no, especially if I believe that it will harm our women and girls. I know this can work against me; a century from now, we'll be remembered through the accounts written about us. Those who are not media-savvy will be erased from public memory. But I forget this almost every time I refuse interviews, so I am at a disadvantage when I desperately need the press. Thankfully, social media allows me to record my work, thoughts and beliefs in my own words, which has the potential to reach larger audiences and even change perspectives.

Of course, several media groups have consistently stood up for our cause and the campaigns that we have initiated. Whether it was NDTV for the #ShameTheRapist campaign or Sakshi TV for #Swaraksha, when the situation arose, they went beyond ordinary news coverage and formulated special programmes to highlight our cause. Senior journalist and businessman Ravi Prakash who used to head TV9 proposed training our survivors as camerapersons. This led to the training of twenty survivors, some of whom now hold senior positions at very reputed television channels. Sakshi TV held a fundraiser for us when our second facility was being built, and a little girl of eight years who was watching the show donated all the savings in her piggy bank, a sum of Rs 8,000. What an amazing gesture! And what an amazing transformation of a young mind! My appearances on the television programme *Satyamev Jayate* hosted by Aamir Khan and the 'Karamveer' episode on *Kaun Banega Crorepati* hosted by Amitabh Bachchan (Yes, the same Mr Bachchan against whom I protested during the Miss World times) made an extraordinary impact on the audience and forced them to consider these causes. Even today, I have people quoting from the *Satyamev Jayate* episode, which happened in 2012, when they try to connect with me. Such is the power of the media. But I have chosen to use it only selectively. It is another matter that when I need them, they don't need me. In the coming years, I will definitely find a balance.

I'm known to reject awards and refuse to make speeches. Once you get a major award, hundreds of organisations offer you smaller ones because you are now visible. I have refused all such awards, not because I think they are insignificant, but because I believe people who are in the early stages of their initiatives deserve them more. I know the pain of not being heard. Awards give you recognition and even more importantly, a platform to shout about your cause. By accepting every small award, I would be denying another worthy person an opportunity to highlight their important work. As for speeches, my great worry is that they'll turn me into someone who is all talk and no action. I am not a motivational orator or even a well-read person, so every time I speak, I parrot the same points. The only invitation I'm happy to take up, no matter what, are requests to speak to stakeholders in the criminal justice system. I think it is the right investment of both my time and life; it directly contributes to changing the perception towards a victim and building a victim-friendly system.

I am sometimes easily misunderstood because of the foolish ways in which I construct an English sentence. For example, I am of the firm belief that I should be available when somebody is in trouble, even if I fail to be there during happier times. One of the weirdest ways I expressed this was when somebody gave me their wedding card. I said, 'All the best, I cannot come to your wedding, but I'll be sure to attend your funeral!' If one of my hapless victims hadn't ranted about this to my staff, I wouldn't have realised my blunder.

Another bugbear is that people want to donate things they no longer have any use for, such as furniture, and are hurt when we don't want it either. We're not a dumping ground for their discards. Why should I accept something from a person who doesn't care if we need or want it? They consider it a benevolent act of charity that people or social workers like me should accept with gratefulness; if we don't, then we have an attitude.

Once, a Non-Resident Indian woman contacted me and said that she wanted to donate laptops. Now this is something that we definitely need since all our systems are more than ten years old, so I invited her over. She brought fifteen brand new boxes and was accompanied by her two teenage daughters and her mother-in-law. As soon as she sat down, she gave me two papers to sign. They basically declared that her daughters had volunteered at our organisation, and had donated these laptops to improve our work. The brand-new boxes were right in front of me, so I grudgingly signed the papers. They were not too keen to see the work we did, and quickly completed their visit and left. Afterwards, I asked our administrative team to open the boxes and list the staff members to whom the laptops could be allocated. Just imagine our shock when we found ancient, second-hand laptops nicely packed in the new boxes. Even worse, only two of the fifteen worked. The rest had to be disposed of as condemned goods beyond repair. How low do people stoop?

On the other hand, I feel that we are doing something vital for society, and that society is morally bound to support causes like ours. I get angry when people make me feel as if they are doing us a big favour by donating to Prajwala, as if I personally created the problem of human trafficking and they are just helping me to solve it.

It's the same thing with volunteers. Each one of them wants to do it within their comfort zones, either virtually, or when they have some time now and then, as if it's a hobby. I think they are trying to assuage some guilt in their mind rather than really support us. There are even those who will just barge into our office without an appointment and then make a long face when they are asked to return based on our availability. One man, claiming that he wanted to volunteer, landed at our campus at 6 p.m. on a Sunday, and when we refused him, wrote a long piece on Facebook accusing us of being opaque and hiding something. There are all kinds around us.

If people wanted to really support us, they would realise we also have some work–life balance to consider. Maybe the children in the shelter, after a busy week of being disciplined, only want to watch films and laze around on a Sunday. Maybe staff members want to wash their clothes and let their hair down. Maybe it is a big logistics nightmare to organise virtual events in a remote village where connectivity is a challenge.

The people who care for the cause and truly believe in our mission take great pains to offer their skills. Brother Narayanan, an eighty-year-old from the Brahma Kumari group, travelled almost 175 kilometres every week for over five years to conduct meditation sessions for our women and girls. He'd seek an appointment through my assistant Nitin to give me some of my favourite prasadam. He could have just walked right into my cabin, but he never took that liberty. Another volunteer is Deepti, a homemaker. She considers Prajwala her religion, and is the first one to ensure that her friends and associates respond to any emergency need of the organisation. She's helped set up our kitchens, and contributed in countless ways to the weddings of our survivors, fairly regular events every year. Thanks to her and her friends, none of our girls has looked like a poor bride who did not have enough of her own. Each of them left with great dignity and pride, secure in the knowledge that people cared for them immensely and showed it tangibly.

Another friend of the cause is Upasana Kamineni Konidela. She would call me up every quarter, jot down the needs of the women and children that nobody else was able to fulfil and then go about making them happen (the requests usually tended to be for feasts of Chinese food or pizza).

I also tend to discourage educational certification through our work. I'm not keen on facilitating a transactional association that only benefits the student and never the mission. It is very difficult for anyone to understand the complicated layers of our functioning in a month, so we end up giving applicants an office assistant's job and then handing over a certificate. I have made exceptions to this rule only for law students, and some of them have indeed contributed greatly. For instance, Anna Wolf, who interned with us for two years, and Kristen Joy Wade, who was a student volunteer for another organisation but ended up becoming one of the greatest friends of the mission. Anna showed me what an ardent learner looks like, happily compromising on personal comfort to learn and contribute.

Kristen is a true believer of the cause, and dreams of a day when a multi-billionaire will spot Prajwala and ensure that we are financially sustained, giving me the opportunity to delink from fund-raising. Thanks to these two, now I am open to paid interns who are willing to commit at least two years of their life to the organisation.

The trust of such people generates hope and confidence in us in a world that's suspicious and cynical about our work.

Like any other person, I also crave power, especially the power to change and influence society. But I have never applied for positions, no matter how prestigious. I have been lucky to be nominated for honorary positions, one in Andhra Pradesh, as a member of the State Commission for Women, which was traditionally only politically nominated, and the position of honorary advisor to the government of Kerala for the Nirbhaya project. Such designations and honours have made me appear to be financially privileged, especially because of the international awards I have received that had cash attached to them. Right from the very first international award, the Perdita Houston Human Rights Award, which connected me to a dear friend, Karen Mulhauser, I have funnelled that cash back into Prajwala, insisting that the transfers be made directly to the organisation. I continue to remain a permanent volunteer of Prajwala, a servant of god doing what I have been sent to do in this world. Among the international agencies that have honoured me, I have greatly benefited, both professionally and personally, from the Vital Voices Global Partnerships and Tällberg Foundation. Both these organisations widened my personal understanding of issues that challenge the world, and have been responsible for my growth as both a woman leader and a humanitarian leader, gaining clearer perspective about solutions for emerging problems. Another great influence in my life is one award that I was nominated for but never got, the Aurora Humanitarian Prize. I was bowled over by the philosophy of the Aurora Foundation. Started by Armenian genocide survivors, it believes in 'gratitude in action', and expects the winner to share the sum that has been awarded with three other organisations in the world. What an absolutely transformative idea—continuing the chain of giving in a world where there is so much competition for resources. By and large, this foundation has made me reflect deeply on whether I've shared the gifts that Prajwala, as an organisation, or I, as an individual, have received to build a safe world.

Giving is not something that is in everybody's DNA, and giving with sincerity is a rarer quality. But there are many who have overwhelmed me with their generosity. One person who deeply moved me with her big heart is Revathy Subramaniam. She offered support for our work, and when I told her about my difficulties in mobilising funds for one of the shelters, she immediately committed to support us from her own personal savings for the next three years. She is not a billionaire or even a businessperson, but she believes she has enough for her sustenance and can give away the rest.

My situation is like Lord Venkateshwara of Tirupati who could not pay back his debts to Lord Kubera. But that is where our similarity ends for, unlike him, who has millions of devotees (including me) helping him repay his debt, I only seem to be falling deeper and deeper in debt to my loved ones who, with their unshakeable faith and unconditional acceptance, have moulded my life.

Two people I will forever remain indebted to and will never able to repay even in a hundred lifetimes are my parents, Raju and Nalini Krishnan. When I was assaulted, they stood by me with their silent strength, never questioning me, never doubting me and never allowing me to fall apart. Never did they say a word about the humiliation they were subjected to because of the choices I made. And then, when I chose to dedicate my life to fight sex trafficking and sex crime, they never stood in my way. I don't remember even a small statement that could have acted as an obstacle in my life. They simply allowed me to chart my own destiny. How many people in this world get such unconditional support, especially when they embark on rough, unchartered waters?

I have mentioned my father multiple places, and the deep bond that I shared with him. But my mother needs a special mention too. My mother is the person whom I think I get some of my best qualities from—compassion, generosity and a sense of fun. While Daddy's whole focus was on ensuring that all of us got a decent upbringing, it is Mummy who taught us the values of generosity. When we were young, I remember how, throughout the year, she would set aside some clothes she thought were 'extra' for us. She would ensure they were stitched properly and ironed neatly before packing them into a bag. Every three years, when we went to Thamarapadam, she would give them to our cousins. Again, with four children, my parents could barely manage our own needs, and yet, my mother found it in her to constantly notice and give away all the 'extra' we had.

When Prajwala was born, one of the first rescues we did was of Viju. I had enrolled Viju in a convent school, and that first summer, Sister Warden refused to keep any children in the hostel. All the parents and guardians were asked to take back their wards. I had no idea what to do with this child. During one of my telephone calls to my mother, I casually mentioned that a friend's daughter needed a place to stay for the summer. My mother did not hesitate even for a second, and told me to bring her home to Bangalore. And that is how six-year-old Viju ended up staying with my parents for that summer. One look at the child, and my mom knew there were no parents in the picture, but she did not ask a single question. Viju was treated as a grandchild. Today, Viju has completed her MSc in pharmacy, is married and has a one-year-old baby. Maybe memories of that summer are part of what makes Viju an exception among our children. She is among the minuscule few who has never dissociated her identity from Prajwala's. She not only insisted that her in-laws know about her roots in Prajwala but also makes sure her child recognises me as her maternal grandmother.

My mother has the amazing gift of being able to accept a person without any judgement, and unconditionally gives love even to strangers. I think some of those qualities have trickled into me as well.

But one of the precious treasures that I have from my mother is to be contented with small joys and find satisfaction in every effort made. Even today, at seventy-three, she is the most fun person to be around, and lives each day as if it is a boon that needs to be enjoyed.

They say that behind every successful man there is a woman. Behind me are these two humans whom I proudly call parents.

Talking about debts, I cannot forget to mention friends like Geeta Sekhon, Aparna Bhat, Bhavana Chiranjay, Lalita Iyer, Jomey Joseph, Geeta Menon, Shoba Veigas, Sharada Manne, Lavanya Ravulapally and Salil Kader. They have spoilt me silly, and ensure that I do not lack anything, whether it be diamonds or Mills & Boons! They make me rich with their love.

Such love makes sense, for I return it equally. But for people like Dr Mohan Reddy, my ENT surgeon, I feel overwhelming gratitude and don't know how to repay all the good they brought to my life. For years he has treated me, carried out a major surgery on my right ear to restore partial hearing, and yet has never taken a single penny for his professional services. I continue to walk into his nursing home NOVA, as I have for the past twelve years, and not a single staff member has ever asked me to pay. I must be doing something right to deserve all this.

How could I have written this autobiography about a life that battles major storms every day? For this I owe Srijith, who introduced me to Manish Kumar Garg and Rajni Nair Deb of Hilton Hotel, Manyata Park, Bangalore. These two beautiful human beings have given me a safe haven cut off from the whole world, adequately fed me and provided the right kind of ambience for me to take a step back and reflect on my life. I am forever indebted to them and Hilton Hotel that my story is finally tangible in the form of this book (even if the walls of Hilton know a lot more than any of you ever will) and will reach the world in my lifetime.

Finally, a group of human beings who make me whole, who touch my core every minute, give me hope every day and lift me up when I am down in the dumps, encouraging me to do better, making me believe my goals are possible and revalidate every moment of my chosen path are the smiles of my children and women.

When Puja, one of my children, completed her masters in social work and found her first job, she gave me her first salary. I cannot describe the pride that flooded my being. While I returned most of what she gave me, I did accept one of the notes and laminated it as my good luck charm. It is the same feeling when my children want to give away their clothes to those who are affected by earthquakes, donate books to children poorer than themselves or decide to reconstruct houses devasted by cyclones. I am witness to the profound generosity of their spirit every day of my life.

When my children reach great heights, I soar in my heart and soul. Today, Durga, my little one, is a doctor. Mary, her sister, has just founded a start-up. Viju works with an international firm. Shaheen is a camerawoman. Bhavani is a chartered accountant, and her two sisters are pursuing nursing and arts. Muskan, Siraj, Naziya, Reshma, Shanaz, Sujatha ... the names are endless. Others pursue vocations such as welding, carpentry, bookbinding, masonry. They are rescue workers, counsellors and more. They stand on their own two feet with dignity. And they are an inspiration not just to women, but to all human beings. I call them 'Aparajita'. Invincible.

To these humans, I owe my life ... for giving it meaning and purpose, for making me believe everything can be overcome through love and faith and for assuring me that nothing is impossible.